PIERS OF HAMPSHIRE
& THE ISLE OF WIGHT

PIERS OF HAMPSHIRE & THE ISLE OF WIGHT

MARTIN EASDOWN *&* LINDA SAGE

AMBERLEY

For Jonty

First published 2011

Amberley Publishing
The Hill, Stroud
Gloucestershire, GL5 4EP

www.amberley-books.com

British Library Cataloguing in Publication Data.
A catalogue record for this book is available from the British Library.

ISBN 978 1 4456 0355 1

Typesetting and Origination by Amberley Publishing.
Printed in Great Britain.

CONTENTS

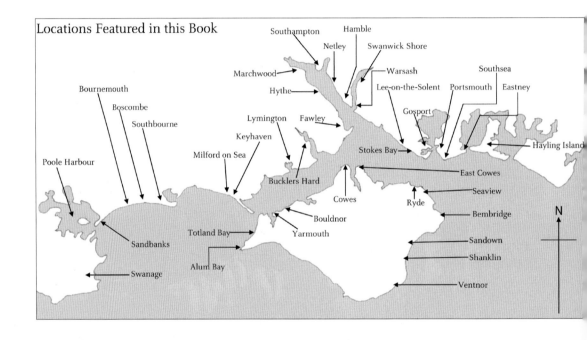

Locations Featured in this Book

INTRODUCTION

Despite their popular association with fun and frivolity, the function of piers as both an amusement centre and landing stage was varied, and nowhere was this more illustrated than on the coasts of Hampshire, Isle of Wight and east Dorset.

Ryde's pier, originally opened in 1814, is usually regarded as the earliest piled pier in Great Britain. The pier was built as a landing stage for the ferries to and from Portsmouth to save passengers having to be brought in at low tide by rowing boat or horse and cart. A lengthening of the structure in 1824 and 1833 enabled it to be used at all states of the tide.

On the other side of the Solent, a shelving area of compacted mud, sand and gravel, known as a 'Hard', had to suffice as a landing stage at Portsmouth until the building of the Victoria and Albert piers in the 1840s. Gosport, which also had a Hard used for the ferry service to Portsmouth, acquired a pontoon pier in 1842 to enable the Ryde steamers to call there.

A ferry service between Southampton and Cowes began in 1823, using quays at both towns. Ten years later, Southampton built a 900-foot-long wooden landing pier, which became known as the 'Royal Pier'. Steamers called at the pier on services along the south coast and also to the Channel Islands and France.

Piers were also erected in the area for naval and military purposes. Gosport became home to a number of naval ancillary depots serving Portsmouth Dockyard and acquired numerous piers and jetties to serve the Priddy's Hard Armaments Depot, Royal Clarence Victualling Yard and Haslar Hospital. Queen Victoria had her own private railway station and pier built in the Clarence Yard for journeys to Osborne House, her home on the Isle of Wight. Following the opening of the large military hospital at Netley in 1863, an iron pier was erected to receive hospital ships and the pier became a favourite relaxation place for the patients.

Indeed, by the 1860s seaside piers were becoming fashionable promenades over the sea, and places of entertainment and recreation, as the popularity of seaside resorts really began to take off. A promenade/pleasure pier became a 'must have' for any self-respecting watering place, and although not all resorts succeeded in building one, nearly one hundred pleasure piers did sprout from the coast of Great Britain. Some of the earliest built landing piers, such as Ryde and Southampton Royal, took on a dual-purpose function as a landing/pleasure pier, and pavilions and other attractions were provided on them. The Isle of Wight, ever-increasing as a popular holiday destination, saw additional piers to the existing one at Ryde being built at Seaview, Sandown, Shanklin, Ventnor, Alum Bay, Totland Bay, Yarmouth and Cowes. Ryde itself gained a second pier, the Victoria, built originally for the Stokes Bay ferry service before it was converted into a bathing station. Generally, these piers were used as both promenade/pleasure piers and landing stages. Two piers were erected at Southsea (the seaside suburb of Portsmouth), known as Clarence Pier and South Parade Pier, and three in the Bournemouth area at Southbourne, Boscombe and Bournemouth. These piers all served much the same dual-purpose function, as did the pier at Lee-on-the-Solent (1888) and Swanage's second pier, opened in 1896.

The railway had reached Southampton in 1840, Gosport in 1841 and Portsmouth in 1848, bringing about faster and cheaper travel to the Hampshire coast. The Isle of Wight acquired its first railway, from Ryde to Shanklin, in 1864, and Bournemouth its first, reluctantly, in 1874. A number of piers were built to serve the railway in Hampshire and the Isle of Wight. In 1863, a new railway to Stokes Bay terminated at the end of a pier, from which a ferry operated to Ryde. The pier, built for the Stokes Bay service at Ryde, the Victoria, proved to be a white elephant and never acquired a railway. However, in 1880 a railway pier was erected alongside the existing promenade and tramway piers at the main Ryde Pier, as part of the extension of the Isle of Wight Railway from St Johns Road. Stations were placed at both the shore end of the pier and the pier head. In Southampton, train services were extended along the waterfront in 1876 to terminate on the Royal Pier, and in 1884 the line to Lymington was extended onto a new pier, from which ferries sailed to Yarmouth on the Isle of Wight. Hythe built a long, iron pier in 1881 to serve the Southampton ferry service, and in 1922 it acquired a charming electric railway, which still operates to this day.

Other pier-like structures to grace the area include the industrial, yacht club and ferry piers of Poole Harbour; the oil terminal jetties at Fawley and Hamble, the ferry pontoons on the Eastney–Hayling Island and Warsash–Hamble routes. Some piers never got off the drawing board; including those for Milford-on-Sea and Swanwick Shore, a second railway pier for Ryde and a railway pier for Bouldnor, which had to make do instead with a small wooden jetty.

The golden age of pier construction lasted from the mid-Victorian era up to the years prior to the First World War. The high cost and sometimes speculative nature of building piers, along with the fact that many resorts already had them, meant that only structures serving military and industrial establishments were built post-1910. A noticeable exception was the rebuilding of the Clarence Pier at Southsea, following its destruction by bombing during the Second World War. Heavy maintenance costs, redundancy, the cessation of pleasure steamer cruises and storm damage have since accounted for the disappearance of some piers.

The Isle of Wight once had ten pleasure/landing piers, but now has only four – at Ryde, Sandown, Totland Bay and Yarmouth – one of which (Totland Bay) is derelict and closed. Ryde continues to be used as a railway and ferry pier, but the promenade deck is now used more by cars than people. Sandown, with its amusement pavilion and small deck rides, is the only fully-fledged pleasure pier remaining on the island. Yarmouth (along with Swanage on the mainland) is constructed of wood and looks much the same as it did when built in 1876. The pier is a listed structure but requires frequent maintenance to combat the effects of the marine worms that eat through its wooden piling. A further pier-like structure on the island worthy of mention is that housing the lifeboat station at Bembridge, which has become something of a tourist attraction in its own right. Originally erected in 1922, and then rebuilt in 2010, a walk along this tall, imposing structure is quite a thrill and not one for the faint-hearted!

Of those piers that have disappeared from the Isle of Wight, the saddest casualty was the elegant chain pier at Seaview, destroyed by storms in 1951 following wartime dereliction. A few years earlier, the pier had become the first to be listed as a structure of historic interest. The pier at Shanklin, which by the 1970s had become a rundown but nevertheless delightful centre of eccentric amusements such as the Disco Granny, was another sad loss when it perished in the Great Storm of 16 October 1987.

In Hampshire and east Dorset, the pier survival rate is better, although Lee-on-the-Solent, Netley, Southbourne and Stokes Bay are amongst those that have gone. Southampton Royal will no doubt soon be added to this list; having lain derelict since the 1980s, parts of which have collapsed into the sea. Elsewhere, the situation is better. Southsea still retains its two piers, of which the Clarence Pier seems to have an assured future as a fairground alongside the sea. The other pier, however, South Parade, is currently under-utilised as its owners struggle to make it pay. The long iron pier at Hythe, with its charming pier train of 1920s vintage, remains busy in its use as a ferry terminal and is one of the most interesting piers remaining in Britain. Swanage Pier is another fine structure, boasting ornate wrought iron deck railing panels, but like its wooden counterpart at Yarmouth it requires constant maintenance to protect the piling against the ravenous attacks of marine worms. Bournemouth and Boscombe still have their piers and recent investment should hopefully give them an assured future for the time being.

The piers that remain continue to be the focal point of their towns and are, on the whole, much cherished. For example, any politician being interviewed at Bournemouth during the political parties' conference season will usually have the pier as a background shot. The fascination of walking over water on a pier remains as delightful an experience as it was when our Victorian forebears built them.

We hope that this book will help convey the often fascinating, diverse and interesting histories of the piers and jetties along the coasts of Hampshire, the Isle of Wight and the eastern part of Dorset. Compared to the numerous books produced on the paddle steamer services that once served the area, books on the piers that served them (with the exception of Ryde and Hythe) are thin on the ground, despite the piers often having the more interesting stories to tell! This book should go some way to helping right that wrong.

HAMPSHIRE

PORTSMOUTH AND SOUTHSEA

Affectionately nicknamed 'Pompey', Portsmouth is the United Kingdom's only island city; being mainly located on Portsea Island. The city was once the country's foremost Royal Navy port and retains strong naval and military links, as well as a thriving commercial ferry port linking it to the Isle of Wight, the Channel Islands and Western Europe.

Southsea is Portsmouth's seaside satellite: once described as its 'breathing space, playground and smartest residential suburb'. The development of Southsea commenced in the early part of the nineteenth century, with housing for dockyard workers built before larger and more elegant residences for the upper and middle classes, with Kings Terrace as the showpiece. On the shore, bathing machines and a bath house were present and Mr Hollingsworth's establishment provided warm baths, a reading room and large assembly room and was visited by the Duke of Clarence in 1824 and King William IV in 1830. Architect Thomas Ellis Owen (*see also Stokes Bay*) further developed Southsea from 1838, with elegant terraces and crescents and the Portland Hotel. In 1861, the Clarence Pier was opened as a landing stage to cross to the Isle of Wight and linked to Portsmouth station by a horse tramway. The second half of the nineteenth century saw the rapid development of Southsea with both large scale residential districts and grand hotels for visitors such as the Queens (1861), Pier (1865), Beach Mansions (1866), Sandringham (1871), Esplanade (1877) and Grosvenor (1880s). In 1879, the South Parade Pier at East Southsea was added, followed by the Southsea Railway to Fratton in 1885. The latter, however, was never a success and closed in 1914.

The inter-war years saw Portsmouth Corporation take on the mantle of developing Southsea as a seaside resort, with the acquisition in 1923, from the War Department, of Southsea Common and the creation of gardens and recreation areas. In recent years, the promotion of Southsea as a leisure area has taken a bit of a back seat to the highlighting of Portsmouth's Historic Dockyard and other waterfront attractions, such as the Spinnaker Tower. Nevertheless, Southsea still has plenty of attractions to offer, including the Pyramids indoor leisure centre and pool, Southsea Castle, Sealife Centre and D Day Museum, along with its two piers and elegant Regency and Victorian architecture.

Eastney – Hayling Island Ferry

A passenger ferry across Langstone Harbour connects the eastern end of Portsea Island, at Eastney, to Hayling Island, saving a 32-mile trip by road. The service, which uses small pontoon piers at both Eastney and Hayling, operates throughout the year, except during the Christmas and New Year's holidays, and is used by commuters, schoolchildren, shoppers and tourists.

The rights of the ferry once belonged to the Duke of Norfolk, owner of the Manor of Hayling Island. Rowing boats were used until the ferry rights were acquired by the Hayling Island Steam Ferry Company in 1901. They acquired a small steamer and built landing pontoons, but the steamer proved to be a failure and the service was abandoned for a time.

The ferry was then operated by George Spraggs, landlord of the Norfolk Inn at the mouth of the harbour, using motor boats. Sadly, in April 1922, Mr Spraggs was drowned whilst trying to rescue his son George who had fallen overboard. His three sons, Cecil, George and Jack continued to operate the ferry for a number of years. In the 1950s, three boats – *Sinah*, *Folkestone Belle* and *Tarpon* – were used on the route.

In 1961, the ferry was taken over by Portsmouth City Council, who added the ferries *Iris* in 1968 and *Irene* in 1976. However, in 1981 they closed the ferry, claiming it was a burden on the rates and the ageing pontoons needed replacing. Hampshire County Council wanted the ferry to keep running and, after promising to subsidise the costs, engaged Messrs Dutfield & Edwards in February 1985 to operate it. New pontoons were built and the vessel *Hayling Enterprise* was used until 2001. In 1989, she was joined by the current vessel on the route, *Pride of Hayling*.

The ferry is now operated by Messrs Edwards & Co. but in November 2010 it had to be suspended following an inspection by the Coastguard, who found defective life jackets and staff members unable to cope with a set of emergency scenarios put to them.

There have been a number of proposals in the past to erect a fixed crossing between the two islands. In 1886, the Portsmouth & Hayling Railway would have branched off the Havant to Hayling Island line near South Hayling (renamed

The Eastney to Hayling Island Ferry boat *Pride of Hayling* at the Eastney Pontoon in 2007.

The pontoon at Hayling Island for the ferry service across Langstone Harbour to Eastney on Portsea Island in 2007.

Hayling Island in 1892) and crossed Langstone Harbour by means of a 900-foot, eight-span viaduct with a swing bridge for both road and rail traffic, before terminating at Fratton station. Wharfs would also have been erected at Hayling. However, the railway plan soon came to nothing, as did a proposal in 1903 to build an aerial bridge 720 feet in length with cable cars.

Southsea South Parade Pier

The instigator behind the proposal for a pier for the eastern end of Southsea was Lt-Col. Edwin Galt, a brewer, wine and spirit merchant who lived in Landguard Villa, Granada Road, Southsea, before moving to Beach Mansions on the seafront. On 27 July 1866, Galt wrote to the War Office proposing that a pier should be built in what was then called New Southsea, but later became known as East Southsea. The plan soon foundered, as it did again in 1871. However, on 2 August 1877, Galt, who had been Mayor of Portsmouth in 1868, wrote to the Board of Trade stating that a pier company was in the process of formation[1]. This was the South Parade Pier Company, incorporated on 13 November 1877, with a capital of £8,000 in 800 shares of £10 each. The Provisional Order to build the pier was placed before the Board of Trade on 23 December 1877 and finally passed by them on 7 August 1878. The area of beach upon which the pier was to be built was leased from the War Department on 29 September 1878, for a term of 99 years, at an annual rent of £10: on condition that all naval, military and civil servants on duty were to have free admission onto the pier. Architect and engineer George Rake of Blackburn, who was residing at St George's, Havelock Park, Southsea, drew up a design for an iron pier, which, due to limits imposed by the Admiralty, was to be 460 foot long. However, the Admiralty eventually allowed a pier of 580 feet in length and a width of 20 feet, widening to 48 feet in the central section. The pier head was to be 150 foot wide, upon which a bandstand was to be placed.

---

[1] Galt was also largely responsible for the opening of the railway to East Southsea from Fratton in 1885.

Southsea South Parade Pier photographed on a fine summer's day *c.* 1901 with lots of activity around the pier entrance and two steamers at the landing stage. Note the advertising panels along the side of the pier, including one for Oxo.

A large crowd watches the destruction of the South Parade Pier head and pavilion during the afternoon of 19 July 1904. The blaze was thought to have been started by a lighted match thrown by one of the fisherman on the landing stage and the funnels of a tug fighting the fire can be seen.

The workmen of contractors T. H. Yelf and Alfred Thorne rebuilding Southsea South Parade for the Portsmouth Corporation in 1907. The pier had been acquired by the corporation in October 1906 after lying derelict since the fire of July 1904.

The mayor and mayoress of Portsmouth touring the South Parade Pier after carrying out its official reopening on 12 August 1908. The pier had cost Portsmouth Corporation £85,000 to rebuild.

Southsea South Parade Pier photographed shortly after it was reopened on 12 August 1908, following a devastating fire four years previously. The pavilion housed a 1,200-seat theatre and a restaurant, and military bands performed in the bandstand at the end of the pier.

An interior view of the theatre in the pavilion on the South Parade Pier, pictured shortly after it was opened on 12 August 1908. The statues situated either side of the proscenium arch are of particular interest.

An aerial view, of the South Parade Pier in the 1930s, showing the three-sided landing stage from where steamer sailings were available to the Isle of Wight.

Southsea South Parade Pier photographed from the air shortly after the ending of the Second World War in 1945. In 1940, a hole was blown in the centre of the pier as a defence measure and the temporary gangway spanning the gap can be seen. The bandstand on the pier head has been removed and the majority of the landing stage stripped of its decking.

The South Parade Pier suffered a second devastating fire on 11 June 1974 when the pavilion was burnt out during the filming of Ken Russell's rock opera *Tommy*. The fire was apparently caused by a lighting gallery being knocked against some curtains, catching it alight and sending sparks up into the roof space, which also caught fire.

Following the fire on the South Parade Pier in 1974, the pavilion was quickly rebuilt and can be seen here in this photograph from November 2010. In 2010, the pavilion housed an amusement arcade, the Albert Tavern and function rooms.

The construction of the pier was begun in 1878 by Messrs Head Wrightson of Stockton, who had previously built piers at Redcar and Cleethorpes, and went sufficiently smoothly for it to be officially opened by the wife of Prince Edward of Saxe-Weimar (Governor of Portsmouth Garrison) on 26 July 1879. The pier head bandstand was replaced in July 1881 by a pavilion, seating 1,500, which was rather unkindly described by the Board of Trade inspector as 'an ugly erection but sufficiently strong for the purpose'. To help support the new building, additional supports were added to the pier head. A landing stage was also provided, allowing steamers to call at the pier on journeys between Portsmouth and the Isle of Wight. In 1885, an application was made to the Board of Trade and Admiralty to extend it by 30 feet. In 1886, the South Parade Pier Company increased its capital to £12,000 to help pay for the work.

Military bands and light orchestras were the staple attractions in the pier pavilion during its early days. In 1885, the pier advertised 'Grand Classical, Operatic, and Miscellaneous Concerts', although The Full Band of the Marine Artillery were the usual fare on offer, admission 3*d*. On 26 August 1886, the 'eminent' Russian pianist M. Vladimir de Packmann appeared in the pavilion. Attractions on the pier in 1894 included the Anglo-Swiss Ladies Orchestra, entrance to the pier and pavilion 6*d*. Church Parade, where everyone liked to promenade on the pier in his or her best bib-and-tucker, was held every Sunday, pier toll 2*d*. The orchestras eventually gave way to concert parties, as evident by this list of entertainments and steamer sailings for Saturday 2 August 1902:

7–9 a.m. – Bathing from the pier head; single ticket 2*d*, monthly ticket 5*s* 6*d*, season ticket 5*s*.

10 a.m. – The S.S. *Solent Queen* to Sandown, Shanklin and Ventnor

10–11.30 a.m. – South Parade Pier Band will play

10.10 a.m. – S.S. *Kitchener* to Sea View and Bembridge

10.30 a.m. – S.S. *Sandringham* to Ryde and Sea View

11 a.m. – S.S. *Bembridge* to Sea View and Bembridge

11.40 a.m. – S.S. *Kitchener* to Clarence Pier, Sea View and Bembridge

11.45 a.m. – Al-fresco concert by Mr Bertram Wallis' Musketeer Concert Party; admission 3*d*, reserved 6*d*

12.30 p.m. – Exhibition of high diving from the pier head by Mr Percy Leslie, the Champion High Diver. He will be in attendance each morning to give instruction in swimming and high diving. Terms – one lesson 3*s*, five lessons 12*s* 6*d*, twelve lessons 21*s*.

1 p.m. – S.S. *Bembridge* to Clarence Pier and Portsmouth Harbour

1.50 p.m. – S.S. *Solent Queen* to Sandown, Shanklin and Ventnor

2.25 p.m. – S.S. *Sandringham* to Sea View and Ryde

2.55 p.m. – S.S. *Kitchener* to Sea View and Bembridge

4–8.30 p.m. – South Parade Pier Band will play

4.30 p.m. – Exhibition of diving from the pier head

5.15 p.m. – S.S. *Solent Queen* to Clarence Pier, Sandown, Shanklin and Ventnor

5.30 p.m. – S.S. *Bembridge* to Clarence Pier, Portsmouth Harbour, Sea View and Bembridge

6 p.m. – Evening excursion to Sea View

8.10 p.m. – A steamer to Clarence Pier and Gosport

9 p.m. – Exhibition of high diving from the pier head

9.15 p.m. – Concert by the Musketeer Concert Party; admission 3*d*, reserved 6*d*

10.15 p.m. – High dive in flames and fireworks from pier head

In 1902, architect G. E. Smith prepared plans to extend the kiosks at the entrance to the pier to provide shops, a toll office, directors' room, reading room, secretary's office, general office and ladies cloakroom. Underneath the new buildings, cellars and ladies and gentlemen's lavatories were to be provided. Plans were also put in place to widen the pier and extend the landing stage.

However, before the improvements could be carried out, the pavilion was completely destroyed during the afternoon of 19 July 1904, by a fire started through a lighted match being thrown away by a fisherman on the landing stage. A large crowd lined the esplanade to view the blaze, which was fought by marine artillerymen from Eastney Barracks with their manual engine, and the Portsmouth Fire Brigade with their motor engine. Two Government tugs sprayed water on the fire from the sea and soldiers from Southsea Fort assisted the firemen. The 'Merry Maker's' concert party, who had been appearing in the pavilion when the blaze started, managed to escape from the pier but the guilty fishermen on the landing stage had to be rescued by boat. By 5.15 p.m. the pavilion was consumed by flames before it dramatically crashed down in a heap.

The South Parade Pier Company initially announced plans to rebuild the pier and widen it, but in December 1905 they announced that it was to be sold to John Franckeiss of Western Parade, Southsea, for £10,250. Eventually however, the pier was acquired on 8 October 1906 by Portsmouth Corporation for £10,782. The winding-up of the South Parade Pier Company was confirmed on 11 December 1907.

Local architect G. E. Smith was engaged to completely rebuild the pier, which was to have an increased length of 610 feet, a width variation of 72–147 feet, and a concrete deck. F. Bevis (landing stage), T. H. Yelf (pier) and A. Thorne (pier head) carried out the work at a cost of £85,000. The Corporation hired 1,500 men at 6*d* each to test the strength of the new structure before the pier was officially opened by the Mayor and Mayoress of Portsmouth on 12 August 1908.

The rebuilt pier featured a large pavilion at the shore end with two halls; one was used as a 1,200-seat concert hall, and the other was a café during the day and a dance hall in the evening. The sea end had a bandstand and the deck was used for open-air dancing and roller-skating. Steamer trips from the landing stage to the Isle of Wight were a further attraction, where a cruise around the island could be taken.

However, the pier sustained losses in its first four years (it was nicknamed the 'White Elephant') until F. G. Robson was appointed manager in 1912. He had previously made a success of the South Pier at Lowestoft and was to do the same for the South Parade Pier until his death in 1936. Robson approached Cosens of Weymouth in 1913 to provide steamer services from the pier, but they declined after deciding to stay loyal to the Clarence Pier. Another factor in their decision may have been the fact that the South Parade Pier was very difficult for steamers to berth during low tide.

Another popular character associated with the pier was Bill Brewington, who started as a deck hand in 1911 and retired as stage manager in 1953 after forty-two years of service. His long career on the pier oversaw the changing face of entertainment: from concert parties such as the Co-optimists to orchestras led by Jack Hylton and Billy Cotton, and from favourite inter-war variety stars such as Arthur Askey to Peter Sellers and Harry Secombe of the Goons. Mr Brewington was at the side of the stage the night that band leader Al Davidson died while his band played on.

However, as the threat of war loomed in 1939, the pier was requisitioned and used as a military depot, putting on hold plans for it to be widened in its centre (which was never carried out). The structure was breached (although it was soon bridged) and gunpowder canisters were placed in position on the deck ready to destroy the pier if the enemy attempted a landing. However, the pavilion at the entrance to the pier stayed open for dancing, except during the periods July–September 1940 (at the height of the invasion scare) and May–October 1944 when the pier was at the forefront of the preparations for the D-Day landings. On the day before the landings, 5 June 1944, Eisenhower visited troops who were to embark from the pier on LCIs 600, 601 and 602.

Upon the resumption of peace in 1945, the pier celebrated a record number of visitors that year (847,000), which allowed the Corporation to record a profit of £25,299. The popular *Showtime* began on the pier in 1946, which four years later could also offer Grand Celebrity Concerts, Eugene & His Serenaders, Gordon Banner and his Hammond organ in the pier café and nightly dancing in the Pier Ballroom. The summer shows of the 1950s on the pier included a host of famous names, featuring:

1952 – Cyril Fletcher & Betty Astell in *Magpie Masquerades*
1953 – Peter Sellers in *Showtime*
1954 – Greatorex Newman's Fol-de-Rols
      Cyril Fletcher
      Eddie Grey & Arthur English in *(K)nights of Gladness*
1955 – Eddie Grey & Arthur English in *Ring Out the Bells*
1956 – Tommy Trinder in *You Lucky People*
1957 – Reg Dixon in *Jump for Joy*
1958 – Jimmy Edwards in *Whacko Southsea*

In addition, a fairly intensive steamer service still operated from the pier during the 1950s. These included British Railways sailings to Ryde, Red Funnel operated services to Shanklin and Southampton, and trips around the Isle of Wight and Portsmouth Harbour and to Bournemouth and Swanage.

In February 1967, ownership of the pier was transferred from Portsmouth Corporation to Fortes (Holdings) Ltd, but in that year the pavilion was damaged by fire and the theatre was removed. By 1970, the pier was offering the following attractions: Gaiety Lounge Cabaret Showbar, Coral Reef Bar, Albert Bar, tea lounge, sun lounge, Golden Goose Family Fun Centre and the Golden Fry restaurant. The Gaiety played host to a number of popular rock music performers, including David Bowie (June 1971), Genesis (December 1971) and Manfred Mann's Earth Band (November 1972).

On 11 June 1974, the pavilion suffered a serious blaze that occurred during the filming of Ken Russell's rock opera *Tommy* and it was burnt out; the damage amounting to £500,000. The fire was apparently caused by a lighting gallery being knocked against some curtains, catching them alight and sending sparks up into the roof space, which also caught fire. As firemen fought the blaze, it was filmed by Russell using a hand-cranked movie camera and footage was used in the film.

Fortunately, the pavilion was quickly rebuilt and soon back in business. The pier changed hands in 1995 when it was acquired by First Leisure, who also owned the three piers at Blackpool and others at Llandudno and Eastbourne. First Leisure subsequently became known as Leisure Parcs and then Six Piers Limited.

In 2008, Six Piers refurbished the Albert Tavern and subsequently spent £300,000 on refurbishing the sub-structure of the pier. However, in 2009, they announced that they would not invest further money on the pier unless it could be recouped by income. The pier's facilities include an amusement arcade at the entrance and children's rides on the pier deck between the pavilion and the jetty, which is used by fishermen. The pavilion contains two function rooms and bars.

Southsea Clarence Pier

Permission was granted to build a pier on the Southsea Clarence Esplanade in 1852, but it was not until 30 December 1859 that the War Office leased the foreshore above the high water mark to the Southsea Esplanade Pier Company, for a term of 99 years, at an annual cost of 5s. The company had been formed by Chairman Emanuel Emanuel along with Messrs G. W. Shepherd, Andrew Neame, Henry Hollingsworth and Alfred Heather, with a capital of £40,000. The pier was to be named in honour of General Lord Frederick Fitz Clarence (1799–1854), Lieutenant Governor of Portsmouth 1847–51. He was one of ten illegitimate children of King William IV and his mistress Dorothea Bland.

Following the granting of the foreshore below the low water mark on 25 December 1860, work began on the pier, which was originally just a basic square wooden structure measuring 130 feet long by 45 feet wide. The pier was opened by the Princess of Wales on 1 June 1861 and immediately proved to be a popular attraction. During the summer of 1862, visitors, each paying 1*d* to enter, generated £538 16*s* 8*d* in income. Ten years later, this had increased to £2,245 16*s* 6*d* and shareholders were receiving yearly dividends between 6 and 10 per cent.

A photograph of Southsea Clarence Pier in 1883, one year after the large pavilion had been opened by the Prince of Wales. The pavilion featured a concert hall, refreshment room and a balcony giving good views of the shipping in the Solent. Note the three cannons lining the esplanade.

The entrance to Southsea Clarence Pier in around 1905, showing the Esplanade Hotel on the right opened by the Southsea Clarence Pier Company in 1865. Electric trams were introduced to Portsmouth in 1901 to replace the horse-drawn trams that used to run onto the pier deck.

A fine real photographic postcard of the beach and Clarence Pier at Southsea, sent through the post on 10 June 1909. The card shows a delightful study of children paddling on the beach, whilst on the pier can be seen the pavilion, extended since 1883.

Southsea Clarence Pier photographed on a fine summer's day during the Edwardian period. A number of ladies can be seen sporting parasols to keep off the sun and the ornate gas lamps typify the elegance of the age. Amongst the flags on view is the rising sun of Japan, then an ally of Great Britain.

An aerial view of Southsea Clarence Pier during the 1930s, showing two paddle steamers at the pier that offered sailings to the Isle of Wight. By this time, the Butlin's Amusement Park had been added to the pier, the centrepiece of which was the Figure Eight rollercoaster.

Following the destruction of the Clarence Pier by bombing on 10 January 1941, work to rebuild it commenced in 1953 but the pier was not reopened until 1 June 1961. A feature of the new pier was the 60-foot-high tower. On the right can be seen one of the trolleybuses that replaced the trams in 1936, but which were replaced themselves by buses in 1963.

The entrance building to Southsea Clarence Pier, photographed in November 2010. The ground floor of the building is home to the Golden Horse amusement arcade and a Wimpy restaurant, whilst upstairs is a children's play area.

The deck of the Clarence Pier is now given over almost exclusively to the popular amusement park, part of which is seen here in this photograph from July 2005.

The pier took over from the Victoria Pier at Portsmouth as the principal point of departure for the Isle of Wight steamer services and remained so until Portsmouth Harbour station was opened on 2 October 1876. A small steam-operated crane loaded passenger's luggage on and off the steamers.

The success of the pier led to the now-renamed Southsea Clarence Pier Company becoming involved in the building of the Pier Hotel (soon to be renamed Esplanade Hotel) in 1864–65, at a cost of £14,700, the laying out of the Landport & Southsea horse tramway in 1865 (which ran onto the pier from Portsmouth Town station)[2], and the adjoining baths and assembly room (1870). Many of the directors of the pier company were also involved in the hotel, tram and bath companies, including Henry Hollingsworth, secretary to the pier company, who was also secretary of the tram and hotel companies (in addition to other business interests that eventually led to his bankruptcy). Wealthy gentleman of leisure and Southsea resident Edward Parson was a director of all four undertakings, in addition to being Chairman of the Portsmouth Liberal Association.

In 1869, the pier was extended to form an unusual hammer-shape 160 feet long and 250 feet wide. Admission was 1d (although naval personnel were admitted free) and facilities comprised of a licensed refreshment room and ladies waiting room in the east tollhouse; a toll takers hut and gentlemen's waiting room in the west toll house; two landing stairs for boats and one landing stair on the north east side for Government boats. The double-track tramway extended almost to the end of the pier, and nearby was a store and a baggage room. During the summer months, military bands played on the pier and good views could be obtained across the Solent to the Isle of Wight. To keep the pier select a uniformed porter was placed at the entrance. In 1872, over 200,000 people paid to go on the pier, while another 23,000 arrived on the horse-drawn trams that ran on it (admission to the pier was included in the price of the ticket). However, the baths situated just along the promenade from the pier proved not to be such a success and, in 1877, the building was converted into a hotel.

In May 1874, the Southsea Clarence Pier Company's attempts to extend the pier's exclusivity and stop the 'promiscuous mingling of the classes around its premises' by erecting barriers across the right of way to the baths and Old Portsmouth led to the infamous 'Battle of Southsea'. Portsmouth Town Council ordered the removal of the barriers, but the company stuck to their guns. The locals, however, took the matter into their own hands and on Tuesday 4 August 1874, a 5,000 strong crowd smashed down the heavy wooden and iron barrier and burnt the timber in view of the assembly rooms. On the following two nights a smaller, but more vociferous, crowd threw stones at the pier, smashing several windows, and also pelted promenaders and the police. It took the police over 2 ½ hours to disperse the fighting mob. However, on Saturday, they returned and by eight in the evening some 4,000 people had gathered at the pier entrance in an ugly mood. The Mayor was forced to read the Riot Act and called upon the crowd

---

[2] The tramway was eventually absorbed into the Portsmouth street system in 1877.

to disperse. They responded by jeering him and setting fire to a barrel, so around 200 soldiers of the 9th regiment were gathered up and, together with police and pier officials wielding truncheons, tried to clear the crowd. However, it was not until midnight that order was finally restored. More trouble was expected the following day, but pouring rain meant all was quiet. On Monday, a smaller crowd gathered outside the pier to listen to speeches by two of the ringleaders – Town Councillors Barney Miller and Manoah Jepps – and cheered what they considered a victory and then left: the Battle of Southsea was over.

In revenge, the Southsea Clarence Pier Company undertook to prosecute six men (including Miller and Jepps) for inciting rioting and conspiracy and another four for rioting. However, the magistrates (who appeared sympathetic towards the defence) adjourned the case and the pier company decided it would be best if they just let the matter rest. One man, Isaac Phillips, was sentenced to three months hard labour for bringing an axe to the battle and being drunk and aggressive, and despite a petition to the Home Secretary calling for his release, he served his time in Winchester Prison.

The disputed rights of way were reopened by the pier company, although they used part of them to extend the pier. For many years a circular painting of the battle was on display in the Barley Mow public house in Southsea, and this can now be seen in the Portsmouth City Museum.

Despite losing much of its Isle of Wight traffic with the opening of Portsmouth Harbour station in 1876, there were still plenty of steamer sailings from the pier. The Isle of Wight Railway offered cheap day return fares between Clarence Pier and Ryde Pier aboard the *Sandown* and *Shanklin* steamers at 1s 6d, with an extra shilling for a seat on the upper decks. On 23 March 1886, the P.S. *Prince of Wales* left Portsmouth Harbour between 8 and 9 p.m. and, when going alongside the pier in thick fog, to embark passengers for Cowes and Southampton, she hit the structure with considerable force, although no one was seriously hurt. The bulwark of the steamer was extensively damaged and the north corner of the pier head had to be re-constructed with a new landing stage. Further work was carried out on the landing stage in 1905, when a new concrete extension to the west was built to accommodate increased boat traffic. In 1908, Cosens of Weymouth ran services from the pier to Brighton, Worthing, Bournemouth and around the Isle of Wight. However, two years later the Southsea Clarence Pier Company refused to allow the Southsea & Solent Steamboat Company and their small steamer *Winifred* to operate a weekday service to Seaview, claiming the route was already catered for.

In August 1882, the Prince of Wales opened a large pavilion on the pier, which housed a concert hall and licensed refreshment rooms. The building was enlarged in 1887 by H. & W. Evans at a cost of £417. In 1885, the War Office leased a further area of the foreshore to the pier company for an extension of the pier, for a term of seventy-three years at an annual rent of £20 5s; a further enlargement of the pier was carried out in 1905. A refreshment kiosk was added in 1908 and three years later an additional iron emergency staircase from the pavilion balcony had to be erected after it was demanded by the Licensing Magistrates.

In 1928, the Southsea Clarence Pier Company acquired the freehold of the land upon which the pier stood from the War Office and the Crown for £1,500 and £4,150 respectively. The company carried out improvements in 1932, when a café, sundeck and concourse hall and shops were added at the entrance. Attractions on the pier in 1938 included the pavilion and ballroom (popular for tea and evening dances), large café and sun deck, Butlin's Amusement Park, licensed refreshment room and round-the-harbour boat trips. However, on 10 January 1941, the pier was almost totally destroyed by enemy bombing.

The first pile of the replacement structure was driven in 1953, although contractors John Hunt of Gosport did not carry out work on the superstructure until 1959. Messrs A. E. Cogswell & Sons designed the pier in association with Mr R. Lewis Reynish, architects, of Portsmouth. Others involved in the pier's construction included J. Croad Ltd of Portsmouth (general construction) and Mouchel & Partners Ltd, London (deck and landing stage). The pier was officially opened on 1 June 1961 and featured a 60-foot-high tower, built around a steel frame.

Now described as one of the largest amusement complexes on the South Coast, the pier houses a fairground and other amusements. In 2002, a 24-metre-high Power Tower ride, the tallest spring tower ride in the world, was added. The ride took over twelve months to build, at a cost of nearly £500,000 and replaced a big wheel that had stood since the 1960s. The current main rides include the Skyways rollercoaster, Cyclone, Disko, Twister and Waltzer.

In 2008, it was revealed that the owners of the pier paid £12,500 to Portsmouth Council in both 2007 and 2008 to keep travelling fairs off Southsea Common.

The pier's other attractions include Pirate Pete's Indoor Adventure Playground, a Wimpy Express restaurant. Adjoining the pier is the hovercraft service to Ryde.

Portsmouth Victoria Pier

The Victoria Pier at the Sally Port was opened on 16 May 1842 on the site of the Powder Bridge and Beef Stage, where supplies, including gunpowder, were landed and stored in the adjoining Square Tower. The pier was used for the steamer service to Ryde and became a stopping point when the Ryde services were commenced from Gosport New Pier (opened in 1843) and the Albert Pier, Portsea, upon its opening on 1 June 1847. Sailings to other south coast ports and resorts, including Southampton, operated from the pier. Royalty also occasionally used the pier, such as Queen Victoria and Prince Albert when they visited the Great Militia Review at Portsmouth Dockyard on 20 May 1856. A penny toll was levied for those who used the pier and military bands performed on it during the summer months.

A dividend of 100 per cent was paid to shareholders in 1860, indicating that the pier must have been a successful structure at that time. However, with the extension of the railway to Portsmouth Harbour station (built adjoining the Albert Pier) in 1876, the popularity of the Victoria Pier declined[3] and, in 1881, the Southampton and Isle of Wight steam packets ceased to call. A proposal in 1857

The Victoria Pier in Old Portsmouth was opened in 1842 and is pictured here *c.* 1910. By this time, steamers had largely stopped calling at the pier and it was left to just fishermen and advertisers such as Chaplin & Company to provide some income for its operating company.

Portsmouth Victoria Pier photographed in November 2010 with just a couple of fishermen using it. The pier had been rebuilt in concrete by Portsmouth Corporation in 1931.

to build a railway to the Victoria Pier, from Portsmouth station, never reached fruition; as did a proposal in 1878 to build a wooden boardwalk, 50 feet wide and supported on iron piles, between the Victoria Pier and Clarence Pier, Southsea. In 1882, the Victoria Pier Company announced that they were going to build baths at the pier, and a design was drawn up by Messrs Rake and Livesay, but once again the scheme floundered.

The deteriorating financial situation of the Victoria Pier Company led to it being reconstituted in 1885 with a capital of £2,000. On 28 October 1886, a special resolution was passed for the company to borrow £750 on the security of debenture bonds, but continuing financial struggles led to the decision to wind it up on 9 June 1896.

The pier was acquired by the Portsmouth Pier Company, which was incorporated on 23 June 1897 with a capital of £1,000 consisting of 200 £5 shares. Following a period of closure after the structure was declared unsafe in June 1897, the pier was reopened in 1898 and a 1d charge was levied to visitors. Further revenue was gained by allowing advertising on the pier. However, steamer revenue was only sporadic and the pier was largely patronised by fishermen. Only 146 of the shares of the Portsmouth Pier Company were ever taken up and in 1914 it was wound up.

In 1925, most of the pier was washed away by heavy seas. Five years later, the Portsmouth (Victoria) Pier Order, 1930, was passed, empowering the Corporation to construct a replacement concrete structure. On 5 May 1931, the Corporation minutes record that the tender of Messrs Frank Bevis Ltd of £4,075 13s 18d had been accepted.

The current pier, which lies close to the entrance to Portsmouth Harbour, is particularly popular with fishermen.

Portsea Landing Stages – The Hard/Gosport Ferry Landing Stage/Albert Pier/Portsmouth Harbour Station

A Hard is an area of foreshore that is sufficiently firm, either naturally or manmade, to be used as a slipway or landing stage for boats. The term is particularly used in Hampshire, in places such as Portsmouth, Gosport, Hythe and Bucklers Hard.

The Portsea/Portsmouth Hard was apparently created by dumping clay in the sea at low tide and then rolling it until it was hard. In later years it was rebuilt in concrete. The Portsea Hard grew in importance as a landing stage following the establishment of the Royal Dockyard by Henry VIII, particularly for the ferry crossing to Gosport (*see the Gosport chapter for a history of the ferry*), and remained the principal landing stage for Portsea until an Act of Parliament, for the building of the Albert Pier close to the Hard by the Portsmouth Harbour Company, was passed in July 1846. The pier was to provide better embarking and landing facilities from the Portsea area for the ferries on the service to Ryde on the

---

[3] Some of the Ryde ferries thereafter ceased to call at the pier.

A view of the Hard at Portsmouth in January 2011 looking towards Portsmouth Harbour station and the Gosport Ferry Pontoon. The lower section of the Spinnaker Tower can also be seen.

Isle of Wight. Work began on the 1,249-foot wooden pier in the summer of 1846 and it was open to traffic on 1 June 1847.

The Albert Pier (also known as the Royal Albert Pier and Portsea Pier) was used by steamers plying between Portsmouth (Albert and Victoria piers), Gosport (New Pier), Southsea (Clarence Pier) and Ryde. The pier was eventually superseded by the extension of the L&SWR and LB&SCR Joint Railway from Portsmouth Town station (opened in 1848 and now known as Portsmouth & Southsea) to the harbour, and the opening of Portsmouth Harbour station close to the pier on 2 October 1876. The last sailings from the Albert Pier were advertised in the summer of 1878. Portsmouth Harbour station was constructed over the harbour on wooden piles, which were later replaced by iron supports. A new ferry landing stage was provided as part of the new works for the Isle of Wight ferries and a floating wooden pontoon was added for the Gosport boats. There was also a slipway for the floating bridge that ran across the harbour from 1840 to 1959 (*see Gosport*).

The Gosport Ferry pontoon was rebuilt in the 1920s and again in 1989/90. Five years later, it was acquired from British Railways by the Portsmouth Harbour Ferry Company.

The Hard Interchange currently provides connecting boat, train, bus and coach services. Portsmouth Harbour station remains busy as the railway connection to the Isle of Wight FastCat services and Gosport ferries with trains running to London Waterloo, Southampton Central, Brighton, Salisbury, Bristol and Cardiff. The car ferry to Fishbourne on the Isle of Wight leaves from the Gunwharf Quay terminal and the continental and the Channel Island ferries operate from the Continental Ferry Port opened in 1976 close to the M275 at North End.

Portsmouth Dockyard South Railway Jetty

Situated in the Royal Dockyard, the jetty was used by the yachts of the Royal Family when they visited Portsmouth, Gosport and Isle of Wight. When the railway was extended to Portsmouth Harbour on 2 October 1876, a branch was built just short of the terminus to cross a corner of the harbour on a steel bridge to the dockyard. A swing bridge allowed vessels to still dock in the adjoining slip. A railway station with waiting room was built and, in 1893, an ornate shelter, which is now a Grade II listed building. The branch across to the dockyard no longer exists.

A postcard issues c. 1910 showing the South Railway Jetty at Portsmouth Dockyard and naval ratings watching a locomotive about to cross the steel bridge, which spans the harbour. In the background can be seen Portsmouth Harbour railway station.

GOSPORT

Portsmouth's position as the home of the Royal Navy led to the development of Gosport, on the other side of Portsmouth Harbour, as a naval satellite town supplying auxiliary services. In 1746, work began on the Royal Naval Hospital at Haslar, which, upon completion in 1860, was the largest brick-built building in the country. In 1752, the navy established a cooperage and brewery at the Weevil Yard in Gosport. Between 1828 and 1832, this was upgraded to house the navy's main victualling and fuel depot (it was said because of excessive thieving at Portsmouth!) and was renamed the Royal Clarence Yard after the Duke of Clarence. At the north end of Gosport was the Royal Navy's armaments depot at Priddy's Hard, opened in 1777.

By 1840, Gosport had a population of some 13,000 and was connected to Portsmouth by both a pedestrian ferry and floating bridge/chain ferry carrying vehicular traffic. On 29 November 1841, the London & South Western Railway opened a line to the town and built an impressive station (designed by Sir William Tite) boasting a magnificent colonnade comprising fourteen bays. The station also served as Portsmouth's rail link until the line from Fareham to the town, via Cosham, was opened in 1848.[4]

The last quarter of the twentieth century saw the decline and closure of many of its naval and military supply establishments, some of which have been opened to the public as tourism and heritage sites, whilst also accommodating new housing. The large Haslar Marina has been developed since 1993, including the provision of a pier in 2001.

Hardway Piers

Situated in the parish of Elson, Hardway retains the feel of a separate community in its own right, and has some interesting buildings lining Portsmouth Harbour. Hardway was so named because of the three Hards that lined the shore. These

---

[4] The railway to Gosport was eventually closed to passengers on 8 June 1953 and goods (beyond Bedenham) on 6 January 1969.

The two piers situated in the Hardway area of Gosport can be seen in this photograph taken in January 2011. The wooden structure in the foreground is used by the Gosport Boat Yard Company, whilst beyond is a steel pier formerly utilised by the Royal Navy Air Sea Rescue base.

were known as Lower Hard (originally Elson Hard and then Sandies Hard), Convict Hard (later Priddy's Hard) and Goliath Hard. The latter was named after a public house and was extended to low water in solid concrete.

An 1881 Ordnance Survey map of the area shows a small pier but this had gone by 1897. Around the turn of the twentieth century, a wooden pier was built near the Jolly Roger public house for ship and engine builders Vosper Ltd, who had a workshop next to the pub.[5] In 1904, the pier was taken over by HMS *Fisgard*, a naval artificers and engineers training unit that utilised old vessels. These included HMS *Audacious* (renamed HMS *Fisgard* I), HMS *Invincible* (*Fisgard* II), HMS *Hindustan* (*Fisgard* III) and HMS *Sultan* (*Fisgard* IV). The pier was later rebuilt with steel girders and railings and the pier head extended to the south.

In 1930, HMS *Fisgard* was moved to Chatham, and in 1942 the pier was utilised by the Royal Navy Air Sea Rescue base established at Moby House (formerly the White Heather public house). Two years later, another pier-like structure was erected to embark troops and vehicles for the D-Day landings, but the remains of this were removed in January 1957.

Following the end of the Second World War, the former HMS *Fisgard* pier was used by sailing clubs, and remains *in situ*, although it cannot be accessed by the public. Nearby is a wooden pier used by the Gosport Boat Yard Company, and there are also slipways used by the Hardway Sailing Club.

---

[5] Vosper Limited were based in Portsmouth and became Vosper Thornycroft in 1966 following a merger. They are now the VT Group.

Top: The former Shell Pier that served the Priddy's Hard Armaments Depot is seen here in January 2011.

Bottom: The remains of Powder Pier No. 2 at Priddy's Hard , photographed in January 2011.

Royal Naval Armaments Depots – Bedenham/Frater/Priddy's Hard

Priddy's Hard was the Royal Navy's principal armaments depot, named after Jane Priddy, from whom the land was acquired for its construction; the first stage of which was completed in 1777. To the north, sub-depots were opened at Bedenham, Frater and Elson, which were connected to Priddy's Hard by a rail system. Other depots were established at Tipner, on the other side of Portsmouth Harbour, and Marchwood, near Southampton. The following piers/jetties were built at the Gosport area depots:

Bedenham – A pier was opened in 1913 for the transhipment of goods to and from Priddy's Hard, supplementing the newly-built Priddy's Hard, Frater and Bedenham Railway. During the year ending 30 September 1918, it was recorded that 205,000 tons of explosives were carried by the railway and 132,400 tons on ships using the pier.

    On 14 July 1950, a spark from a shell being lifted up from a lighter set fire to cordage and ropes on the pier and led to an explosion that completely blew the middle out of it and also damaged buildings in the area. The pier was patched up and continued in use but later became derelict. The railway to Bedenham continued in use until the 1990s.

Frater – A small jetty was erected on the creek abutting the depot.

Priddy's Hard Forton Lake Rolling Stage – This pier was built in 1849 for the laboratory unit before being converted in 1860 to handle explosives and other cargo. The structure was known as the 'Rolling Stage', as it could be retracted in and out on wheels (like the adjoining Forton Bridge). However, it was rarely used after 1879, following the erection of the Powder and Shell piers, and was removed.

Laboratory Jetty – Erected in 1860 to replace the jetty on Forton Lake converted into a rolling stage. This structure was itself replaced by the Shell Pier in 1879.

Priddy's Hard Powder Pier No. 1 – Constructed in 1876 out from the northern arm of the Camber-facing Portsmouth Harbour to serve the newly-built E Magazine. The pier was built of iron piles and wooden decking, and terminated in a head facing north upon which a small examining shed was erected. An 18-inch gauge tramway commenced from the pier to transport the armaments and supplies around the depot.

The pier was eclipsed by the opening of Powder Pier No. 2 in 1899 and was demolished *c.* 1918. However, a tiny fragment of one of the wooden supporting piles can still be seen off the Camber.

Priddy's Hard Shell Pier – The provision of a new shell store led to the building of this pier in 1879 on the site of the Laboratory Jetty. In 1899, the pier was lengthened and an additional structure was built alongside it on the southern side. Both of the depot's tramways, of 18-inch and 30-inch gauge, ran out onto the piers. The southern pier was demolished in the 1950s but the other still remains. It is not accessible to the public but can be viewed through the fence by the entrance to Explosion! The Museum of Naval Firepower opened in March 2001, following the closure of the depot in 1988. The museum was acquired in 2009 by the Portsmouth Naval Base Property Trust.

Priddy's Hard Powder Pier No. 2 – Built in 1899 to serve a new magazine complex, only the pier head and a few iron piles can still be seen.

Forton Lake Jetty – The small concrete structure is used for the waterbus service that serves Portsmouth Historic Dockyard, Gunwharf Quays, Royal Navy Submarine Museum and Explosion!

Royal Clarence Victualling Yard

On 13 September 1845, the railway was extended from Gosport station for 600 yards into the Royal Clarence Yard, at the suggestion of Prince Albert, to enable a private station to be established for the Royal Family during their visits to Osborne House on the Isle of Wight. A large station, known as 'Royal Victoria' was built on a 520-foot platform, and a covered gangway led to a small pier from which the Royal Yacht *Alberta* sailed to the island. The pier was built northwards extending from the entrance to the goods pier. Nearby was another pier where fuel was shipped in and out of the yard. This had a double track line connected to the railway that ran into the yard, but wagons could only be fly-shunted as the pier could not take the weight of a locomotive.

A small pontoon pier, erected in the Royal Clarence Victualling Yard in 1845, for the private use of Queen Victoria and her family when sailing to and from Osborne House on the Isle of Wight aboard the Royal Yachts.

Following Queen Victoria's death at Osborne on 22 January 1901, her body was brought back to the mainland on 1 February aboard *Alberta,* to the Clarence Yard Royal Pier and Station. The body lay overnight in the station waiting room, under guard, before it was taken aboard the funeral train to Victoria station in London. The station platform had to be extended by 50 feet to accommodate the train, which left the station eight minutes late. This was because the distinguished dignitaries aboard (who included the new King Edward VII and the German Kaiser), seated according to royal protocol and rank, had been directed to the wrong seats due to an official not realising that the train was reversing at Fareham and the front carriage would become the back carriage and vice versa. However the time was made up on the journey and the train actually arrived at Victoria two minutes early. The funeral cortege, with the Royal coffin aboard a gun carriage, then made its way through the streets of London before boarding another train at Paddington bound for Windsor Castle. On arrival at the castle and following a remembrance service in St George's Chapel, the Queen's body was placed in the Albert Memorial Chapel to lie in state before it was placed beside her beloved Albert at the mausoleum at Frogmore.

Following the decision of Edward VII, in 1902, to effectively abandon Osborne House and give it to the nation, the Royal Pier in the Clarence Yard was used only sporadically as the Royal Family tended to use the South Railway Jetty in Portsmouth Dockyard. Eventually, the Royal Pier was removed, although the fuel pier can still be seen.

A fine postcard view of Gosport Hard following the improvements of the 1920s, which included a new landing pontoon for the Portsmouth ferry, added in 1925. Five vessels are moored at the pontoon and beyond them can be seen the floating bridge/chain ferry that operated between 1840 and 1959.

The Gosport Ferry Pontoon photographed in November 2010. Dating from the 1980s, the pontoon is due to be replaced in 2011. Two of the ferries can be seen: *Portsmouth Queen* in the foreground and either *Spirit of Gosport* or *Spirit of Portsmouth* behind.

Gosport Hard and Ferry Pontoon

The service between Gosport and Portsmouth is the busiest short route ferry crossing in the country, making some 67,000 trips each year and carrying around three million foot passengers. The short, five-minute ferry journey saves a twenty-mile trip by road.

The local watermen and their wherries had transported passengers and goods across Portsmouth Harbour between slipways (known locally as 'Hards') for centuries, but their trade grew following the establishment of Portsmouth as a Naval Base during the reign of Henry VIII (1509–47) and the settlement of naval personnel and dockyard workers in Gosport. In 1602, Stephen Riddleston and John Jeffries of Gosport held the ferry rights (and had done for some time), for which they paid a rent to the Crown, but this was challenged by three other Gosport residents. The case was taken to the Court of the Exchequer, which ruled that the rights of the public ferry service be given exclusively to the inhabitants of the Borough of Gosport. Two prominent residents of the town would regulate the ferry and be responsible for keeping order, safety and fares. In addition, there should be twenty serviceable boats for passengers and three for horse traffic. Fares were not properly regulated, however, until an Act of Parliament was passed in 1809 in a bid to stop overcharging, although a fixed fare schedule was not put in place until 1835.

A serious competitor to the watermen's ferries, a floating bridge, began running between Gosport and Old Portsmouth on 4 May 1840. Operated by the Port of Portsmouth Floating Bridge Company, and constructed by Acramans of Bristol to a design by J. M. Rendel, the bridge was 100 feet long, 60 feet wide and was powered by two steam engines driving oak cogs engaged on iron chains laid across the harbour. The bridge, which was named *Victoria*, proved to be immediately popular, not only as it made the transportation of vehicular traffic and goods easier, but it enabled the citizens of Portsmouth to easily connect to the railway opened to Gosport in November 1841. During the first six months of operation, 220,000 passengers, 13,965 carriages, 3,964 horses, 1,763 cattle and the Royal Mail coach for London were all carried on the twelve-minute crossing and, as a result of its success, a second bridge, named *Albert*, was soon added. In 1860, extensive repairs and improvements were carried out to Gosport Hard and four years later *Victoria* was replaced by a new bridge, christened *Alexandra*.

The watermen tried to counter the threat of the floating bridges by introducing fast steam launches, which gained back some of the foot traffic from the bridges. In 1875, the Gosport watermen organised themselves into the Gosport & Portsea Watermen's Steam Launch Company in a bid to provide a regular and reliable service. Following the opening of the railway extension to Portsmouth Harbour in 1876 and the provision of a free public landing stage, the Gosport ferries were able to operate their boats close to the new harbour station. However, in 1883 a rival appeared for the Gosport Company: the Port of Portsmouth Steam Launch & Towing Company, who in addition to providing passenger ferries also offered a towing service for sailing vessels in and out of the harbour. Eventually, following much rivalry, the two companies came to an agreement in 1888 to pool and share the ferry takings. The standard single ferry fare of ½d remained so until 1921 when it was increased to 1d. A few watermen continued to operate on their own, particularly at night when the two companies operated no service. The Floating Bridge Company also operated their own steam launches and in 1891 added the new bridge *Duchess of York* after *Albert* had sunk at its moorings.

In 1922, Gosport Council commenced work on major improvements to the waterfront, which included a new Ferry Gardens, esplanade, quay and steel sectional pontoon. The pontoon was opened in 1925 but partially sank during a storm two years later and was not fully operational again until 1930.

By the 1950s, the floating bridges were showing their age and becoming unreliable due to the build up of sandbanks in the harbour off Gosport, which made it difficult for them to dock. As a result, local businesses deserted the bridges, while foot passengers preferred the ferries because they took them to the dockyard, harbour station and closer to the city centre. The bridges began to lose money and, on 15 December 1959, they suddenly ceased operating and never resumed.

The formal merging of the Gosport and Portsmouth companies took place in 1963 and they became known as the Portsmouth Harbour Ferry Company. At the time, each company had four vessels: Gosport – *Ferry Queen* (introduced in 1959 and the first diesel vessel on the route), *Ferry Prince*, *Ferry Princess* and *Ferry Belle* and Portsmouth – *Vadne*, *Vita*, *Venus* and *Vesta*. Four of the vessels – *Ferry Belle*, *Ferry Prince*, *Ferry Princess* and *Vadne* were disposed off and the others were largely restricted to excursion and relief duties, upon the introduction of *Portsmouth Queen* and *Gosport Queen* on 29 October 1966. The two new vessels could each carry 500 passengers and had a covered area for motorcycles and bicycles. In 1971, they were joined by the *Gay Enterprise* (changed to *Solent Enterprise* within a few years), which was mainly used for relief duties and for cruises around Portsmouth Harbour, the River Hamble and the Isle of Wight.

In 1982/83 Gosport Council rebuilt their landing stage in concrete with a fully enclosed walkway. This was later wrecked by a storm in December 1989, and the ferry had to be temporarily transferred to the Royal Clarence Yard for several weeks until the pontoon was rebuilt. Meanwhile, in 1984, the Portsmouth Harbour Ferry Company had acquired the Portsmouth pontoon from British Railways and, in 1989/90, built a new landing stage and brow.

In 2001, the new ferry *Spirit of Gosport* was introduced, followed by the *Spirit of Portsmouth* in June 2005. They joined the *Portsmouth Queen* and *Gosport Queen* as members of the current fleet, although the latter was not operating in 2010. The ferry is currently operated by Gosport Ferry Limited; a subsidiary of the Portsmouth Harbour Ferry Company, which itself is a wholly owned subsidiary of Falkland Islands Holdings following a £10 million takeover in 2004. The service operates 364 days a year and carries around 3.8 million passengers, bicycles, motor cycles and wheelchairs annually on the five-minute crossing. Sailings commence at 5.30 in the morning and continue at 15 minute (7½ minutes at peak hours and on Saturdays) intervals until midnight. In 2010, the ferries had a 99.8 per cent reliability rating.

A new ferry pontoon is due to be placed at Gosport in early 2011. As part of the agreement for them to use the Gosport pontoon, the Portsmouth Harbour Ferry Company contributes towards the maintenance costs.

Gosport New Pier

The New Pier was authorised in 1842 as a landing stage for the steamer service to Ryde. Designed by J. M. Rendel, Engineer for the Gosport floating bridge, the pier consisted of an iron walkway with a wooden deck leading to a floating pontoon. Messrs Fox of London commenced building the pier in August 1842 and it was completed the following year.

For four years, between 1843 and 1847, the pier was used as the terminus of the Ryde steamer service, which also called at the Victoria Pier in Old Portsmouth. Following the opening of the Albert Pier at Portsea in 1847, the Portsmouth and Ryde Steam Company's packets commenced their sailings from there, calling at Gosport New Pier and Portsmouth Victoria Pier on their way to Ryde.

The number of vessels calling at the pier declined during the 1850s until, under some pressure from the Admiralty, the Portsmouth and Ryde Steam Company announced they would no longer call at Gosport. The pier was officially closed on 24 June 1862 and, in February 1863, tenders were invited for the removal of the structure, which had suffered storm damage during the previous winter. The demolition of the pier was supervised by the Admiralty and some of the ironwork was auctioned off on 7 May 1863. A further auction of the remaining materials took place on 18 June 1863.

There was some agitation for a replacement pier and, in December 1867, it was reported that drawings for a new pier were available for inspection. In December 1871, a meeting was held to discuss applying for a Provisional Order for a Gosport Pier and Wharf scheme, but nothing came of the proposal. No replacement steamer pier was to be built and the people of Gosport had to travel to Portsmouth or Stokes Bay to catch the Isle of Wight ferries.

In 1867, a pier for the Coastguard was opened close to the site of the New Pier and this was used until the 1880s to auction off vessels.

Haslar Marina Millennium Pier

The pier was built in 2001 by Mildren, at a cost of £450,000, as part of the Haslar Marina which had opened in 1993. The marina is one of the largest in the area, capable of holding nearly 700 boats. An old Trinity House Lightship acts as the marina's clubhouse. The pier, which has a solid concrete base, has proved to be a popular angling centre and offers a fine walk out into Portsmouth Harbour.

By the entrance to the pier is a mosaic commemorating a defence chain that used to stretch across the harbour at this point, and the Timespace sundial,

A view of the Haslar Millennium Pier at Gosport in January 2011. The pier was erected as part of a marina development in 2001.

inspired by Albert Einstein's Theory of Relativity and erected in 2000 as part of the Renaissance of Portsmouth Harbour Millennium project.

Haslar Hospital Jetty/Fort Blockhouse Pier/HMS *Hornet* Petrol Pier

The foundations of the Haslar Naval Hospital were laid in 1746 and by the time of its completion in 1762 it was the largest brick-built building in the kingdom, capable of holding 1,800 patients. A jetty was built to receive the hospital boats that ferried the sick patients to the hospital from the fleet at anchor in Spithead and Portsmouth Dockyard, and also to take delivery of supplies, including munitions. Rails were laid from the jetty to the hospital receiving room to transport the sick by means of wheeled ambulances, pushed along the track by sick berth staff. In addition, an 18-inch narrow-gauge railway commenced from the jetty, transporting munitions to Fort Gilkicker and Fort Blockhouse, and also possibly patients to the Zymotics Isolation Hospital.

The Haslar Conservation Area was founded in 1990 to look at ways of preserving and developing the former naval areas of the Haslar Naval Hospital, Fort Blockhouse, HMS *Hornet* and the Victorian Gunboat Yard. In 2001, Haslar

The jetty that once served the Haslar Hospital at Gosport now forms part of the Submarine Museum. The jetty is seen here in January 2011 with part of HMS *Alliance* visible on the left.

Hospital was designated a Grade II listed building, but was closed as a hospital in 2009. The jetty survives as part of the Royal Navy Submarine Museum, opened in 1980, and can be visited free of charge as it is not one of the chargeable attractions of the museum. During the summer, it is used by the Water Bus that connects the waterside attractions of Portsmouth and Gosport. The jetty still features some of the narrow-gauge railway track and, on the path leading to the hospital, a section of the ambulance tramway track can also be seen.

At the nearby Fort Blockhouse, a small pier was built for the Royal Engineers Submarine Mining School in 1873, which was extended along the shore in 1882 and had rails to transport mines across the site. The ironwork of the lattice girders and supporting piles can still be seen under the platform. In 1905, the Submarine Service Base, known as HMS *Dolphin,* was established on the site and, in the following year, they extended the pier in ferro-concrete creating a small enclosed harbour. During the 1960s, the jetty was widened and remains to this day, although the submarine base was closed in 1998.

The adjoining blockhouse, known as Blockhouse 2, was also once used for submarines, and in 1910 a petrol pier was built, which turned at a right angle about a third of the way along. In 1921, a Coastal Motor Base was established on the site, which became known as HMS *Hornet* in 1925. The base was closed in 1956 but the pier can still be seen.

STOKES BAY

A quiet bay to the south of Gosport, Stokes Bay, was developed in mid-Victorian times with a series of defensive moats and ramparts (known locally as 'Palmerston's Follies') and a railway and pier that offered a ferry service to the Isle of Wight. There was also an attempt to turn the area into a fashionable watering place when, in 1827, property developer Robert Cruickshank acquired land at Alverstoke, close to Stokes Bay. Cruickshank engaged architect Thomas Ellis Owen (*see also* Southsea) to design an elegant crescent of Regency houses, and the Anglesey Hotel was opened at one end of the crescent in 1830. Gardens were laid out in front of the crescent and a library and two bath houses (one each for ladies and gentlemen) were provided.

Cruickshank named his new watering place 'Angleseyville' in honour of the Marquis of Anglesey, one of the heroes of the Battle of Waterloo. In 1830, Princess Victoria, accompanied by her mother the Duchess of Kent, stayed there and she was taken around the Royal Clarence Yard at Gosport, where in 1845 she would acquire her own railway station and pier for her trips to Osborne House. Cruickshank added other attractions: a racecourse, bathing machines on the beach and entertainers. However, following his death in 1853 the resort did not develop further. The wealthy of the area tended to turn their back on Angleseyville in favour of Southsea where Ellis Owen's architecture really flourished.

The beach of Stokes Bay was developed as a recreational area in the 1920s when a promenade, tennis courts, putting greens and refreshment rooms were built. The bay remains a popular rendezvous during the summer, but is otherwise often quiet.

Leather's/Submarine Mining Establishment Pier

The introduction of steam propulsion by the Royal Navy led to the abandonment of the booms and chains that protected harbours and ports, requiring a new form of defence. Since 1863, a joint naval and military committee had been experimenting with submarine explosives, and they recommended that the Royal Engineers should be responsible for their design, construction and operation. The first submarine mining company was formed in 1871 and in 1878 the Portsmouth

Company of the Southern Mining Militia was stationed at Fort Monckton between Gosport and Stokes Bay. The Portsmouth Company was superseded in 1884 by the 4th Company Gosport Submarines Mines.

In 1890, it was felt that an additional mining school was needed in the area and one was established west of Fort Gilkicker, close to Stokes Bay Pier. The site chosen was where, in 1863, the building yard of contractor John Towlerton Leather[6] had been leased from Crown land for his construction of the six Spithead forts and a number of shore batteries. A slender iron pier, complete with crane, was erected to land the Cornish granite and Portland stone used to build the forts. On 28 February 1863, the pier was used to receive the passengers of the steamer *Gareloch*, which had been barred from using the main Stokes Pier by contractors armed with clubs who had not been paid for building it. Swimming contests were also held from the pier, such as in June 1867, when they included diving off the end of the pier, and swimming to the railway pier. The pier was taken over by the Submarine Mining Establishment and was used mainly for training purposes. A narrow gauge railway was built by the Royal Engineers to connect the two mining establishments.

In 1905, the decision was taken that all underwater defences should be taken over by the Royal Navy and the Submarine Mining companies of the Royal Engineers were abandoned. The Royal Engineers School of Electric Lighting moved into the Stokes Bay establishment to train in the use of electric searchlights for defence but had little use for the pier and, on 12 July 1914, work began on its demolition.

The Electric Lighting School remained at Stokes Bay until the 1950s and the abandoned buildings remained extant for a further twenty years. Today, pieces of concrete rubble show where it once stood.

Railway and Ferry Pier

The crossing of the Solent, between Portsmouth and Ryde, by the Port of Portsmouth & Ryde United Steam Packet Company, was often the target of much criticism regarding its services and the condition of its boats. The earliest proposal for a crossing to the island from Stokes Bay was made by the London & South Western Railway in 1846. Their 'Gosport Pier and Branch Railway' was to be a mile long and would terminate in a wooden pier about 900 feet long. It was thought that both the railway and pier would be used by Queen Victoria to access Osborne House[7]. Nonetheless, the plans were quickly dropped as L&SWR concentrated its efforts on reaching Portsmouth and battling with the Great Western Railway in other parts of Hampshire.

---

[6] John Towlerton Leather (1804–85) was an eminent civil engineer and contractor who completed a number of contracts for the Admiralty in addition to building the Spithead Forts; including the Portland Breakwater and extensions to Portsmouth Dockyard (with George Smith). He was also the founder, in 1864, of the Hunslet Engine Company.

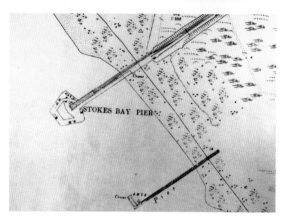

Above: the Submarine Mining Pier at Stokes Bay: in the background is Fort Gilkicker. The iron pier was erected in 1863 as a landing stage to receive materials for the building of Spithead forts and was demolished in 1914.

Right: An 1898 map showing both the railway/ferry and Submarine Mining Establishment piers at Stokes Bay. The submarine mining base has been blanked out on the map for security reasons.

A postcard showing Stokes Bay Pier and Beach *c.* 1910. The pier was 600 feet long and featured a covered platform station at the end and a three-sided landing stage. The Submarine Mining Establishment Pier can also just been seen on the other side of the railway pier.

The Pier & Beach, Stokes Bay   12

Families on the beach at Stokes Bay pose for the photographer in the 1920s. The pier was now under the control of the Admiralty, who added a building on to the pier head. A train can just be seen parked outside the pier head station.

An aerial view of
Stokes Bay showing
the three-sided pier
head, covered railway
station and the
building added on
the pier head by the
Admiralty.

A derelict looking
Stokes Bay Pier
pictured towards the
end of its life. Work
began on demolishing
the pier in 1972 and
it was completed
three years later.

A view taken on
Stokes Bay Pier
looking towards the
covered platform
station.

However, in 1854 the scheme was revived by the Stokes Bay & Isle of Wight Railway Telegraphic Steamboat Company, which was registered on 21 November and planned to run a chain ferry (otherwise known as a floating bridge) to the Isle of Wight from new piers to be built at Stokes Bay and Ryde. By the following year, the company had changed their name to Stokes Bay Railway & Pier Company and were registered with a share capital of £24,000 in £10 shares. The railway was estimated to cost £13,200 and the pier £7,000. The L&SWR once again announced their opposition, but on 14 August 1855 the Stokes Bay Railway & Pier Act was passed after the Stokes Bay Company agreed to let other ferry companies (particularly the Port of Portsmouth & Ryde Steam Packet Company) use the pier. The Act authorised the construction of the 850-foot pier (later reduced in length to 600 feet) and a 1.75 mile railway to run onto it, branching from the London & South Western Railway's line to Gosport. The floating bridge would measure 120 feet long by 20 feet wide and would be powered by two engines driving the screw propeller. Vehicles and livestock would be loaded via a ramp from the pier to a central roadway on the bridge located between two passenger saloons. At the first AGM of the company, held at the Anglesey Hotel on 3 October 1855, the expectation was raised that the Royal Family would use the railway and pier following interest in the project by Prince Albert. The engineer for the project was named as Hamilton Fulton and the appointed contractors were Messrs Smith and Knight, who had tendered £16,200 to build the railway and £8,000 for the pier.

However, the Act only authorised the works at Stokes Bay, so an associated company, the Isle of Wight Steam Bridge Company, was formed in November 1855 with a capital of £20,000 to handle the works at Ryde (*see the Ryde Victoria chapter*). The Bill for the floating bridge was placed before the House of Commons on 18 February 1856 and again a week later but then opposition from the Admiralty, who claimed the chains would injure their vessels in Spithead, caused it to be abandoned.

A revised plan was soon proposed by the Stokes Bay Railway & Pier Company and the now renamed Isle of Wight Ferry Company to run a conventional ferry service between the new piers at Ryde and Stokes Bay. The change of propulsion from floating bridge to steam ferry led the Port of Portsmouth & Ryde Steam Packet Company to oppose the scheme (they had supported the floating bridge in exchange for landing rights at Stokes Bay Pier) and lined up alongside them were the Ryde Pier Company, Portsmouth Corporation and the Ryde Commissioners. The latter withdrew their hostility after safeguards were given over their interests for Ryde Esplanade and, despite the opposition, the Bill received the Royal Assent on 21 July 1856.

In April 1858, a joint working board was set up with the Isle of Wight Ferry Company, who had commenced their works at Ryde. In contrast, difficulty in raising the necessary capital meant little was happening at Stokes Bay. However,

---

[7] However, the Queen rarely used the Stokes Bay pier and railway, preferring her private pier and station in the Royal Clarence Yard, Gosport, although large quantities of her baggage and supplies were sometimes sent via Stokes Bay.

an agreement was reached on 9 March 1858 with the London & South Western Railway for them to work the railway in perpetuity at a yearly rental of £1,600 (soon increased to £1,800) and a year later, in March 1859, the new contractor, Thomas Brassey, finally commenced work on the pier and the railway. Brassey was a respected railway contractor with a high reputation who had built several railways for the L&SWR including the direct line to Portsmouth. By the end of 1860, Brassey had presented bills to the tune of £11,363 and indicated that he was prepared to accept shares in the cash-strapped company in lieu of some of the payment.

The work continued apace and, on 5 January 1863, Captain Tyler, a Government inspector, came to inspect the railway and pier although they had not been fully completed. Tyler recommended that additional piles be added to the pier head and the platforms lengthened on the incomplete station. However, Brassey, who had not been paid for some time, ordered his men to down tools. Matters reached a head on 28 February 1863 when the 45-ton iron paddle steamer *Gareloch* (which was 140 feet long and could carry 300 passengers) was unable to land passengers on the pier during the first test crossing from Ryde due to Brassey's men barring the way with clubs. The steamer had to unload instead on Leather's Pier nearby (later the Submarine Mining Establishment Pier), built for workers on the Spithead fortification works. A further test crossing was made on 30 March 1863 when the pier was this time accessible and Captain Tyler declared that the railway and pier were fit for opening. In a spirit of reconciliation, the contractors invited the directors of the company to a formal lunch.

A description of the pier was given in the *Portsmouth Guardian* on 30 April 1863:

'The pier, which is reckoned will be accessible for steamers at all seasons and in any weather, is about 600 feet in length. On it is a commodious shed capable of receiving a train of five railway carriages so that passengers can step straight out of the train under shelter and close to the water's edge. There are also commodious waiting rooms for ladies and gentlemen, along with the requisite offices. The pier head is admirably adopted for a promenade and has a superficial area of nearly 4,000 square feet available for that purpose.'

A ramp led down from the pier to a three-sided landing stage, capable of accommodating three steamers, but was rarely, if ever, utilised.

The service between Stokes Bay and Ryde, along with the Stokes Bay railway, was officially opened on Easter Monday, 6 April 1863, although the new Victoria Pier at Ryde would not be finished until 1 November 1864 and the existing pier at Ryde had to be used for the time being. The company played up the fact that the crossing, at fifteen minutes, was shorter than that from Portsmouth and that 'unsavoury town' was avoided. On 1 May 1863, the *Chancellor* (170 feet long, able to carry 700 passengers) entered service alongside *Gareloch*. The fifteen-minute crossing was operated with five sailings daily from Ryde and seven from Stokes Bay, with two sailings each way on Sundays. However, the latter were soon withdrawn from 1 August 1863. The fares for the crossing were 1s single and 1s 6d return (first class) and 9d and 1s 2d return (second class). *Chancellor* broke her back on rocks at the new harbour at Ventnor on 1 July 1863, and in the following month *Gareloch* was temporarily put out of action, and the Stokes Bay–Ryde route had to be worked by the Portsmouth and Southampton companies. *Gareloch* returned and in 1864 was joined by the small 100-foot steamer *Transit*. She continued the ill-luck of the company's fleet when, in June 1864, whilst berthing at Stokes Bay, a stoker crushed his head against the pier piling whilst stretching out his arm to save a passenger who had fallen into the sea. *Gareloch* was withdrawn in February 1865 and her replacement – a steam tug called *Ursa Major* – was found to be unsuitable after a few days' service.

The Stokes Bay Railway & Pier Company were by now in serious financial trouble, with debts of over £15,000. On 13 May 1865 it was acquired, along with the Isle of Wight Ferry Company and Ryde Victoria Pier, by the Ryde Pier Company for £23,000. Following the purchase, the Stokes Bay steamers were almost entirely re-directed to the main pier at Ryde and the steamer *Her Majesty* became the usual vessel to be introduced onto the route.

All the trains using the Stokes Bay line had to reverse at Gosport until a spur to connect it directly to the Fareham line was opened on 1 June 1865. At the same time, a station was opened just south of the triangle, originally called Stoke Road, but quickly renamed Gosport Road and Alverstoke, and sometimes just plain Gosport Road. Protracted negotiations with the War Office over the lease of land at Stokes Bay prevented the acquisition of the railway and pier by the L&SWR until 1875, when they paid £40,000. A further £658 was spent on improvements to the pier. The pier station, along with Gosport Road, came under the responsibility of the stationmaster at Gosport. During the 1880s, there were five steamer services daily in each direction, with three on Sundays, which were usually met by a train waiting on the pier. The 2½ mile crossing took fifteen minutes to complete and cost 1s for first class and 9d second class. The L&SWR liked to advertise the Stokes Bay crossing as the 'Family Route'.

The pier also took on the guise of a pleasure pier, with the introduction in the summer of 1867 of band concerts on Saturday afternoons by the Portsmouth Division of the Royal Marines. The decision to have the concerts had been taken following their success on Ryde Pier. A special train was even laid on from Fareham and Fort Brockhurst for those wishing to hear the music. The concerts were also held in 1868, when the Royal Marines performed pieces by Mozart, Beethoven, Mendelssohn, Rossini and Gungl. Refreshments were available for both railway customers and those who used the pier as a promenade and to listen to the bands. A bottle of iced ginger beer for example, cost 3d. Bathing also took place from the pier, although there were complaints during the summer of 1870 that people undressing on the pier and by the bathing machines on the beach were driving customers away from that 'agreeable promenade' (the pier) and the police had to be called. During the Royal Naval Reviews at Spithead, viewing places on the pier were at a premium and in 1885 cost 5s each.

The acquisition of the pier by the Admiralty was considered on a number of occasions. On 24 August 1870 the *Hampshire Telegraph & Sussex Chronicle* reported: 'INCREASED ACCOMMODATION FOR NAVAL STEAMERS – It is understood the Government have under consideration the proposal to extend the Stokes Bay Pier into the deep water of the Solent, so as to enable the largest ironclads of the Royal Navy to lie alongside the proposed landing place at low water.'

The Royal Family's journeys to and from Osborne House on the Isle of Wight were usually via the pier at the Royal Clarence Yard, Gosport, but on occasions the pier at Stokes Bay was also used. On 7 August 1871, the Duke of Edinburgh and the Crown Prince of Germany landed at the pier from the Royal Yacht *Elfin*, and Queen Victoria landed at the pier on 24 December 1882 during a visit to the Royal Naval Hospital at Haslar.

Further rebuilding was carried out on the pier in 1896, at a cost of £6,610, to renew the ironwork and enable the steamers to have easier access to the landing stage. Whilst the work was being carried out, a temporary platform of 420 feet in length was provided just north of the pier and connected to it by a temporary viaduct. A through train service from London Waterloo to Ryde via the pier was introduced, which took two hours forty-five minutes. Nevertheless, by this time, the Stokes Bay–Ryde route was in decline: the opening of the railway to Portsmouth Harbour in 1876 having diverted most of the traffic away. The service was reduced to summer only from 1902, and was closed altogether in 1913. The railway limped on for a further two years until closure on 30 October 1915.

From 1913 until 1916, the pier was used by the Royal Thames Yacht Club as a base for its annual regatta before it was leased to the Admiralty in June 1918. Four years later, in March 1922, they officially acquired the pier (along with the railway south of Gosport Road station) for use as an experimental torpedo research station named HMS *Vernon*. Additional buildings were added to the pier and they were used in the preparation of torpedoes for test runs and the recovery of dropped torpedoes.

After the Second World War, the pier was used for a time by the Royal Navy's degaussing service. By the 1960s, it had become derelict and buildings and the decking were removed to prevent people climbing onto and vandalising the pier. In July 1965, services to the Isle of Wight briefly returned to Stokes Bay (but not the pier) when Hovertravel Limited commenced a hovercraft service to Ryde. However, it was not well patronised and ceased at the end of the 1967 summer season.

Work began on removing the pier in 1972 and it took place over a three-year period, with the Royal Engineers blowing up the structure using various explosives until the last substantial remains were removed on 18 July 1975. However, remains of the supporting piles continued to cause a hazard to shipping and, between 1985 and 1987, ninety of the pile bases along with two crane bases were largely removed by the Royal Engineers based at the Marchwood diving establishment. Despite this, at very low tide, traces of the supports can still be seen and they are marked to shipping with buoys. A slipway at the end of Military Road indicates the site of the pier and much of the Stokes Bay branch is now a public footpath.

LEE-ON-THE-SOLENT

Lee-on-the-Solent is a small resort to the south-west of Gosport and was a personal creation of wealthy doctor John Newton Robinson of Newton Manor, Swanage. The area's potential as a resort was noted by Robinson's son Charles whilst he was cruising on his yacht in the Solent in 1884. Both father and son were keen sailors and members of the Cowes Yacht Club. Contracts were soon drawn up with agents acting for the local landowner, the Earl of Southampton, and a limited company was formed to develop what was just a tiny hamlet. The name of the new resort was coined by Robinson's agent Herbert Hannen.

Plots were laid out, which were developed by builders with substantial villas offering fine views of the Solent and the Isle of Wight, and parades of shops, a promenade, hotel and pier were built. A main piece of the jigsaw in Robinson's plans was the Lee-on-the-Solent Light Railway, built by the Lee-on-the-Solent Railway Company – of which he was the main shareholder. The line opened on 12 May 1894 and ended its journey at Lee from Fort Brockhurst with a station close to the pier entrance. In 1923, the line was taken over by the Southern Railway but it was never particularly successful and was closed to passengers from 1 January 1931 and goods from 30 September 1935.

Lee-on-the-Solent was never developed on a large scale and settled down to become a small resort. A push to send it into the big time was made with the construction of the Lee Tower complex in 1935 but the innovative building became a white elephant for much of its time and was demolished in 1971. Today, Lee is an attractive residential area.

Lee-on-the-Solent Pier

The pier at Lee-on-the-Solent was conceived in 1884 as one of the key points in John Robinson's plan to develop a new seaside resort. The pier was to replace a small wooden structure already in use, and the site for its construction was conveyed to Robinson for a nominal rent of 1s if demanded.

The Provisional Order for the construction of the pier was granted in 1885 and the design of Messrs Gailbraith & Church for a pier 750 feet in length was chosen.

Lee-on-the-Solent Pier was opened in 1888 as part of the development of a new seaside resort and is pictured here *c.* 1910 in its original form. The pier was 750 feet long and featured a bandstand and small pavilion on the pier head, and an attractive gabled toll house building. The photograph was taken close to where the railway station stood.

The pavilion on the pier at Lee-on-the-Solent played host to concert parties such as the Joy Bells, who appeared there in 1908, providing a mixture of light music and mirth.

A postcard scene taken from the roof of the Lee-on-the-Solent Pier Pavilion, *c.* 1914, looking along the pier to the shore. In the foreground is the bandstand and steps to the landing stage whilst the narrowness of the pier deck is clearly seen. On the right of the picture is the railway station, opened in 1894 but closed to passengers on the last day of 1930.

The Pier Pavilion at Lee-on-the-Solent as featured on a picture postcard from the 1920s. By this time the bandstand that stood in front of it had been incorporated into the building. It is said that in 1911 Noël Coward appeared in a talent show in the pavilion.

The fire on 19 June 1932, which destroyed the pavilion on Lee-on-the-Solent Pier. The blaze was thought to have been caused by faulty electrics and a group of fishermen trapped on the landing stage had to be rescued by speedboat.

A postcard sent in 1936 of the sea end of Lee-on-the-Solent Pier after the pavilion fire of 1932, showing that the building was not replaced.

In 1935, the shore end of the pier was totally transformed with the construction of Lee Tower, which was opened on Boxing Day of that year. The building housed a cinema, dance hall, restaurant, lounge bars and roof terrace, along with a 120-foot-high tower.

In 1940, a breach was blown in Lee-on-the-Solent Pier as a defence measure and, subsequently, the shore end of the pier was washed away. This postcard view shows what remained of the pier in the 1950s until it was finally cleared away in 1958. Both the swimming pool and Lee Tower have also gone; the latter in 1971 after proving to be a costly white elephant.

The shore end of the pier was approached from Marine Parade and an attractive gabled entrance building was constructed, resting on an abutment of Portland cement concrete. The deck of the pier was twelve feet wide for a length of 600 feet, widening out to 34 feet at the 150-foot-long pier head. This came to house a small pavilion (known as the 'Golden Hall') and bandstand. The superstructure of the pier was described as consisting of 'cast iron screw piles, driven in about an average of 9 feet into the sea bed, support the superstructure, which consists of wrought iron piles, strongly braced together with angle-iron bars, and united longitudinally by wrought iron lattice girders, which carry the joists of the deck. The whole is surmounted by a neat iron railing. At the seaward extremity are timber fender piles, and along the eastern side of the pier-head extends a landing stage for steamers and boats, composed of massive timber piling, well braced, and abutting against iron screw piles driven diagonally, to take the thrust of vessels coming alongside, and relieve the main structure from strains thus arising.'

The appointed contractor, Mr F. Bevis of Portsmouth, commenced work in 1886 and, by the autumn of 1887, the pier was virtually complete, save for the entrance building. Mr Horace A. Alexander, architect, of 72 Cannon Street, London, submitted the design for the entrance building, which was erected by Mr Wareham of Titchfield at a cost of £334.

Robinson had personally financed the £8,500 cost of erecting the pier and, in autumn 1887, he formed the Lee-on-the-Solent Pier Company with a capital of £12,500 in £5 shares to acquire and work it. A share in the company was payable with a £1 deposit on application, £1 on allotment, £2 at the expiration of two months from the date of allotment and a balance of £1 when called up. The directors of the company were named as Sir John Charles Robinson, his son Charles Edmund Robinson (a Barrister-at-Law), Horace A. Alexander, Alfred Ernest Petrie and Thomas Andrews Raynes, who was Chairman of the Ventnor Local Board. The share capital was slow to be taken up though, and the pier remained the virtual personal property of Robinson. In 1904, it was conveyed to the Lee-on-the-Solent Pier Company, whose shares were entirely held by Robinson and his family!

The Pier Pavilion was used by concert parties such as the Joy Bells and Noel Coward is reputed to have appeared in a talent show on the pier in 1911. Boat trips were also available from the landing stage and, in the early years of the twentieth century, the New Launch Company from Portsmouth ran their steam launch *Venus* from the pier from May until the end of September. Eight trips ran daily between Lee and the Clarence Pier, Southsea. The ride took forty-five minutes and the return fare was 1s. However, the main steamer companies in the area did not call at the pier. During the First World War, King Albert of the Belgians was landed at the pier. In March 1923, the Lloyd's Motor Packet Service was introduced by Lloyd's of Southampton, between Southampton, Lee-on-the-Solent and Cowes.

In 1929, Albert Bradley became the youngest Pier Master in the country when he was appointed to look after the pier. On 19 June 1932, Bradley was at the pier when smoke was seen coming from the pavilion. He called the local telephone exchange, who alerted an RAF fire crew at a nearby base. Stepping inside the burning pavilion, Bradley found the restaurant manageress Mrs Brickwood dazed and managed to get her outside, in spite of his trousers being alight. A group of fishermen found themselves trapped at the end of the pier and had to jump into the sea, where Commander Miller rescued them in his speedboat. The pavilion was beyond saving and a portion of the deck was hacked away to prevent the fire from spreading along the pier. The damage to the pier was estimated at £3,500 and the Harry Lawrence Dance Band lost all their instruments, valued at £500. A faulty electrical connection that joined the navigation light and pavilion radio was said to have been the cause of the blaze.

The pavilion was not rebuilt and the pier was now used just as a promenade and for fishing. However, in 1935 the pier owners, Solent Properties and its subsidiary company the Lee Tower Company, commenced building the imposing Lee Tower entertainment complex at the entrance to the pier, which necessitated the sweeping away of the old gabled entrance building. The Lee Tower housed a cinema, dance hall, restaurant, lounge bars, roof terrace and a 120-foot-high tower, and was opened on Boxing Day 1935 by Admiral Sir Arthur Wanstall, assisted by the Mayor of Gosport. The cost of erecting the building sent the Lee Tower Company into liquidation in 1937.

A new landing stage, erected at the pier by Messrs Yates, Cook & Darbyshire, was completed in December 1935. The old landing stage remained *in situ* for a further two years until its removal by the Risdon Beazley Marine Trading Company. However, the pier was in receivership and negotiations were opened in 1938 for Gosport Council to acquire it. However, the coming of the Second World War curtailed these and in 1940 the pier was breached for defence purposes. Heavy seas then proceeded to wash away much of the shore end of the structure. The Lee Tower, meanwhile, was camouflaged to prevent it being used as a landmark by the Luftwaffe.

After the war, the pier was acquired by Gosport Council, who announced plans to renovate it. However, the money acquired from the War Damage Commission was spent elsewhere and the remains of the pier were cleared away in 1958. The Lee Tower did reopen after the war but never paid its way. In 1958, the cinema was closed and the complex was used for all-in wrestling and ten-pin bowling before it was demolished in 1971.

WARSASH AND HAMBLE

Warsash is an attractive maritime village situated on the east bank of the mouth of the River Hamble, favoured as a yachting marina and home to the Warsash Maritime Academy, part of Southampton Solent University, which utilises a former Admiralty pier. A small ferry connects Warsash with Hamble-le-Rice on the opposite bank of the river, which is home to a large fuel terminal.

Admiralty Pier, Warsash

A pier was built at Warsash by the Admiralty for the Royal Naval Air Service in 1913, which was 915 feet long and encased in concrete for two-thirds of its length, with the remainder consisting of 12-inch timber piles. The public were originally allowed to use the pier, but by 1920 were prevented from doing so as the area was in use by the Air Ministry and they were in dispute with landowner Commander Chilcott. There was talk of the pier being disposed off but it was still in use for the landing of boats and, in 1938, it was reconstructed in concrete. During the Second World War, the pier and naval base was known as HMS *Tormentor*.

The pier is now used by Warsash Maritime Academy – a faculty of Southampton Solent University – in the education, consultancy, research and training in the international shipping and offshore oil industries. The pier head features two totally enclosed lifeboats on outrigger davits, one semi-enclosed lifeboat on a single pivot gravity davit, and a slewing single arm davit for Davit Launched Liferaft operations and the launching and recovery of rescue boats. In addition, there are two open lifeboats (kept in the water) and a pontoon for transfer and throwover liferaft exercises.

Warsash – Hamble Ferry

There are a number of jetties at Warsash, including one for the ferry service across the River Hamble to Hamble-le-Rice. In 1897, Fareham Rural District Council proposed building a pier from the Hard for the ferry service but changed their minds.

A pier was built for the Admiralty at Warsash in 1913, which was reconstructed in concrete in 1938 and used during the Second World War as a naval base known as HMS *Tormentor*. The pier is now used by Warsash Maritime Academy – a faculty of Southampton Solent University – in education, consultancy, research and training in the international shipping and off-shore oil industries.

An interesting postcard showing the naval ratings based at TS Mercury at Hamble, about to dive off the jetty *c*. 1910. This shore-based naval training centre for boys entering the Royal Navy moved to Hamble in 1892 and was closed in 1968.

The small jetty at Warsash used for the ferry service across the River Hamble to Hamble-le-Rice. The old concrete waiting shelter, and the ferries themselves, are painted in a vivid shade of pink. The photograph was taken in November 2010.

The ferry can carry up to twelve passengers per journey and operates on demand. The boats, as well as the Warsash Ferry shelter, are painted in a vivid shade of pink. The landing stage at Warsash is a simple wooden jetty laid on concrete supports, whilst that at Hamble-le-Rice consists of a steel lattice bridge leading to a floating pontoon.

Hamble Fuel Terminal

The B.P. Fuel Terminal at Hamble was opened in 1924, and a pipeline under Southampton Water connects it to the oil refinery at Fawley. An iron and steel jetty, to receive the oil tankers, was built upon opening and was extended in 1943/44.

NETLEY

Netley (sometimes known as Netley Abbey) is a village on the east bank of Southampton Water, which was once home to the large Royal Victoria Military Hospital – the site of which is now part of the Royal Victoria Country Park. The village's main attraction is Netley Abbey, which is the most complete surviving Cistercian monastery in southern England.

Royal Victoria Hospital Pier

The original pier at Netley was a 300-foot wooden structure erected by Major Ravenhill of the Royal Engineers to enable Queen Victoria to disembark on 19 May 1856. She came to lay the foundation stone of this first purpose-built army hospital, brought to bear following the medical failures of the Crimean War.

Set in 200 acres, the massive three-storey-high main building, which was over a quarter of a mile long, was not completed until March 1863, at a cost of £350,000. Built to house 1,000 patients, the grand design of the building was soon criticised for being impractical. Both Florence Nightingale and Lord Palmerston were amongst the critics who agreed with the sentiment 'the comfort and recovery of the patients has been sacrificed to make a building that would cut a dash when looked at from Southampton Water'. On 31 July 1864, the Prince of Wales landed at the hospital's pier from the Royal Yacht *Fairy* to lay the foundation stone for a memorial to the medical officers who fell in the Crimean War.

In 1865, the wooden pier was replaced by a 570-foot cast iron structure designed by the prolific pier engineer Eugenius Birch. The pier was 15 feet wide and featured an enlarged area on the pier head and two shelters at the entrance. Benches were provided for patients who enjoyed relaxing on the pier. The new pier received a royal visitor on 6 August 1867 when Queen Victoria visited the hospital aboard the Royal Yacht *Alberta*. Excursion vessels also occasionally used the pier, such as on 12 September 1872, when the steamer *Princess of Wales* landed visitors from the Portsmouth area to view the ruins of Netley Abbey.

The original plan for the pier envisaged a structure double the length of that constructed and, as a result, the shorter pier failed to reach deep water, causing great

The Pier. R.V. Hospital. Netley. B.4.

The Royal Victoria Hospital at Netley was completed in 1863 as the army's first purpose-built military hospital and, two years later, an iron pier was built to receive patients arriving by hospital ships. The pier was 570 feet long and designed by Eugenius Birch; responsible for such noted pleasure piers as Brighton West, Blackpool North and Eastbourne. This postcard of the pier was issued *c.* 1910.

After 1901, the pier was rarely used as a landing stage and it became largely used as a relaxation area for the hospital patients. This postcard shows the pier head crowded with men, some of them in special bed carts.

A delightful postcard of the Royal Victoria Hospital as seen from the pier on a snowy day in January 1918.

A postcard of the entrance to Netley Royal Victoria Hospital Pier, posted on 14 May 1914. A shelter similar to those at the entrance was placed at the pier head along with a couple of small cranes.

difficulty to hospital ships landing patients. This led, in 1901, to the abandonment of the pier as a landing stage and all troops from overseas were disembarked at Southampton Docks and taken directly to the hospital's own railway station. The pier was left *in situ* however, as it was a popular recreation area for the hospital patients. Locals from Netley village were also sometimes allowed to use the pier and it was the prime vantage point during the Netley Regatta.

In common with its seaside cousins, the pier was breached as a defence measure during the Second World War. However, at the conflict's end, the pier was sadly not thought worthy of restoration and all the remaining spans had been removed by 1955. An information board giving details of the pier is sited at its former entrance.

The hospital itself only outlived the pier by a few years, in spite of its proud war record. During the First World War, 50,000 patients had been treated there, which was surpassed during the second great conflict when it was in the hands of US forces who, it was said, liked to drive their jeeps along the corridors! However, the hospital was now deemed uneconomic to run and was largely closed in 1958. A fire damaged the main building in June 1963, which led to its demolition in 1966. The only buildings to survive were the asylum (which became a Police Training College in 1978), officer's mess (converted into luxury apartments) and the Royal Chapel (now a museum). In 1979, Hampshire County Council purchased the grounds and in the following year opened them to the public as the Royal Victoria Country Park.

SOUTHAMPTON

Southampton is the largest city in Hampshire and one of the biggest commercial ports in Europe, with strong associations with the large cruise ships that have used it down the years, particularly the ill-fated *Titanic*. What is lesser known is that Southampton was a favoured place for sea bathing in the late eighteenth/early nineteenth centuries, after Frederick, Prince of Wales, bathed there in 1750. A spa was also developed following the discovery of a spring in 1755 containing compounds of iron and sulphur, and the water was pumped into a fountain with a fluted pedestal. Hotels, gardens, indoor baths, assembly rooms and subscription libraries were opened in the area around the River Test but by 1818 the resort was in decline and was eventually killed off by the expansion of the commercial docks. Nevertheless, for many years the city could boast of a fine promenade/pleasure pier, the now derelict Royal Pier.

Itchen Pier

During the early 1860s, the steamers of the Southampton & Isle of Wight Royal Mail Steam Packet Company occasionally called at this obscure pier in addition to the Royal Pier. The pier proved to be short-lived and the area began to be developed from the 1870s, with quays for commercial goods traffic.

The Itchen Ferry connected the western and eastern suburbs of Southampton and this was joined by a Floating Bridge/Chain Ferry, which was opened on 23 November 1836. The ferry, which is featured on a painting by L. S. Lowry, was finally closed on 11 June 1977 upon the opening of the Itchen Bridge.

Town Quay

The Town Quay was first recorded as Watergate Quay, in 1411, which was located at the foot of the High Street close to the town walls. The quay was used for importing French wine and exporting wool, and a fifteenth-century wool house still survives nearby. In 1623, the quay was the original departure point for the Pilgrim Fathers and a memorial can be found today on the quay.

The Town Quay at Southampton as pictured on a postcard sent to Swansea on 21 June 1917. The quay was busy with coastal trade at this time, but this largely ended with the opening of the Western Docks in 1932. The horse carriages in the foreground are standing on the railway line around to the Royal Pier.

The Town Quay is now used as the terminal for the ferry services to Hythe Pier and the Red Funnel Red Jet Hi-Speed services to Cowes. This photograph of the quay was taken from a departing Hythe ferry in November 2010. During the late 1980s, the quay was extensively redeveloped with a 117-berth marina, offices, cafes and restaurant, in addition to two new berths for the Hythe and Cowes ferries.

During the eighteenth century, continental goods traffic from the Watergate Quay declined in favour of London and it became derelict. In 1803, the newly-formed Harbour Commissioners demolished the remains of the old quay and built the Town Quay on the site. In addition to the goods vessels, passenger steamer services began to operate from the quay, including those of the Isle of Wight Steam Packet Company (later the Southampton, Isle of Wight & South England Royal Mail Steam Packet Company, and then Red Funnel) in the 1820s. However, the opening of the nearby Royal Pier in 1833 led to many of the passenger steamer services being transferred there.

In 1846, the quay acquired the clubhouse of the Southern Yacht Club and, in the following year, a customs house. At the same time, a wagon tramway pulled by horses was provided to connect the quay to the station of the London & Southampton Railway by means of a wagon turntable. A direct connection between the railway and tramway was provided in 1871 and the tramway was upgraded to take small steam locomotives six years later.

The first jetty was added to the quay in 1853 and this was extended to provide nine berths. During the late Victorian era and first quarter of the twentieth century, the quay remained busy with coastal trade. In the 1920s, a floating pontoon was added to the quay, but upon the opening of the Western Docks in 1932 and the upgrading of the Eastern Docks all of the goods traffic moved away, leaving the quay to be largely used by the passenger ferries.

The Town Quay is now used as the terminal for the ferry services to Hythe Pier and the Red Funnel Red Jet Hi-Speed services to Cowes. During the late 1980s, the quay was extensively redeveloped with a 117-berth marina, offices, cafes and restaurant, in addition to two new berths for the Hythe and Cowes ferries. In November 2010, owners Associated British Ports announced plans to transform the quay in 2011 with the addition of a wide pedestrian boulevard running the length of the quay, providing extensive views across the port and waterfront.

Royal Pier

The origins of the Royal Pier at Southampton lie in an Act of Parliament passed in 1803, which empowered the Southampton Harbour Commissioners to administer the affairs of the port and improve quay facilities in the lower town. One of the aims of the commissioners was to provide a landing pier for steamer services to France, the Channel Islands, Isle of Wight and Weymouth and the design of Messrs Doswell for a pier 900 feet in length was accepted. The contractor William Betts completed the pier in 1833 and it was officially opened by the Duchess of Kent and her daughter Princess Victoria, for whom the pier was named 'Victoria Pier' in her honour.

Sailings from the pier were undertaken by a number of different companies, including the Southampton, Isle of Wight & South of England Royal Mail Steam Packet Company. During the summer of 1835, the *Apollo* sailed to Le Harve, and

Southampton Royal Pier in the 1880s, with the railway track and station to the left and the promenade deck on the right. At the entrance to the pier is the parcel office and cloakroom for the Southampton, Isle of Wight & South of England Royal Mail Steam Packet Company, whose steamers ran from the pier.

25 SOUTHAMPTON. — Royal Pier — LL.

This postcard from *c.* 1907 shows the railway station on the Royal Pier (with two trains in the platform) and the pavilion added as part of the improvements of the 1890s. It can be seen that horses and carriages were allowed onto the pier through their own entrance.

An Edwardian postcard of the ornate pavilion and bandstand on Southampton Royal Pier erected in 1894. Benches line the outside of the pavilion and three mutoscopes are propped up against the bandstand.

The staff of the refreshment room on the Royal Pier pose for the photographer *c.* 1910.

A view along the Royal Pier in 1923, two years after the railway services to the station on the pier had ceased. The damage to the pier, which forced the closure of the line, can be seen. Also noticeable are the cars parked on the pier and the line of mutoscopes, sweetmeat and weighing machines.

In 1930, the 'wedding cake' gatehouse, designed by Edward Cooper Poole, was added to the entrance of the Royal Pier and seen here shortly after it was opened. By this time the defunct railway station had been cleared away except for one of the canopies.

This aerial view of the Royal Pier from the late 1940s/early 1950s shows the extensive area of landing stages available for the steamers that ran to Portsmouth, the Isle of Wight, Bournemouth and Swanage.

The gatehouse of the Royal Pier, photographed in November 2010, in use as a Thai restaurant. The heraldic lions seen on the roof were rescued from the original gatehouse when it was demolished in 1930.

Aside from the gatehouse, the remainder of the Royal Pier has lain derelict since the 1980s. This photograph from November 2010 vividly shows the sad fall from grace of this once fine structure.

in the following year the iron paddle steamer *Forester* provided an hourly service to Hythe and also sailed to Cowes, Ryde, Portsmouth and Lymington. In 1838, the *Atalanta* ran to the Channel Islands, whilst *Camilla* operated to St Malo. An advertisement by the Commercial Company in 1841 stated that their vessels sailed from the pier to Le Harve, Guernsey, Jersey, Plymouth, Torquay, Weymouth, Swanage and Yarmouth. Brighton and Southsea were amongst the other places served from the pier.

Upon the arrival of the London & Southampton Railway (soon to become part of the London & South Western Railway) in 1840, passengers were conveyed to the pier by horse bus until a horse tramway was laid to connect the railway station to the Town Quay and Royal Pier in 1847. The tramway was connected to the railway by a wagon turntable (although it could not be used by passenger trains) and in 1851 was leased to L&SWR.

The pier was constructed with a straight neck leading to a pier head angled at 45 degrees. A floating bridge and pontoon were placed at the angle in 1864 but was moved six years later to allow for the construction of a single platform station for the tramway service, which was directly connected to the railway in 1871. Five years later, steam hauled trains were allowed on the line and onto the pier (replacing the horse tramway), although there were limitations to the weight of the train and a speed limit. Three small condensing locomotives – *Southampton*, *Cowes* and *Ritzebuttel* – were acquired to work the pier line.

Queen Victoria used the pier during her visits to Southampton when sailing from Osborne House. On 4 April 1864, the noted Italian patriot Garibaldi landed at the pier to be met by large crowds, banners and Italian flags and a full Italian band playing their national anthem.

In 1888, the pier's entrance booths were replaced by a new gatehouse, which was enlarged six years later. The new entrance was the start of a radical transformation of the pier during the early 1890s. In 1891, work began on rebuilding the pier in iron and extending the pier head. The Prince of Wales Steps were added in 1891 and the formerly open platform of the railway station was rebuilt with two platforms housing canopy shelters, opened on 2 June 1892. That same year saw the docks purchased by the L&SWR. One side of the pier was converted into a pleasure pier with the addition of a pavilion and refreshment rooms on an enlarged pier head. The pier's major refurbishment was concluded with the addition of a pontoon on the site of the old pier head in 1898, which allowed two boats to be berthed at the same time. The new pier was blessed with the name 'Royal Pier'.

The three locomotives used on the line to the pier began to be replaced in 1900 when *Bretwalda* replaced *Ritzebuttel*. The following year saw *Cowes* replaced by *Clausentum*, while *Southampton* was reduced to a standby engine. In 1902, *Bretwalda* was relocated to Bournemouth and, four years later, Class C14 motor tanks took over the pier route. They, in turn, were replaced by railmotors in 1909.

The Pier Pavilion became a popular centre of entertainment following its opening in 1894. Concert parties and light musical concerts were a staple attraction, although exhibitions and meetings took place. On 1 October 1897, a luncheon was held in the pavilion in honour of King Chulakongkom I of Siam, who was celebrating 29 years on the throne. The king was in Southampton to inspect renovation work on his yacht *M. Chakrkri* by Messrs Day, Summers & Company and suggested that the Hythe Ferry could be replaced by a bridge! The pavilion also housed a popular tea room and, from 1908, roller skating during the winter.

The outbreak of the First World War saw railway passenger services to the pier cease on 1 October 1914. During the war, the line was used to move troops but became damaged by ship collision and was never reinstated, leading to the official closure of the Royal Pier station in 1921.

The ferries, however, continued to operate from the pier to the Isle of Wight and other south coast destinations, and the pavilion remained a popular entertainment venue. The Anglo-Indians were a feature in the pavilion during the 1918 season, followed by the Gay Gondoliers the following year. The Vaudeville Follies also appeared in the pavilion, which was extended and remodelled in 1922.

In 1930, the pier gatehouse was demolished to make way for a new 'wedding cake' gatehouse designed by Edward Cooper Poole. The new building incorporated from its predecessor six cast-iron heraldic lions, with shields bearing the coat of arms of Hampshire, and was set back from the road to allow for a bigger forecourt. The 1930s saw the pier house become a novel attraction when a Supermarine S.B.6 flying boat was housed adjacent to it as a tourist attraction. On 29 September 1931, Flt Lt G. R. Stamforth set a new world speed record in Southampton Water in the craft, which was to prove the prototype for the legendary Second World War Spitfire fighter plane. During the war, in which the Spitfire was to make its name, the pier was requisitioned by the military.

Following the end of the Second World War, the pier was reopened in 1947 and ferry services resumed. Vehicles were side loaded onto the ferries until 1950, when a ramp was provided to allow them onto the converted landing craft *Norris Castle*. Excursion ferries ran to Ryde and Southsea. The pavilion was reopened in 1947 by Mecca Entertainment and in 1963 they converted it into a ballroom at a cost of over £100,000. The venue instantly became one of the top attractions in the town and manager Len Canham brought many top singers and bands to the pier, some of whom he managed himself. The popular group Dave Dee, Dozy, Beaky, Mick and Tich began their career on the pier. Johnny Dymond, who later had a stint at BBC Radio One, was appointed resident disc jockey in the ballroom from 1963 and became known for his fine line in patter and flashy suits to match. The pavilion was also used for wrestling and attracted many of the top names such as Mick McManus and Jackie Pallo.

However, the ballroom's popularity was eventually eclipsed by that of the Top Rank Suite and the pier and pavilion were closed on 31 December 1979 for being no longer 'viably maintainable'. Part of the structure was used from 1984 by Red Funnel Ferries for parking, and in 1986 the gatehouse was reopened as a pub/restaurant by First Leisure, who laid out a conservatory area on part of the pier deck. First Leisure announced plans for further development of the pier but these were cut short when the pavilion and bandstand were destroyed by fire on 4 May 1987. A further fire in 1992 destroyed much of the pier neck and damaged the pub conservatory, leaving the structure virtually unrecognisable as a pier.

In June 2008, the gatehouse was reopened as a Thai restaurant but the pier itself continued to badly deteriorate and, in June 2010, a 98-foot section of it collapsed into the sea, at a time when Southampton City Council announced it was seeking proposals to transform the deck area into an attractive waterfront district.

HYTHE AND NEW FOREST WATERSIDE

Hythe is a small town in the waterside area of the New Forest with a long pier from which the ferry to Southampton operates. The pier has been one of the finest vantage points to watch the arrival and departure of the great liners to and from Southampton, attracting many ship-watchers to the area. A marina is a recent addition to the town, which is gaining a reputation for affluence.

In addition, the Western side of Southampton Water has seen pier and jetty structures erected at the Royal Naval Armaments Depot and Military Port at Marchwood, the oil refinery at Fawley and the popular tourist spot at Buckler's Hard.

Marchwood Royal Naval Armaments Depot

The Royal Naval Armaments Depot at Marchwood was opened as a sub-depot of Priddy's Hard in 1815 for the storage of gunpowder and, later, munitions. A rolling stage, featuring a raised planked barrow way, was built out to a landing stage in deep water. This was later replaced by a more traditional iron pier structure, which did not survive the site's decommissioning and closure in 1961. Some of the shore structures that have survived, such as the Officer's Quarters and barracks, have been given a Grade II listing and converted into housing. The Marchwood Yacht Club also occupies part of the site.

Marchwood Military Port

A military port was established at Marchwood, in 1943, to ferry equipment and troops to the Normandy Landings the following year. The site, which is the sole military port in the United Kingdom, remains in use, but in October 2010 it was announced that it is likely to close within the next four years and be sold off to a private operator.

The port is home to the Royal Fleet Auxiliary (RFA), Landing Ship Logistic (LSL) and army vessels under the command of the Royal Logistic Corps (RLC)

An aerial photograph of the Royal Naval Armaments Depot at Marchwood in the 1940s, showing the pier, which no longer exists.

and has three principal jetties for their use. The largest is 220m long and 33m wide and is capable of accepting vessels up to 16,000 tonnes. It has a sophisticated Ro/Ro facility capable of handling vessels with various ramp configurations, and the jetty also has two 35-ton rail-mounted cranes and railway access. The second jetty, built during the Second World War, is 190m long, has rail access and is capable of accepting vessels of up to 8,000 tonnes with limited Ro/Ro facilities. Finally, there is a subsidiary jetty of 117m that is used to berth military landing craft and smaller vessels.

Hythe Ferry and Railway Pier

Hythe is derived from the Anglo-Saxon word *Hith* or *Hyth*, meaning a sheltered landing place and by 1575 a ferry service was in operation between Southampton and Hythe. The watermen with their wherries carried out the ferry duties for many years, although in 1830–32 the wooden paddle steamer *Emerald* was also providing a service. In 1836, the iron paddle steamer *Forester* was providing an hourly facility to the Royal Pier in Southampton. An Act of Parliament was gained in 1844 by the Hythe Hard Company to build a landing hard, which was opened the following year at a cost of £7,000. Although an improvement on what there had been before, the Hard still often gave passengers wet feet on their way to and from the ferry.

The paddle steamer *Gipsy* commenced a service to Southampton from the new Hard, but this was discontinued after a couple of years due to a lack of patronage. Eight years were to lapse before another effort was made to provide a steamer for the crossing when, on 17 July 1855, the Hythe & Southampton Steam Ferry Company was incorporated with a capital of £2,500 in 500 shares of £5 each. They placed an order for a new paddle steamer from the Northam shipyard of Day, Summers & Company, but in the meantime purchased the Thames paddle steamer *Prince Alfred*. She was placed on station following a trial run to Beaulieu on 26 February 1856 and generally received favourable comments. However, she

Opened in 1881 for the ferry service to Southampton, Hythe's 2,100-foot-long iron pier is seen *c.* 1905 on this postcard sent on 1 June 1910. Note the two boys pulling the luggage hand cart.

An interesting study of the entrance to Hythe Pier *c.* 1905, showing barrels and other goods being loaded onto carts which were pushed along the pier whilst members of the pier staff happily pose for the photographer.

Hythe Pier in 1905 showing a young lady holding one of the luggage carts and, in the distance, what looks like a group of soldiers marching towards the ferry.

Hythe Pier has been an excellent vantage point to view the big liners moving in and out of Southampton and this postcard, used in 1918, shows the *Olympic* (the sister ship of the ill-fated *Titanic*) on her way out to the sea.

This postcard, sent in 1915, shows the luggage tramway added on the north side of the pier in July 1909. The ferry seen on the left was *Hampton*, which was introduced in 1894 and remained in service until 1938.

In July 1922, a 2-foot gauge tramway powered by a 250v DC third rail was opened on the pier. Two Brush locomotives and four carriages were acquired to operate the service, which levied a charge of 1*d* for passengers.

The sea end and landing stage of Hythe Pier in the 1950s with the train waiting for any passengers to arrive off the ferry. The vessel is *Hotspur II*, which entered service in 1932, and was sold in 1978 and renamed *Kenilworth*.

The train trundles along Hythe Pier on 6 June 1959 with a folded-down pram seen on the luggage trailer.

Now operated by White Horse Ferries, the entrance to the pier is seen in November 2010. On the right can be seen the train in the platform.

Still using the locomotives and carriages from 1922, the Hythe Pier train stands at the sea end platform in November 2010 awaiting passengers from the ferry boats.

Hythe Pier and landing stage seen from a ferry arriving from Southampton in November 2010. The vessel moored at the stage, *Hotspur IV*, has been at Hythe since December 1947.

spent only one year in the hands of the company as, following the delivery of the *Lady Elizabeth* from Day, Summers & Company, she was sold on 29 January 1857 to Mr N. Harvey of Fawley. He continued to run the vessel on the Hythe route for a short period that year but she was laid up and left to rot before being sold for scrap in 1861.

The Hythe & Southampton Steam Ferry Company's spanking new steamer *Lady Elizabeth* (named after Lady Elizabeth Drummond, wife of local landowner and leading shareholder in the company Alfred Drummond) sadly proved to be a complete failure. The vessel was too large to dock at both Hythe and Southampton and passengers had to come ashore in small boats, in the process getting their feet wet. Customers soon deserted the steamer in favour of the watermen, who were able to offer a dry journey. The *Lady Elizabeth* was soon disposed of after the company took delivery of a smaller and more suitable steamer named *Louisa*. However, despite her suitability for the route, *Louisa* failed to turn round the fortunes of the company, which was dissolved on 9 November 1861.

Louisa was sold to William Winckworth of Hythe, the Secretary of the defunct Hythe & Southampton Steam Ferry Company. Unlike the company's shareholders, he still had faith in the ferry service as a paying concern and ordered the *Frederica* from Messrs Day, Summers & Company. She commenced her duties in 1863 and proved to be a success, allowing the ferry service to pay its way for the first time and also enhance the fortunes of the Hythe Hard Company. On 24 May 1872, Winckworth sold his ferry interests, along with the *Frederica*, to Frederick Fry.

Nevertheless, the problem of wading through water at the Hard for customers to reach the steamer had not gone away and in 1870 the Hythe & Southampton Pier & Steam Ferry Company was formed to provide a pier for the ferry service. On 1 February 1871, the Hythe Pier Order was granted to build a pier 2,000 feet in length, designed by Mr Greathead and incorporating a railway. However, the scheme foundered, leading to the formation on 15 December 1874 of a new company headed by Edgar Drummond and including Lord Montagu of Beaulieu. This was the Hythe Pier & Hythe & Southampton Ferry Company, which, as its name implies, was also to take over the existing ferry service provided by Frederick Fry (and lease it back to him) and the interests of the Hythe Hard Company. The Hythe Pier Order was issued in 1875 but legal difficulties (particularly with the Southampton Harbour & Pier Board) meant that the Bill was not given the Royal Assent until 4 July 1878.

The design of the pier was now undertaken by Mr James Wright, engineer for the Hythe Pier Company, and John Dixon, an experienced pier engineer and contractor who had previously worked on piers at Douglas and Llandudno. Dixon was largely paid for his work with 1,000 shares in the company. Wright and Dixon designed a pier 2,100 feet in length and 16 feet wide, standing four feet above the high water mark. Cast iron screw piles and columns, forty feet apart, would support wrought iron lattice girders and cross bracing, upon which the wooden decking was placed.

The appointed contractors were Messrs Bergheim, who had submitted a contract price of £7,700, and they commenced work in October 1879 whilst also busy erecting piers at Hornsea and Bournemouth. All went smoothly and the last pile was driven in on 29 June 1880, leaving just the deck fittings to be carried out. The official opening of the pier was carried out on New Year's Day 1881, by J. H. Cooksey, the Mayor of Southampton (who had travelled over by launch from the Royal Pier), in company with the Chairman of the Hythe Pier Company Edgar Drummond, James Wright and Frederick Fry, lessee of the ferry operation. The pier was bedecked with flags and bunting and was surrounded by a flotilla of boats in the water. A refreshment tent was placed on the pier head to refresh the crowd listening to the Band of the 1st Hants Volunteer Engineers. Following the official opening, the dignitaries retired to the Drummond Arms for a dinner.

The principal function of the pier was always as a landing stage for the ferry to Southampton Town Quay and it never housed any amusements. However, the Hythe Regatta was centred on the pier, which hosted a band concert and refreshment tent on such occasions and, in 1894, a clubhouse was erected on the pier head for the Hythe Sailing Club. The pier was also used as a marine promenade and a vantage point to watch the big ocean-going liners sailing in and out of Southampton, including the *Titanic*, *Olympic*, *Queen Mary*, *United States* and *Queen Elizabeth II*.

On 30 July 1885, the pier was damaged by the schooner *Annie* midway on the northern side but repairs were quickly put in hand. Two years later, the ferry service was leased to James Percy for a sum of £665 per annum, who acquired the existing ferry boats *Frederica* and *Louisa* from Mr Fry for £475. Percy was a direct descendant of Henry 'Hotspur' Percy, the famous medieval soldier, and in 1889 named the first ferry built for him (by Messrs Willoughby Brothers of Plymouth) *Hotspur*. She replaced the ageing *Louisa* and, in 1894, *Frederica* was also finally retired upon introduction of *Hampton*, built by Day, Summers & Company. The fares charged for the ferry around this time were 10d return and 6d single for first class, 7d return and 4d single for second class. The watermen continued to provide their service to Southampton after the pier opened but eventually realised they were fighting a losing battle.

Hailed as the 'Gateway to the New Forest' the pier was visited by royalty on 13 August 1888 when the yacht *Elfin* docked with Prince Henry of Battenburg and Princess Alice of Hess on board. The pier was further visited by European royalty on four occasions during the Edwardian period: by King Alphonso XIII of Spain on 27 April 1906; Kaiser Wilhelm of Germany on 6 December 1907; Princess Beatrice of Battenberg on 25 August 1909 and Prince Henry of Prussia on 9 July 1911.

During the 1890s, four shelters were added to the pier for the comfort of the ferry passengers and, in 1896, the deck was re-planked at a cost of £1,500. The luggage of the ferry passengers was transported up and down the pier in hand carts until a tramway was erected on its north side by local undertaker Edward Kingham in July 1909. Additional sidings were laid the following year.

Upon the death of James Percy on 17 May 1915, the ferry passed into the hands of William Percy and his General Estates Company, for a yearly lease of £850. The pier and ferry continued to operate throughout the First World War, although on 26 August 1915 the pier was hit by the sailing barge *Itchen*, fortunately sustaining only minor damage. In October 1915, the motor launch *Hamble*, capable of carrying fifty to sixty passengers, joined *Hotspur* and *Hampton* on the ferry service. However, the three craft struggled to cope with the popularity of the route and the Great Yarmouth screw steamer *Southtown* was transferred to Hythe in September 1918.

The General Estates Company made a loss during its two years of operating the pier (£223 in 1915 and £148 in 1916) but finished with profits of £55 in 1917 and £204 in 1918. In the latter year, receipts of £108 were received from passengers, £101 from goods traffic and £106 from rates on vessels. The largest item of expenditure was £189 on salaries. During the same period the pier's owners, the Hythe Pier & Hythe & Southampton Ferry Company Limited, made profits of £236 in 1915, £158 in 1916, £99 in 1917 and £163 in 1918.

Following the end of the war, a number of significant improvements were carried out to the pier. A refreshment room was added on the pier head in 1919 and in the following year the original toll house on the pier head was replaced by a new ticket office. The old Hythe Sailing Club building was modernised by its new lessees, the Royal Motor Yacht Club, to house a dining room, bar, bathroom and four sleeping cabins.

The biggest alteration to the pier was the decision of the General Estates Company in 1922 to replace the luggage tramway with a 2-foot gauge railway laid on the south side, powered by a 250V DC third rail. To operate the line, two Brush locomotives (a third was used for spares), built in 1917, were acquired from the MOD Avonmouth mustard gas works and converted from battery to third rail operation. Four carriages, built by Baguley of Stoke-on-Trent, were supplied by the Drewry Car Company, and a tank truck was obtained to transport fuel oil to the ferry boats. Two luggage trucks were retained from the old tramway. The line was opened in July 1922 and a fare of 1d was levied for passengers who used it. In 1923, the Hythe Pier & Hythe & Southampton Ferry Company Limited sensibly shortened their name to the Hythe Pier Company.

In 1926, a new semi-diesel engine vessel was ordered by the General Estates Company from Messrs J. Samuel White & Company. She entered service on Easter Monday, 18 April 1927 as *Hotspur*, entailing the retirement of its namesake, which was renamed *G.E.C.* The old vessel was put up for sale but there were no takers and she was left to rust into oblivion. Ten years later, two new ships were added to the fleet: *Hotspur II*, a new twin-screw diesel vessel, which entered service in November 1936, and *Hotspur III*, purchased as *Carrick Lass* from Scotland and commencing operations in January 1938. This led to the retirement of *Hampton* and its final journey to a breakers yard in Holland.

During the Second World War, the pier and ferry continued to operate, albeit with a reduced service. On 4 June 1944, the pier was honoured with a visit by King George VI who enjoyed a ride on the train, although in the following year the structure was damaged after being hit by an LCP (Landing Craft Personnel). Repairs were soon carried out and in 1947 the pier head and landing pontoon were reconstructed. The pier head also came to house a restaurant and buffet following the conversion of the Hythe Sailing Club building. By now, the old *Hotspur* was pretty well worn out and, in December 1947, she was replaced by *Hotspur IV*, built by the Rowhedge Ironworks Company (as were *Hotspur II* and *Hotspur III*).

One of the largest crowds ever to assemble on the pier formed on 8 July 1952 to witness the liner *United States* returning from her maiden transatlantic voyage, having captured the Blue Riband for the fastest crossing from the *Queen Mary*. The crowds returned to the pier the following year to view another liner, the *Olympia*, which had run aground close by on 13 December 1953. The vessel was promptly pulled clear into the main shipping channel by three tugs. The pier itself had a close shave during the afternoon of 9 July 1958, when the Panamanian passenger liner *Arosa Kulm* ran aground very close to the pier head. On 13 September 1962, the pier railway suffered a rare derailment as the train returned to the entrance station, which was found to have been caused by a wooden wedge placed deliberately on the track.

During the 1960s, the entrance to the pier was modernised and the shelters on the deck removed. Further modernisation was carried out in 1970–71 and repairs had to be carried out following a small fire on 4 August 1976, as deck planks had to be ripped out to prevent the blaze spreading along the pier. The pier decking was renewed in 1982 and a structural survey revealed that the pier needed extensive restoration; this was carried out in 1985–88 by Clifford & Partners at a cost of £290,000.

The operation of the ferry and railway passed, on 1 February 1977, to Southern Coastcrafts Limited, and later that autumn the decision was taken to order a new ferry from Marine Services Ltd. However, the shipyard company went into liquidation within a few months and the second-hand Portsmouth ferry *Southsea Queen* was acquired instead for £160,000. She arrived at Hythe on 14 June 1978 and was renamed *Hythe Hotspur* before being put on mainly cruise and charter work and deputising for *Hotspur III* and *Hotspur IV* on the ferry service when necessary. *Hotspur II* was sold for £27,000 to the Clyde Marine Motoring Company and, after being renamed *Kenilworth*, was put on the Gourock–Kilcreggan service. In 1981, another new vessel was ordered by the General Estates Company, this time from the Arun Yacht & Boat Company of Littlehampton, half of which was to be paid for by a grant from Hampshire County Council. Named *New Forrester*, she quietly entered service on 20 August 1982, replacing *Hotspur III*, which was broken up. The council also assisted in the cost of replacing corroded ironwork and other repairs needed to the pier during ongoing work in the 1980s.

In 1991, the operation of the ferry passed to Derrick Shipping, trading under the name Waterfront Ferry. However, two years later they went into liquidation and the pier, ferry and railway were taken over by White Horse Ferries. In 2002, Hampshire County Council announced that they would continue to provide financial assistance to ensure the future of the ferry operation.

The pier suffered a further ship collision on Saturday 1 November 2003, when the dredger *Donald Redford* went right through the structure shortly after a ferry carrying football supporters had docked. A gap of 80 feet was left in the pier and the ferry service had to be temporarily transferred to the Hythe Marina. Repairs were carried out at a cost of £308,999 and the pier was reopened on 7 January 2004. The Master of the dredger was subsequently sentenced to eight months in prison after pleading guilty to causing damage to the pier under the influence of drink.

The pier and its railway remains a delightful throwback to a bygone age and it is recognised by the Guinness Book of World Records as having the oldest continually operated pier train. The ferry provides a half-hourly service to Southampton Town Quay and, in 2010, the entrance fee to the pier was £1.10, which includes a journey on the train (the train is free to ferry passengers). To help pay for the pier's upkeep there is a 'sponsor a plank' scheme in donations scales of £30, £60 and £90.

Fawley Oil Refinery

The Esso refinery at Fawley is the largest in the United Kingdom and was opened in 1921. The site features a mile-long marine jetty terminal with sixteen berths that handles 2,000 ship movements and 22 million tons of crude oil and other products every year.

The mile-long marine jetty terminal that serves the Esso refinery at Fawley. The jetty has sixteen berths which handle 2,000 ship movements and 22 million tons of crude oil and other products every year.

The small river steamer *Duke of York* calls at the Buckler's Hard Jetty *c.* 1920. Trips from Bucker's Hard along the River Beaulieu can still be taken.

A photograph taken on the landing stage of the jetty at Buckler's Hard in July 2000.

One of the private jetties along the River Beaulieu that serve yacht clubs, marinas and houses.

Buckler's Hard

The delightful maritime village of Buckler's Hard, created in the eighteenth century by the second Duke of Montagu on his Beaulieu Estate, has a jetty that serves boat cruises along the Beaulieu River. There are also a number of private jetties along the river serving yacht clubs, marinas and private housing.

Originally a major shipbuilding area, supplying three vessels that fought at the Battle of Trafalgar, Buckler's Hard is now a popular tourist destination and yachting centre.

LYMINGTON

Lymington is an ancient town on the west bank of the River Lymington that was famous for the production of salt and shipbuilding, but is known now for its yachting marinas and ferry service to the Isle of Wight. The town has received the accolade of being the best town to live in on the coast due its good transport links, low crime rate and beautiful situation.

Railway and Ferry Pier

The Lymington to Yarmouth crossing, at 3½ miles, is the shortest ferry route to the Isle of Wight from the mainland and in the opinion of many also the most relaxing and convenient. Boats had sailed between the two towns for centuries and on 5 April 1830 the locally owned and built *Glasgow* commenced the first regular steam service. In addition to calling at Yarmouth, the vessel sometimes also ran to Cowes, Southampton and Portsmouth. However, tidal restraints at Lymington Town Quay meant that passengers were sometimes ferried out to the steamer even at high tide. From May 1836, goods and livestock were ferried separately from the passengers on tow boats pulled by service steamers or chartered tugs. In 1841, the Solent Sea Steam Packet Company (later the Solent Steamship Company) was formed to operate the route and they ordered the steamer *Solent*, which became the principal vessel on the route, relegating *Glasgow* to operate just the Lymington-Yarmouth ferries.

On 12 July 1858, the privately owned Lymington Railway reached the town via a branch from Brockenhurst on the London & South Western Railway's line from London to Bournemouth. In anticipation of the increased traffic the railway was expected to bring, the two-year-old steamer *Red Lion* was purchased from the Admiralty. Three years later, *Solent* was withdrawn and replaced in November 1863 by a larger vessel of the same name. She was joined by the iron hulled *Mayflower* in July 1866.

In 1861, the railway company opened a small jetty downriver from the Town Quay, easing somewhat the problems of access to the town at low tide. On 23 March 1878, the Lymington Railway was acquired by the L&SWR and, six

A steamer approaches Lymington Pier in the 1920s with a train waiting at the platform. The pier had been constructed by the London & South Western Railway in 1884.

The Isle of Wight car ferry *Freshwater* discharges its cars and passengers on the slipway beside the pier in the 1960s. *Freshwater* entered service on 21 September 1959, operated until 1973 and had a capacity for 620 passengers and 26 cars.

A train operated by South West Trains enters the station on Lymington Pier in November 2010. One of the current car ferries can be seen moored by the old slipway.

In January 1976, a new £250,000 terminal was opened on reclaimed land just to the east of the pier along with a £100,000 link-span to allow easier berthing and loading/unloading. To accommodate the link-span, the pier was shortened by about 60 feet. This photograph of a car ferry arriving at Lymington was taken in November 2010.

years later, on 1 May 1884, they constructed a half mile branch from the town station to a new pier, thus allowing sailings to Yarmouth to be undertaken at all states of the tide. The L&SWR also took over the steamer services by acquiring the Solent Steamship Company's vessels *Solent* and *Mayflower* along with four tug boats, for £2,750. The first purpose-built L&SWR vessel for the route, costing £6,000, was the steel hulled *Lymington* in 1893, followed by *Solent* in 1902.

In addition to Yarmouth, the Lymington boats were also extended to Totland Bay, and occasionally Alum Bay, who both had small piers to receive the steamers. However, the services to Alum Bay were never resumed after the First World War whilst those to Totland Bay ceased in 1927 as they were not paying their way.

In 1923, the railway, pier and ferries became part of the newly-formed Southern Railway. On 3 May 1927, they launched the largest steamer to be built for the route, the 264-ton *Freshwater*, at a cost of £22,500, which necessitated the dredging of the channel and pier berths at Lymington. The demand to carry cars on the route was ever-increasing and they were towed across by a tow boat from a slipway at Lymington Town Station Wharf, which also handed goods traffic to the island. Nevertheless, there were demands for a proper car ferry and the baton was initially taken up by the newly formed Isle of Wight Ferry Company. They planned to build piers and slipways at Keyhaven (just to the west of Lymington) and Fort Victoria (near Yarmouth) and run a car ferry service using two old vehicle ferries retired from the Mersey Ferry following the opening of the Queensway Mersey Tunnel in 1934. The Southern Railway entered into negotiations with the company but quickly realised that the finance for the venture would not be forthcoming and announced plans to provide the car ferry themselves. New slipways were built adjacent to Lymington Pier and at Yarmouth Harbour to take the new car ferry *Lymington*, which began running on 1 May 1938. The ship could take up to twenty cars and was powered by the revolutionary Voith-Schneider propulsion units, which enabled her to be manoeuvred in any direction and earned her the nickname of the 'crab'. The new ferry was an immediate success; carrying 4,000 cars in her first year compared to 2,500 in 1937.

During the Second World War, the ferries continued to operate, although night time sailings were prohibited. *Freshwater* was requisitioned by the Royal Navy and *Lymington* largely carried on the service, complete with a Lewis gun for protection. This was brought into action during the evening of 10 August 1942 to fight off a Heinkel. In preparation for the D-Day landings, *Lymington* was required to operate the service from the Town Quay whilst the car ferry slipways were doubled in size to allow simultaneous loading of two tank landing craft.

Upon nationalisation of the railways in 1948, the diesel-electric paddle vessel *Farringford* was introduced to partner *Lymington*. *Solent* was retired at this time, although *Freshwater* remained in service for a further eleven years. By 1955, 42,000 cars were being carried annually on the route, necessitating the need for a third car ferry. The new Voith-Schneider-propelled *Freshwater* entered service (replacing its paddle steamer namesake) on 21 September 1959 with a capacity of 620 passengers and 26 cars. The three vessels remained in service until 1973 when the C Class ferries, named *Caedmon*, *Cenwulf* and *Cenred*, were introduced. They could each carry 750 passengers and 52 cars and carried 179,000 cars and a million passengers during their first year of operation. *Lymington*, *Farringford* and *Freshwater* all ended up in the hands of Western Ferries in Scotland and, except *Farringford*, were used on a twenty-minute crossing on the Firth of Clyde.

The railway to the pier was electrified on 2 June 1967 and major improvements were carried out at Lymington when a new £250,000 terminal was opened in January 1976. The terminal was placed on reclaimed land just to the east of the pier, along with a £100,000 link-span to allow easier berthing and loading/ unloading. To accommodate the link-span the pier was shortened by about 60 feet. Yarmouth received its new terminal and link-span on 20 September 1983.

Wightlink now operate the crossing, which takes about thirty minutes each way. In 2008, they replaced the C Class ferries with the Wight Class *Wight Light*, *Wight Sky* and *Wight Sun*.

ISLE OF WIGHT

RYDE

Ryde has long been known as the 'Gateway to the Isle of Wight', with its lengthy pier dating back to 1814. The opening of the pier assisted the island's development as a popular holiday destination, along with Queen Victoria's acquisition of Osborne House near Cowes in 1845. Ryde was a fashionable resort even before the opening of the pier, having been developed with many fine houses by local landowners William and Jane Player from 1780. The town flourished during the Victorian era but its popularity as the island's favoured watering place was eventually challenged by the isle's other main resorts of Sandown, Shanklin and Ventnor, which had better beaches. Evidence of Ryde's once grand status as a resort can still be seen in its central and seafront areas.

Ryde Pier

Boats known as a 'Ryde Wherries' were providing a fairly regular service on the 4 ½ mile crossing between Ryde and Portsmouth by the seventeenth century. In 1796, the large sailing vessel *Packet* was introduced to provide a daily return trip and, in 1811, Messrs Bazley were providing two return journeys daily at a fare of 1s per person. However, these services were largely dependent on a high tide at Ryde where a gently shelving beach left a half mile expanse of mud at low tide. When the tide was out, vessels had to anchor half a mile offshore and passengers were brought in by rowing boat and horse and cart. The solution was a low water landing pier and, in 1812, some of Ryde's most prominent citizens formed the Ryde Pier Company, led by the Chairman Hon. Charles Anderson Pelham. Shares in the company were issued in amounts of £20, £30, £50 and £100, with a share of £50 and £100 giving you a seat on the board.

A design for the pier was submitted by architect John Kent of Southampton, who proposed a stone structure. His plan was given to naval architect Sir Samuel Bentham, who made some changes before both the original and amended plans were placed in front of Sir John Rennie, the distinguished railway and harbour engineer. He recommended the construction of a timber pier and Kent resubmitted a new design for a timber pier 1,600 feet in length with the first 300 feet to be

This engraving shows Ryde Pier in 1828, four years after the structure had been extended to 2,040 feet. The landing stage was enlarged in 1827 to accommodate two vessels at a time and an open deck steamer can be seen approaching the pier.

On 29 August 1864, a horse tramway was opened at Ryde, laid upon a new pier that adjoined the promenade and landing pier. The tramway cost £22,500 to build and consisted of two running lines with crossovers and a run-round loop joined to a turntable at the sea end, where two platforms were provided. In 1886, the tramway was converted to electric operation.

A photograph of Ryde Esplanade station and pier taken shortly after the opening of the railway from Ryde St Johns Road to Ryde Pier Head in 1880. On the left is the booking office for the station, which, as can be seen, had two platforms, a signal box and semaphore signalling. Also of interest is the ornate kiosk in the foreground.

Ryde Pier Head station photographed not long after it opened in July 1880. The double track railway along the pier culminated in three lines at the pier head with two platforms, one of them an island platform, and station buildings at right angles to the line of the railway. Note the sailor standing on the tramway pier looking through his telescope.

A fine, expansive view of Ryde Pier *c.* 1905 showing the promenade pier on the left, tramway pier in the centre and railway pier on the right. On the pier head the pavilion can be seen, added in 1895, and in the foreground are the tollbooths for the promenade pier. The advertised refreshment rooms are situated in the Ryde Esplanade station building.

Ryde Pier photographed from the Western Esplanade in around 1905, with the promenade pier in the foreground. The piling of the shore end of the pier had been rebuilt in iron during the 1880s but wooden supports can still be seen on the remainder of the pier. On the extreme right is the pier head of the Victoria Pier with its bathing station.

A postcard of a paddle steamer approaching Ryde Pier sent on 24 June 1907. Over twenty sailings a day between Ryde and Portsmouth were operated by the pier's owners, the LB&SCR and L&SWR Joint Railway Committee.

Crowds on the promenade pier at Ryde look down upon the boatmen assembled for the annual Ryde Regatta in 1908. The building on the left with the roof balcony was the pier head entrance to the tramway.

An aerial view of Ryde Pier, *c.* 1930, showing the extensive landing stages available. On the left is Ryde Pier Head station and in the centre the pavilion, which was erected on its own piling away from the main decks of the pier. Next to it is the station for the tramway.

The electric tramway and pavilion on Ryde Pier, photographed in 1964. Sadly, within seven years both had gone: the tramway closed on 27 January 1969. The pavilion was demolished two years later.

A postcard view across Ryde Pier towards the mainland *c.* 1973. The ex-London Underground tube trains seen on the pier had been introduced on the Ryde Pier Head–Shanklin service in 1966. One of the British Railway diesel motor vessels can be seen approaching the pier; they were put in service between 1948 and 1951.

In the summer of 2010, the promenade pier at Ryde was closed due to rusting steelwork under the structure. Repair work was carried out during the autumn and winter of 2010/11, during which time pedestrians were rerouted onto a temporary walkway laid on the supports of the old tramway.

A photograph taken in November 2010 shows one of the ex-LT tube trains travelling along Ryde Pier. The train is in the colours of Island Line, operated by South West Trains. The photograph was taken from the former tramway pier, in use as a temporary walkway whilst repairs were being carried out to the promenade pier.

Ryde Pier Head station photographed from the former tramway pier in November 2010 with only the island platform remaining in use. Beyond the station is the Costa coffee shop building opened in 2009.

carried on brick arches. The pier was to be 12 feet wide, increasing to 20 feet at passing places for carriages where landing steps were to be placed, and was to be built on the site of Mr Cooper's jetty. This had been erected in 1796 to transport livestock and supply fresh water to ships.

The new design was duly approved, and contractor George Jukes laid the foundation stone on 29 June 1813. Whilst building the pier, Jukes discovered that longer piling was needed for the seaward end and allowances for these had not been made in the contract price. He was advanced £600 in December 1813 (on security of his equipment) but experienced financial problems throughout the undertaking of the contract. However the first thirty-three bays of the pier were completed to allow for the pier to be opened on 26 July 1814. The remaining thirty bays (which brought the pier's length up to 1,740 feet) were completed by 1816, by which time £16,000 had been spent on its construction.

The company recouped some of the costs of the pier's construction by initially charging a 1d promenade toll (soon increased to 2d) and a landing toll for vessels. A landing stage was not initially provided for the steamer traffic and only a flight of stairs was placed at the end of the pier. The sea bed was dredged from the pier to the low water mark to allow for the small steamer *Britannia* to commence a twice daily service between Ryde and Portsmouth on 19 May 1817. Unfortunately, the vessel, which was designed to work in the Thames Estuary, could not cope with the rough sea conditions and the service was discontinued after only four weeks. To add to the company's woes, 750 feet of the pier was extensively damaged by a storm in March 1818. The structure was repaired, but the company found itself in financial difficulties and shareholders were reluctant to dip further into their pockets. Furthermore, in 1821 John Kent took the company to court claiming that he was owed £1,097 4s 6d. However, he lost the case and ended up in prison for debt.

A description of the pier at this time was given in Horsey's *Beauties of the Isle of Wight*:

Ryde, which in the course of a few years has become one of the most beautiful watering places in the south of England, was originally an insignificant fishing village; placed on the shores of the Solent, opposite to Stokes Bay, in the coast of Hampshire, it commands a most delightful sea view. The peculiarity of Ryde (being the nearest landing place from any part of the opposite coast) is gradually giving it a commanding character as it affords the greatest facility for commercial pursuits or visits of pleasure; and has become the most direct communication from the metropolis of the kingdom to the capital of the island. One of the most attractive objects of a public kind is the pier. This ornament to the town forms a beautiful marine promenade running from south to north, a distance of 1,740ft, and varying in its width from twelve to twenty feet. There is an iron railing on each side, which extends the whole length of the pier; and seats are placed in different parts for the accommodation of visitors. The upper part of this fine promenade is finished in a greater style of elegance than the lower. It has an arched gateway at the entrance, and a very neatly constructed lodge for the toll keeper. The descent to the water is very easy. A small flight of steps conducts to a lower basement, from which an arm stretching out on each side affords a very convenient landing. Those who delight to inhale the sea breeze will find this a most propitious spot in the neighbourhood. Here, hour after hour may be passed, without being sensible how rapidly time is gliding away. The vivacity which characterises the company – the ocean spreading its fine blue waves in the front; the fishermen at the foot of the pier, occupied in their marine employments; the vessels sailing at short distances; the boats moving in each direction calmly and swiftly over the bosom of the deep – form a very beautiful scene. On returning to the pier, immediately opposite, the town rises in all its simple character to view; while on each hand the woods, and cliffs, and seats which skirt the shore, form a very beautiful and enchanting scene. On this delightful promenade, persons may regale themselves as frequently as they please, by the payment of an annual, quarterly, monthly or weekly subscription. Those who do not subscribe, have a toll of two pence demanded each time they enter the pier.

The fortunes of the Ryde Pier Company began to improve during the early 1820s as traffic to and from the pier picked up. This allowed them to extend the pier in 1824 to 2,040 feet and, in the following year, the Portsmouth & Ryde Steam Packet Company commenced using it with four sailings daily by the steamers *Union* and *Arrow*, augmented by *Lord Yarborough* in 1826. The pier head was enlarged in 1827 by Thomas Dashwood to cater for two steamers at once, which allowed the Southampton-based steamers *George IV* and *Earl of Malmesbury* to use the pier. A further extension to the pier, to 2,250 feet, was carried out in 1833, which meant that it was now available to use at all states of the tide. The contractor, Mr Butt, also drove nails into the pier's wooden piling in a bid to protect them from the voracious appetites of marine worms. Access to the pier entrance was also improved, when, in 1829, a 25-foot causeway was built to it from George Street.

A warning lamp was added to the end of the pier in 1836 to act as a navigational aid for shipping. Nevertheless, it failed to prevent the collier *William of Cowes* crashing into the pier and removing 60 feet of it during a storm in February 1838, with all hands presumed lost. In 1841, a music licence was granted to the pier and this led to the opening of a small pavilion the following year. At the same time the pier tolls were also reduced in a bid to encourage more locals to use it. The pier always proved to be at its most popular with locals during the annual Ryde Regatta.

The pavilion of 1842 was added on an enlarged triangular-shaped pier head, designed by Thomas Hillyer and erected by James Langdon, which could berth up to four vessels. A Gosport–Ryde service was commenced in 1842 and improvements at Portsmouth with the building of a new Victoria Pier at the Sally Port in 1842 and the Albert Pier, Portsea, in 1847/48 led to a better service to that town. On 28 August 1843, Queen Victoria landed at the pier, although following her purchase of Osborne House in 1845 she usually travelled to the island via Gosport and East Cowes, where the Trinity Pier was erected. In 1850, the Portsea, Portsmouth, Gosport & Isle of Wight Steam Packet Company, with their vessels *Prince of* Wales and *Princess Royal*, began using Ryde Pier in direct competition with the Portsmouth & Ryde Steam Packet Company, who responded by launching *Her Majesty*, the first iron steamer on the route. *Her Majesty* soon set a new record crossing time on the route of around fifteen minutes. The fierce competition between the two companies resulted in fighting amongst the rival crews and confusion for passengers, necessitating the placing of policemen to keep law and order. The rivalry almost led to the bankruptcy of both companies and, in June 1851, they voted for amalgamation to become The Port of Portsmouth & Ryde United Steam Packet Company. This came into being on 1 January 1852 and during its first summer provided eleven weekday services between Ryde and Portsmouth, eight of them calling at Gosport, using the five vessels *Her Majesty*, *Union*, *Princess Royal*, *Prince of Wales* and the unpopular *Prince Albert*, nicknamed the 'Old Tub' due to its ability to induce seasickness amongst its passengers. The vessel was eventually relegated to goods and towing duties in 1861 after the acquisition of a second iron paddle steamer, *Prince Consort*, two years earlier. The opening of the Clarence Pier at Southsea in 1861 led to the steamers calling there in addition to Victoria and Albert piers. The Clarence Pier was connected to Portsmouth by the Landport and Southsea Tramway, and gained the majority of the Ryde patronage until the extension of the railway to Portsmouth Harbour and the opening of a passenger station on the site of Albert Pier on 2 October 1876. The vessels of the Southampton, Isle of Wight and South England Royal Mail Steam Packet Company (later Red Funnel) also called at the pier on their way from Southampton to Portsmouth and Southsea via Cowes and Ryde.

The increased patronage of the steamer services to the pier resulted in it being widened to 20 feet throughout in 1851–53, and there were calls for the Ryde Pier Company to lay a tramway to transport passengers and their luggage. In 1857, they wrote for advice to James Walker, Engineer of Southend Pier, where a tramway was already in operation, but decided to enlarge the pier head first and awarded the contract to James and John Langdon. Work began during the winter of 1859/60 but was delayed by bad weather and damage to the pier by storm-damaged vessels. By the time of its completion in 1861, the pier head had been doubled in size with a 280- by 120-foot triangular platform, featuring an attractive iron balustrade by Messrs Mew and Thorne, with landing stages on four sides. An attractive new pavilion was designed by William Harvey with refreshment and waiting rooms, leading to the old pavilion being moved to a new site on the pier. Band concerts, along with sacred concerts on Sundays, were a feature of the pier head during the summer months.

Thoughts now turned to the provision of the tramway and, in 1861, the Ryde Pier Company paid the Crown Commissioners £50 to gain ownership of the seabed upon which a new tramway pier was to be built alongside the original pier (£21 was also paid to gain legal ownership of the seabed under the original pier).

The Langdon brothers were once again awarded the contract and by September 1862 they had driven in all 386 piles for the tramway pier. To help pay for the new pier, the company took out a £1,000 mortgage with the North British & Mercantile Insurance Company with an interest of 4 ½ per cent per annum. The tramway was largely completed by 2 July 1863 when a horse pulled a luggage van along it. Steam traction was envisaged for the tramway and, in November 1863, Messrs Manning, Wardle & Co. were contracted to supply a locomotive. Named *Vectis,* the engine arrived at the pier on 14 March 1864 along with Mr Wardle to handle it, but after two trials it was decided that the engine caused too much vibration to the pier structure and it was returned on 4 May, having cost £152 to hire. There was no alternative for now but to open the tramway using horse power, which duly occurred on 29 August 1864, with fares set at 4*d* for first class and 2*d* for second.

The tramway and the pier upon which it stood cost the Ryde Pier Company £22,500. The tramway consisted of two running lines with crossovers and a run round loop joined to a turntable at the sea end, where a siding branched off to the north-east landing stage. Platforms were provided at the sea end terminus and a triangular platform serving both tracks was built at the pier entrance. Initially, only one carriage was provided, until a second arrived in 1865, allowing both lines to be worked as independent single lines. A horse bus ran between the pier and the Eastern Railway (soon to be renamed Isle of Wight Railway) at St John's Road, which had been opened to Shanklin on 23 August 1864 (an extension to Ventnor was carried out two years later). The bus remained in service until an extension of the tramway to the station was opened by the Ryde Pier Company on 1 August 1871, at a cost of £32,783.

Improvements were also carried out to the entrance to the pier. In 1867/68, two octagonal toll houses replaced the old toll house and an unsightly building used for luggage and stores. Stairs behind the new toll houses led to stores vaults and an underground passage. An arched covering was added at the entrance in December 1868, at a cost of £2,246. In February 1872, work was completed to provide gas lighting along the whole length of the pier, which was now brightly lit up at night. The cost of a stroll along the pier at this time was 2*d*.

At the sea end of the pier, steamer traffic arriving at Ryde was ever increasing and, by the mid-1860s, fifty vessels a day were docking at the pier head. The pier was temporarily used for the new Stokes Bay to Ryde service operated by the Isle of Wight Ferry Company, from 6 April 1863 until the company's own pier at Ryde, the Victoria Pier, was opened on 1 November 1864. However, the company, along with its associated Stokes Bay Railway & Pier Company, soon foundered and all its assets were acquired by the Ryde Pier Company for £23,000 on 13 May 1865. They transferred the Stokes Bay service back to the main Ryde pier and the Victoria Pier became a bathing station. From 1866, Messrs Cosens of Weymouth commenced an increased service to the pier and, in 1873, a new half-hourly service to Southsea Clarence Pier was commenced from the pier by the Southsea & Isle of Wight Steam Ferry Company using the vessels *Ventnor,*

Shanklin, Southsea and *Ryde*. Their policy of offering cut price fares forced the Port of Portsmouth & Ryde United Steam Packet Company to reduce their prices, but in 1877 the Southsea company were acquired by the Portsmouth company, who by this time had added four vessels to its fleet: *Princess of Wales* in 1865, *Duke of Edinburgh* and *Princess Alice* (1869) and, in 1876, *Heather Bell* (which was the largest vessel to be used on the route). *Albert Edward* joined the fleet in 1878 (replacing *Princess Royal*) and was the first of the company's vessels to be powered by compound engines. *Alexandra* was added the following year before the company was acquired by the Joint Committee of the London & South Western Railway and London, Brighton and South Coast Railways, for £38,000, on 31 March 1880.

Plans to extend the Isle of Wight Railway to the pier were stalled by the Ryde Pier Company until a scheme for a new pier and railway at Ryde was put forward by the Ryde New Pier & Railway Company in 1875. The new company received the support of the mainland London, Brighton & South Coast Railway (who, along with the London & South Western Railway, jointly managed railway operations at Portsmouth) and parliamentary approval was gained in preference to the Ryde Pier Company's alternative plans. The Ryde Pier Company then wrote to the L&BSCR and L&SWR Joint Management Committee offering to sell or lease them their tramway from Ryde Esplanade to St John's Road. Keen to gain a foothold on the island, the mainland companies agreed on 10 May 1876 to withdraw their support for the New Pier scheme, on condition the RPC present a new Bill to Parliament to build a railway from the St John's Road to Ryde Pier that would be acceptable to them. A formal agreement was reached between the RPC, LB&SCR, L&SWR and Ryde Corporation for the RPC to relinquish the tramway extension from the pier to St John's Road so it could be upgraded by the L&SWR and LB&SCR Joint Railway to a full railway extension of the Isle of Wight Railway. A major part of the works would involve building a railway pier alongside the existing tramway and promenade piers, along with new esplanade and pier head stations.

The work on the new railway and pier commenced in July 1878, with the construction of two tunnels under the esplanade and a single line of the railway between Ryde St John's Road and Ryde Esplanade, completed and opened on 5 April 1880. Work on the pier and Ryde Pier Head station was completed by the summer, enabling it to open for business on 12 July along with double track working along the whole line. An inspection of the pier by the Board of Trade gave details of its construction:

'The length is entirely on a viaduct consisting of twelve spans of 40 feet and 43 spans of 20 feet. The 40ft spans are covered by wrought iron girders, two for each line of railway supported on columns or piles of wrought iron known as Hughes' Piles filled with concrete and driven to a depth of around 30 feet into the ground. These piles are stated to have been tested by having 50 tons of dead weight placed on each pile. The 20 feet spans are wrought iron girders supported on cast iron screw piles each with three blades with wrought iron partly filled with concrete.'

The pier head was constructed with wooden piling and seven landing stages with stairs. The double track railway along the pier culminated in three lines at the pier head with two platforms, one of them an island platform, and station buildings at right angles to the line of the railway. The LB&SCR and L&SWR Joint Committee operated all the ferry services from the pier, initially by acquiring seven paddle steamers from the Port of Portsmouth & Ryde United Steam Packet Company. However, they soon introduced their own purpose-built, faster vessels, beginning with the double-ended P.S. *Victoria* in 1881, at a cost of £17,300. She was joined in 1884 by the *Duchess of Edinburgh* and *Duchess of Connaught*, which each had a passenger capacity of 551 as compared to 426 for *Victoria*.

With the railway complete, the focus now turned on the horse tramway, now just running on the pier itself. In 1880, an experiment took place to adapt the two tramcars to run on steam raised by coal gas and the Ryde Gas Company erected a small gas holder by the pier gates. However, the experiment proved unsatisfactory and by January 1881 the tramcars had been converted to run on steam by coke burning. Unfortunately, this caused the temperatures inside the cars to become overbearingly hot and passengers began to forsake the tramway for a short journey on the competing railway, leading to the eastern track being taken up in the winter of 1883. Cinders from the steam boiler also led to small fires on the wooden decking and during the 1885 season horse traction made a brief return. The steam cars were sold to the Ryde Gas Company, and the Ryde Pier Company engaged Siemens to electrify the tramway, which opened on 4 June 1886. The clean and efficient electrified tramway proved to be a success, leading to the reinstatement of the eastern track in 1890 and the installation of a larger generator to power both tracks the following year.

The new railway pier was badly damaged during the evening of 17/18 January 1881 when the colliers *Havelock*, *Lucknow* and *John Ward* smashed against it during a snowstorm. Repairs were swiftly carried out but the pier received further damage on 24 October 1881 from the barge *Alpha*, and then in the following year by the *Hopewell* on 26 March 1882 and *Gloworm* on 25 September. The old wooden piling of the promenade pier was beginning to show its age and, in 1884, 600 feet of the shore end was reconstructed by F. Baddley in iron, with another 600 feet completed by 1888 when attractive shelters were added along the promenade deck. The 1890s saw further improvements. In 1893–95, Richard St George Moore extended the pier head and a large pavilion was erected upon it by Messrs Roe and Grace in 1895 at a cost of £5,358. The pavilion was a two-storey octagonal building with a concert hall seating 700, reading and refreshment rooms and an upstairs sun lounge. The work continued with the provision of new iron railings and shelters in 1895 and new piling under the pier head in 1896/97. The tramway pier was then rebuilt in wrought iron by Frederick Grace of Southampton in 1898/99 at a cost of £14,655.

Concert party shows soon became a feature of the pavilion, particularly those run by the eccentric Reuben Moore. During one afternoon, when business was slack, Moore hired a man to jump off the pier during a performance and feign drowning. By means of a prearranged signal, Moore suddenly stopped singing *On with the Motley*, left the pavilion and jumped into the Solent to rescue the 'drowning man'! This made headlines in the local papers and led to increased numbers visiting the show. In 1908, a maple floor was laid in the pavilion so it could be used for roller skating during the winter, and outside on the pier head, an impressive range of slot and gaming machines was provided. The Royal Victoria Yacht Club and Vectis Rowing Club were both based on the pier and between 1869 and 1922, as was Ryde's RNLI lifeboat.

By 1912, the Joint Railways Committee was operating twenty-six sailings to Ryde on weekdays and thirteen on Sundays in response for the ever-increasing popularity of the island as a holiday destination. The three original steamers *Victoria*, *Duchess of Edinburgh* and *Duchess of Connaught* had been withdrawn from service: *Victoria* in 1899 and the other two in 1910. Seven main vessels were on duty in 1912, namely, *Duchess of Albany* (1889–1928), *Princess Margaret* (1893–1928), *Duchess of Kent* (1897–1933), *Duchess of Fife* (1899–1929), *Duchess of Richmond* (1910–19) and *Duchess of Norfolk* (1911–37). Amazingly, the old Portsmouth Company's steamer *Alexandra* was also still in service, but she was sold in February 1913 to the Bembridge & Seaview Steam Packet Company (who sold her on to Cosens of Weymouth the following year). The increasingly unproductive service to Stokes Bay Pier was finally withdrawn in 1913, having been a summer-only since 1902.

The First World War saw passenger services from the pier curtailed, and the four most modern vessels of the Joint Committee were requisitioned by the Royal Navy for use as minesweepers. They all returned after the war except the *Duchess of Richmond*, which struck a mine in the Mediterranean on 28 June 1919.

In 1921, work began on refurbishing the pier, with F. Bevis of Bournemouth renewing the decking and wooden piles at a cost of £12,731. Once this was completed, work was started in October 1922 by A. Jackaman & Company, rebuilding the wooden pier head in ferro-concrete using 309 new piles of 60 feet in length. The total cost of this work was £27,881.

The days of the pier being under the control of the Ryde Pier Company were coming to an end. In 1923, all of the island's railways came under the grouping of the newly-formed Southern Railway, which wanted total control of the pier to avoid the payment of tolls to the Ryde Pier Company. In 1924, the promenade and tramway piers were sold to the SR for £84,000 and the RPC was wound up. Steamer services from the pier also came under the control of the railway and new steamers were introduced, named largely after Wight locations, beginning with PS *Shanklin* in 1924, thereafter *Merstone* (1928), *Portsdown* (1928), *Southsea* (1930), *Whippingham* (1930), *Sandown* (1934) and *Ryde* (1937). In 1927, a car ferry service commenced from Portsmouth to Fishbourne, west of Ryde, using the purpose-built vessel *Fishbourne*. She was joined by *Wootton* in 1928 and *Hilsea* in 1930.

The SR had little interest in operating the promenade pier and its pavilion, and in August 1927 it was leased out to Ryde Corporation at an annual rent of £2,000. Summer shows in the pavilion continued to be popular, particularly Clarkson Rose's *Twinkle*. In addition to the Portsmouth ferries, which were by now carrying over a million passengers annually, pleasure cruises were also operated from the pier, including a 'Round the Island' cruise that called at many of the island's piers.

During the Second World War, anti-aircraft guns were placed on the pier, which led to it being attacked by German bombers. Fortunately, little damage was sustained to the structure and it remained open to transport people to and from the island. On 1 April 1944, Ryde Corporation surrendered their lease of the promenade pier.

Two of the SR steamers, *Portsdown* and *Southsea*, were mined during the war, but the other five returned and by the summer of 1946 they were working flat out as the holiday traffic returned to the island with a vengeance. This reached its height during the summer of 1947 when huge queues lined the pier to board the steamers. In addition to the Portsmouth and Southsea services, there were also sailings to Southampton, Bournemouth and occasionally Brighton. The SR ordered two new twin-screw diesel ships, but before they were delivered the railways were nationalised on 1 January 1948 and British Railways took over both the steamer services and the pier. The new vessels *Sandown* and *Brading*, entered service at the end of 1948 and in 1951 they were joined by a new *Shanklin*. Its old namesake was withdrawn from service, along with *Merstone*.

Following the end of the war, the pavilion became a ballroom. The pier's other facilities included the Ocean Restaurant, First and Last bar, amusements and a skating rink. However, as most people who used the pier were just passing through, it was difficult to make them pay. In the late 1950s, the pavilion was largely turned over to amusements, although there was also the Seagull Restaurant and short-lived cabaret shows. Sadly, the attractive pavilion, along with other Victorian buildings, was demolished in the early 1970s to make way for more car parking on the pier head. The era of the pier as an entertainment centre was at an end: even the promenade deck was given over largely to car traffic to and from the pier head.

The 1960s saw great changes to the railway and tramway on the pier. By 1966, only the line between Ryde Pier Head and Shanklin remained open, and this was converted for use by ex-London Transport tube trains. The electrification of the railway was the death knell for the pier tramway, which ran for the last time on 27 January 1969. One of tramway carriages can be seen at the Isle of Wight Bus Museum in Newport. The decade also saw the withdrawal of the last three SR paddle steamers: *Whippingham* (in 1962), *Sandown* (1966) and *Ryde* (1969). The three remaining motor vessels were upgraded and, in 1966, new mechanical gangways installed at Portsmouth and Ryde Pier greatly sped up the unloading and loading of the ships. A rival to the ferries commenced in July 1965 with the opening of a fast hovercraft service to Southsea using the George Street Slipway, which in its first two years of operation attracted over half a million passengers. BR responded with a hovercraft service from the pier beginning 1 April 1968 although the two craft proved initially to be mechanically troublesome leading to erratic sailing times.

On the night of 9 March 1973, the MV *Shanklin* ploughed into the promenade side of the pier during thick fog. A few minutes later a taxi driver taking a fare along the pier drove over the gap and fell into the sea, fortunately without injury. Repairs were quickly carried out and the pier was given Grade II listed status.

In 2003, following the privatisation of the British Railways ferry services and the transfer of the Ryde ferries to Wightlink Limited, there were proposals to transfer some of the car ferry traffic from Fishbourne to the pier. A new pontoon would have been provided and the promenade and disused tramway decks would have been given over entirely to car traffic. Opposition to the scheme meant it was put on hold. In 2009, berthing facilities for the new Wightlink catamarans were upgraded and a new coffee shop and waiting room were added to the pier head. However, other parts of the pier are in a less healthy condition, as evidenced during the summer of 2010 when the pier was closed to cars, to allow the rusting steelwork under the structure to be replaced during the winter of 2010/11. Whilst the work was taking place, the promenade pier deck was closed and pedestrians were rerouted onto a temporary walkway laid on the supports of the old tramway.

Nearly two hundred years from when it was opened, the Wightlink catamarans *Wight Ryder I* and *Wight Ryder II*, each seating 260 passengers, still connect Ryde and its 2,305-foot pier to Portsmouth, taking twenty minutes to do the journey. Ryde Pier remains a major gateway for passenger traffic to and from the Isle of Wight.

Victoria Pier

The Isle of Wight Steam Bridge Company was incorporated in November 1855, with a capital of £20,000, to provide a floating chain bridge ferry service from Ryde to Stokes Bay in association with the Stokes Bay Railway & Pier Company, who were to handle the works at Stokes Bay (*see also the Stokes Bay chapter*). However, the Ryde Board of Commissioners opposed the scheme because of the works to be carried out in the town, which included a solid horizontal approach projecting into the sea for a length of 600 feet before sloping down to a length of 2,420 feet to enable the floating bridge to land at all states of the tide. The bridge itself would measure 120 feet in length by 20 feet wide and have a central roadway for vehicles and livestock between two passenger saloons. Two engines on either side of the bridge would power the screw propeller, enabling it to have an independence of movement.

At the same time as the floating bridge plan, there was a further scheme in Ryde to provide a breakwater or tidal basin at an estimated cost of £1,200 for goods vessels, which had to unload their cargo onto the beach. This idea never got off the drawing board.

2102 Ryde: Pier from Royal Esplanade Hotel.

Above: The Victoria Pier at Ryde, photographed *c.* 1890, with its attractive wrought-iron railings. Following its short-lived use as a landing stage for the Stokes Bay ferries, the pier was used as a bathing station until 1912 when it was declared unsafe and closed. Within a few years large parts of the pier had been washed away.

Left: A rare postcard sent on 13 February 1902, showing bathers using the facilities at the end of the Victoria Pier in Ryde.

In contrast to the corporation's view, the people of Ryde gave their support at a public meeting to the floating bridge scheme and the Bill was read in the House of Commons on 18 February 1856 and again a week later. However, the Admiralty then declared their opposition, claiming the bridge and chains would cause a hindrance and interfere with the navigation and anchorage of naval vessels. In response, the promoters brought forward an amended scheme which envisaged using steamers rather than a floating bridge and changed their name to the Isle of Wight Ferry Company. This placated the opposition of the Admiralty and Ryde Town Commissioners (whose interests had been safeguarded at Ryde Esplanade), but now the Ryde Pier Company, Portsmouth Corporation and the Port of Portsmouth & Ryde Steam Packet Company all voiced their opposition to the scheme. Nevertheless, the Bill received the Royal Assent on 21 July 1856 and in February 1857 the Isle of Wight Ferry Company opened an office in Ryde where shares could be applied for. In the meantime, the plans were altered to build a pier 2,040 feet in length rather than a slipway, which could accommodate a railway as well as those wishing to promenade. The main body of the pier was to be 600 feet, leading to an incline plane and pier head where boats could land at all states of the tide. The pier was to project from a new quay and docks, 120 feet wide and 100 feet in length, which was to be erected abutting from the esplanade. In April 1858, a Joint Board was formally established between the Isle of Wight Ferry Company and the Stokes Bay Railway & Pier Company.

The project was finally commenced by contractor Mr Bennett of Pimlico in October 1857, but was beset by rough seas damaging the work carried out and water filling up in the basin behind the sea wall. In addition, there were constant battles with the Ryde Commissioners over the works and the stagnant, foul water collecting in the basin. They accused the Isle of Wight Ferry Company of tampering with the sea wall and demanded £3,000 in compensation. To add to the company's woes, a further bill to extend their powers met with local opposition and was defeated.

By the end of May 1859, the quay was virtually complete and consisted of a sheltered harbour, two basins and storage sheds. Messrs Langdon & Son now commenced work on the pier, which was to be a straight structure of 1,000 feet in length (which meant it would not be available at low tide) consisting of cast-iron screw piling and wrought-iron cross girders supporting a wooden deck with a 16-foot centre roadway for carriages and two seven-foot walkways either side. A small, octagonal toll house would front the entrance to the pier and waiting rooms would be placed on the pier head. Work on the pier progressed well and by the end of June the support piling had been sunk for a distance of 500 feet. As it neared completion, however, the pier was wrecked during a severe gale on the night of 25/26 October 1859, which left gaps of 220 feet, 200 feet and 100 feet in the structure; it was further damaged on 1 November. It appears that the pier had been built lower than the existing pier at Ryde, which had left it prone to damage by heavy seas.

The decision was taken in January 1860 to totally rebuild the pier using longer piles to increase its height above high tide level by four feet. By April, a slipway had been completed in the outer basin of the dock, but then the company hit more legal trouble when it was sued by Dr Lind, Lord of Ashey, for £5,500 for erecting their 'obnoxious and unsightly works' on land not indicated in their plans. More legal action occurred after the company attempted to take over the George Street Slipway in August and placed obstructions across it, which were removed by the commissioners. The Ryde authorities also succeeded in blocking the construction of three further quays.

Progress on building the pier proved slow and by the beginning of 1863 only half of it had been erected. The associated Stokes Bay Pier had been completed and services were commenced between Stokes Bay and the existing Ryde Pier on Easter Monday, 6 April 1863, using the company's vessel *Gareloch*. She was an iron vessel of forty-five tons and 140 feet length, with accommodation for 300 passengers; previously in the service on the Clyde. By the summer of 1864, the Isle of Wight Ferry Company was in dire financial straits, not helped by the expenditure of £10,000 during the various legal disputes it had been involved in. In a bid to raise further capital, the company promoted a Bill to raise an additional £46,000 but it proved to be a failure. Eventually, the Ryde Victoria Pier (as it was christened) was opened on 1 November 1864 to a length of 970 feet. Passengers landing at the pier from the Stokes Bay service were ferried along the pier to the railway station in three omnibuses and six cabs.

Despite the dredging of a channel at its landing stage, the pier could only be used at high tide and attempts to lengthen it were doomed due to lack of capital. On 18 February 1865, the Stokes Bay steamer services were transferred back to Ryde Pier and in the following month the Isle of Wight Ferry Company, along with the Stokes Bay Railway & Pier Company, was wound up due to debts of £12,000. The assets of the company, including the ferry service and the Victoria Pier, were sold to the Ryde Pier Company on 13 May 1865 for £23,000. They transferred the Stokes Bay ferry service to the main Ryde Pier and initially intended to demolish the Victoria Pier, but changed their minds and proposed that it should be used to land goods and a tramway would be provided for that purpose. However, the pier ended up being used as a bathing pier and in 1868 the bathing accommodation was enlarged, as reported by the *Isle of Wight Observer* on 30 April:

ENLARGED BATHING PLATFORM – The bathing accommodation at the end of Victoria Pier has been extended to double its former dimensions, and a new tariff has been issued. The charge is to be sixpence for a single bath, and threepence after 5 o'clock in the evening. The season ticket is a guinea. The bathing on the sand when the tide is suitable will be most safe and pleasurable, the temperature will be delightful to the body, and the yellow sands a carpet to the feet. The directors hoped to have had the same accommodation on the west side of the pier for ladies, but owing to representations made to them, the Lords of the Admiralty put a stop to the works, on the ground that they would be an obstruction to navigation.

On 8 September 1877, the Portsmouth barge *Emma* hit the pier, causing considerable damage. In May 1882, the pier was let to William Harvey and, following further damage caused by the vessel *Medina* in October 1882, repairs were carried out by Isaac Barton, who also installed hot and cold baths. Following Harvey's death in January 1885, the Ryde Pier Company formed a Baths Committee to run the baths and employed local ladies to oversee them. The baths were featured in the an article in the *Isle of Wight Observer* on 19 December 1885:

OZONE IODISED BATHS – We feel sure it is not generally known that there is growing up in our town an institution which bids fair to become one of the principal attractions of Ryde as a health resort. We allude to the Ozone Iodised Baths, which have been established by the Ryde Pier Company on the Victoria Pier. These medical baths have been originated by Dr Alexander Davey and Mr W Gibbs, and are conducted under their superintendence. These baths combine all the advantages of Carlsbad and Droitwich, and are strongly impregnated with iodine in its natural and most efficacious state. They are especially recommended for gout, rheumatism and liver complaints. They also have a most powerful effect on the skin: it is in fact through this organ they produce such beneficial results. It is not more than nine months since these baths were commenced, but during that time more than a thousand persons have benefitted from their use. Many of the patients coming from a considerable distance, have returned to take another course of the baths from which they have derived so much benefit. Altogether the success of the undertaking and the benefits derived have exceeded the most sanguine expectations of the promoters. Unfortunately the position of the baths at the end of the Victoria Pier is not calculated to tempt invalids during the winter months, but in spite of this drawback and the late inclement weather, bathing still continues to a very great extent. We hope that long before another winter Ryde Pier Company will be able to erect a largely increased number of Baths, with superior accommodation, and in a more suitable position at the south end of the Pier. If the Pier Company will do this in a spirited manner, from what we have seen, we do not doubt the result financially, or the benefit that will be derived by the unfortunate sufferers. We wish the promoters every success for we are certain that the success of the Ryde Pier Company in this matter will be attended by a considerable benefit to the town generally.

The pier and its baths were also described in a Victorian guide to Ryde:

The Victoria Pier constructed in 1859, and intended to rival the Old Pier, is now used exclusively for bathing purposes. There are graduated enclosures for ladies and gentlemen, and both hot and cold ozone baths are to be had. It is a somewhat shivery walk down the steps from the dressing rooms to the water, but otherwise a very enjoyable dip is to be had, and even non-swimmers may enjoy the novelty of disporting themselves a quarter mile out to sea without the risk of being drowned.

During the winter of 1894/95, the pier was damaged by storms, with piling and slipways washed away. Repair work was carried out during the first half of 1895, as reported by the *Isle of Wight Observer* on 25 May 1895:

THE RYDE PIER BATHS – The baths on the Victoria Pier have been closed for a week or two. Considerable damage was done to the Pier by the storms of last winter. Several piles were washed out and two slipways carried away completely. As considerable work was necessary to repair damages, and to make the baths suitable for the coming season, advantage was taken of the circumstance to thoroughly improve the bathing accommodation. Under the superintendence of Mr H. Roberts the secretary and manager of the Pier, a number of additions have been made to the gentlemen's side. The little dressing rooms have been completely refitted in a more comfortable style, and additional accommodation has been afforded for quite 100 bathers. The platform in front of the dressing boxes has been widened, and in other ways the comfort of bathers has been studied. An addition, which we believe will be appreciated, is a fresh water shower bath, so that those who come out of the sea will now be able to wash off the salt water if they desire to do so. It must not be supposed that the damage referred to has interfered with the warm sea baths, etc., which have been proved to have such fine medicinal properties. These have been available all through the winter, and the alterations only necessitated discontinuing them for about a week. The Bathing Pier will be opened in a few days, and we believe the alterations made will meet with general approval. The Pier Company are certainly to be congratulated on their spirited efforts to cater for the convenience of the bathing public. We paid a visit to the Victoria Pier a few days since and were struck with the clearness of the sea, the bottom being clearly visible in 10 or 15 feet of water. There were then a number of beautiful medusa or jellyfish floating about, which sailors say is a sign of approaching hot weather.

In 1901, Ryde Corporation made an offer to the Ryde Pier Company to buy the Victoria Pier, but the sale fell through after the two parties failed to agree on what land should be included. The pier continued in use for bathing but, in September and October 1903, the bathing stages and cabins were damaged during storms. They were repaired but the pier was proving to be a strain on the finances of the company and its maintenance began to be neglected. In 1912, the baths were leased to Mr Grace, who had to spend £300 to make them fit for use, but his lease expired in October 1913 and it is unclear whether they were opened the following year.

The Ryde Pier Company decided to demolish the dilapidated pier and announced plans to build a new bathing station along the west side of Ryde Pier. Ryde Corporation opposed the plans and offered once again to buy the Victoria Pier, which it was thought they would shorten and use either as a goods landing stage or a walkway to a new bathing pool. The pier company's sale price of £1,500 was rejected by the corporation but during lengthy negotiations the company agreed to include in a sale the right of way in Quay Road. An agreement was finally reached whereby the corporation would pay £1,000 and the costs of an Act of Parliament to transfer ownership to them, which occurred on 3 August 1916.

The poor condition of the pier soon led the corporation to realise they would have no use for it. Parts of the structure collapsed into the sea during gales and by 1918 only the iron piles remained standing, which were removed soon afterwards. In 1920, the Ryde Pier Company finally received their £1,000 from the corporation.

Appley Pier

In 1873, Sir Willam Hutt MP of Appley Tower wrote to the Board of Trade asking for permission to erect a private pier of 200 feet to replace an existing pier about a 100 feet eastward of the site of the new one. The pier was completed that year by a Mr White, but only to a length of 100 feet.

Sir William died on 24 November 1882, with Lady Hutt passing away on 26 September 1886. Thereafter, the pier was little used and the silting up of mud and sand made it impossible for boats to use. By 3 November 1911, it had been removed.

Appley could have had a far grander pier. In 1874, the Ryde Pier Company put forward a proposal to construct a new railway from St Johns Road station to a pier at Appley beach by tunnelling under Appley Hill. However, the heavy expense involved meant the idea soon foundered.

The small private pier at Appley Castle, Ryde, built in 1873 for Sir William Hutt MP and demolished in 1911.

SEAVIEW

Seaview is a small village resort near Ryde, which has remained something of a quiet backwater compared to other parts of the island. The village was described as 'a pleasant retreat for those who are fond of a quiet seaside nook away from the bustle and gaiety of Ryde' and was noted for its fine bathing and good sands. For seventy years, its claim to fame and pride and joy was a very elegant suspension pier, one of only three suspension or chain piers built in the British Isles.[8]

Seaview Pier

The Sea View[9] Pier and Improvement Company was formed by the local landowner (of the Seagrove Estate) Squire Glynn on 20 December 1877, with an initial capital of £6,000 in £10 shares and the aim of providing a pier to capture some of the steamboat traffic operating from nearby Ryde to the mainland. An Act of Parliament for the scheme was passed in 1878 and the design of engineer Frank Caws was accepted. The Caws family owned much of the land in Sea View, and Frank, who was based in Sunderland, was an expert on suspension bridges; with his brother Edward he designed a suspension pier with very few support piles to lessen the pier's resistance to heavy seas and the necessity of driving them into the difficult rocky foreshore. The pier was to consist of five suspension spans, three of 200 feet, two of 140 feet and eight suspension cables, consisting of seven strands of forty-eight galvanised steel wires that were rested on saddles and free-moving rollers on top of the four timber towers. The deck would be suspended from the cables by flat bar galvanised hangers and kept in constant tension by the counter and upward pull of the cables and hangers, or by straining it from both ends. The timber used in the construction consisted of pine, beech, elm and deal. The pier was to jut out from a prominent headland, which ensured that those who used the pier would obtain splendid views of Spithead.

---

[8] The other two chain piers were both built by Captain Samuel Brown at Trinity, Edinburgh, in 1821 and Brighton in 1823.

[9] The resort was initially spelt as two words 'Sea View' until around 1904.

The graceful chain pier at Seaview, seen here on a postcard *c.* 1905, was one of only three chain/suspension piers erected in the United Kingdom. The pier was 1,050 feet long, largely built of timber and had unusual curved decking.

This excellent postcard view of Seaview Pier was taken from the Pier Hotel and was sent as a postcard on 7 June 1906. One of the two tollhouses at the entrance doubled as a general waiting room and seating was provided in the open timber framing of the towers.

Members of a bathing club pose for the photographer on the pier head at Seaview *c.* 1910. The glass-fronted building on the left was erected for the Sea View Sailing Club in 1894. The other round building has a fine looking amusement machine.

The elegant outline of Seaview Pier as seen from the entrance *c.* 1910. The notices on the tollhouse include an order about behaviour on the pier issued by the Pier Master George White, and details of steamer sailings.

A postcard sent in 1926 showing the curved nature of the pier deck, and the Pier Hotel on the shore. The gentleman walking along the pier is probably the Pier Master.

The very sad sight of Seaview Pier following its destruction by storms on 27–29 December 1951. The remains were demolished early in 1952.

On 6 September 1879, William Pearson of Sunderland was appointed contractor to build the pier at an agreed price of £3,000, of which £480 was to be taken up in the company's shares. If the work was completed by 1 June 1880, Pearson would be paid £2,205, and a further £315 would be given after twelve months satisfactory use of the pier. Pearson commenced work almost immediately, but by the following June the pier was nowhere near finished and Pearson was sacked by a frustrated Caws, who used the following contractors and suppliers to help complete the pier: Mr Barnes of Haslemere (beech cable anchorages), Messrs Armstrong Addison & Company of Sunderland (pitch pine and other timber), Messrs R. Johnson and Nephew of Manchester (cable wires), Messrs Glaholm & Robson of Sunderland (cable spinning), Mr Henry Tomkinson of Sunderland (galvanised ironwork), Mr Arthur Creath of Nettleston (ironwork) and Messrs Dashwood & Company of Ryde (elm and other timber). As the work progressed, it became clear that the pier would cost more than the original share capital allowed and the company increased it to £10,000 in £5 shares. However, only £6,075 worth of shares was taken up and both Caws and Squire Glynn (who had built the sea wall, embankment and road to the pier) had to be paid mostly in shares rather than cash. On 7 June 1881, the pier was formally opened, although it was not fully completed until the following year.

The pier was immediately heralded as a thing of beauty, yet there were some concerns that it looked too fragile to withstand gales and heavy seas. Early concerns were raised when the pier was seen to oscillate when it was crowded with people, but the adjustment of the wire stays appeared to cure the problem. The *Isle of Wight Observer* commented on the pier: 'This delightful little structure, which has received such econuims from professional engineers, was opened on Monday last, a great many excursionists landing upon it. In spite of its fragile appearance, the pier is said to be very firm.' The completed pier was 1,000 feet in length and 15 feet wide and was noticeable for its curved deck spans. A small pavilion was provided on the fan-shaped pier head, which stood in a sufficient depth of water to accommodate up to three steamboats even during the lowest spring tides. Two tollhouses were built at the entrance, one of them doubling as a general waiting room, and seating was provided in the open timber framing of the towers. A one penny toll (increased to 2d in 1894) was charged to use the pier, although those partaking of a bath or sedan chair paid 4d and those on a bicycle 3d. If 'Rover' was out for walkies he was charged 1d!

The pier received the royal seal of approval in August 1881, when the Prince and Princess of Wales disembarked at it from the steam yacht *Helen*. In the mid-1880s, a regular steam service by Brading Harbour Company began operating between Bembridge, Portsmouth and Southsea, calling at Sea View, and following improvements to the pier head and landing stage in 1889 (which increased the pier's length by 50 feet) the Southsea & Ventnor Steamship Company's Vessels *Island Queen* and *Bembridge* called. The *Dandie Dinmont*, an unreliable steamer belonging to the Southsea, Ventnor, Shanklin & Sandown Steamboat Company, was an occasional caller. So too were the *Winnie* and *Prince*, which it is believed used the pier in 1894. From 1898, only *Bembridge* remained from the fleet of the Southsea & Ventnor Steamship Company, but in 1899 she was joined by additional steam launches, which led to receipts rising to £937 and a 4 per cent dividend being paid to shareholders.

In 1893, the pier was repainted at a cost of £45 and a successful season paid a 3 per cent dividend to shareholders. A small glass-fronted round house was placed on the new pier head in 1894 by the Sea View Sailing Club, but a wet season saw a drop in receipts and the company's report stated 'your directors are confident that, until the company can charter or purchase a steamboat, the pier can never be such a success from a financial point of view, as was anticipated when the company was formed.' The company regularly had to pay out for what the directors called the 'constant, necessary repairs required to keep the pier in satisfactory order.' Despite its fragility, the pier made a good impression on the 1897 *Ward Lock Guide* for the island: 'The pier makes an agreeable promenade – the switchback-like arrangement of the flooring adding something of a novelty.'

A good season in 1900 enabled both a 4 per cent dividend to shareholders to be paid out and the pier head to be enlarged in 1901 at a cost of £505 by Edward Hayden of Ryde. Three mutoscope machines were leased that year from the London-based South Coast Mutoscope Company, with the pier company gaining 20 per cent of the gross takings. In 1904/05, electric lighting was installed along the pier by the Isle of Wight Electric Light & Power Company at a cost of £41. At the same time, the pier was strengthened with the addition of ten wire stays (five on each side of the pier), which were pegged into the beach 20 feet from the structure.

However, since 1900, the company was no longer paying dividends to its shareholders due to the continued heavy expenditure on maintenance and repairs to the fragile pier structure. To compound matters, both the Southsea and Ventnor steamboat services using *Bembridge* and the steam launches to Portsmouth provided an unreliable service from the pier. In 1903, a winter service between Seaview and Portsmouth quickly foundered due to the difficulty of landing at the structure in rough seas and the hopes of the pier competing with Ryde in providing intensive and reliable boat services were never realised. An attempt to provide a satisfactory service to Portsmouth and Southsea was made in 1914 with the formation by members of the Seaview Pier Company of the Seaview Steam Packet Company, who purchased the steamer *Alleyn* for £2,250. A service was commenced to Portsmouth Harbour via Southsea South Parade Pier in May 1914; however, the company soon got into dispute with the competing Bembridge & Seaview Steamship Company, who, as the Southsea & Ventnor Steamship Company had unreliably served Seaview Pier until 1913. They were now operating *Lord Kitchener* and *Alexandra*, the latter having been acquired in 1913 as a replacement for *Bembridge*. The Seaview Pier Company argued that the *Alexandra* was too big to call safely at the pier, and the vessel never did in fact call as she was quickly replaced by the equally large *Mermaid*. The pier company responded by charging landing rates according to the tonnage of each vessel, but the Bembridge company refused to pay and both sides sought legal advice. In the meantime, the two companies ran their services to and from the pier until some sort of agreement was finally brokered when the Bembridge Company agreed to pay the tonnage dues owed.

Upon the outbreak of the First World War in August 1914, the Bembridge Company immediately ceased their services, but the *Alleyn* operated for a further month and took twenty village recruits for the army to the mainland. The vessel needed £800 worth of repairs before she was passed as seaworthy for the 1915 season, but in the event she didn't run as the Admiralty ordered that all boat services from the pier be suspended to enable shipping lanes to be free for vessels vital to the war effort. The *Alleyn* was sold off to Mesopotamia (for a heavy financial loss to its owners) and for much of the Great War the pier was closed. The pier was reopened in 1919 without any regular steamer services, although a national rail strike affected sailings to Ryde and Gosport-based steam launches ran between Seaview and Southsea South Parade piers. A service of small boats (known as the 'V' boats) did operate from the pier to Portsmouth and Southsea (Clarence Pier) between Easter and autumn throughout the 1920s and 1930s, and vessels of the Brading Harbour Company called. The main function of the pier was now as a bracing marine promenade to enjoy the invigorating air and splendid views. However, this failed to bring in the necessary income for the cash-strapped Seaview Pier Company, which in 1925 folded following the death of Squire Glynn and had to be reformed the following year with new shareholders. They carried out much needed repairs to the pier including twelve new piles fitted to the pier head and a strengthening of the sea wall.

Upon the arrival of the Second World War, the pier was closed to the public once again and was taken over the by Royal Navy, who used it amongst other things to practise for the D-Day invasion of Normandy. Sadly, by the end of the war, lack of maintenance and heavy handed usage by the navy had caused the pier to become very dilapidated. The Seaview Pier Company had gone into liquidation and the pier was put up for auction in November 1947 with the following description: 'Believed to be the only remaining Suspension Pier in England and extending seawards for a distance of approximately 1,000ft, with a depth of water at the seaward extremity of about 6ft to 7ft at mean low water springs. Owing to no soundings having been taken recently, this depth cannot be definitely stated and must only be regarded as a rough guide. The Pier itself has fallen into disrepair during the war and will be sold as it stands, with no guarantee as to the state of repair or its safety.'

The pier, along with its surrounding land, was acquired for £775 in 1947 by A. J. Figgis, who announced his attention to restore it. Government bureaucracy and a repair bill of around £6,000 soon changed his mind and in July 1948 he announced that the pier was to be demolished. However, the pier was then sold to Messrs Horwich Brothers who owned the Pier Hotel.

By the late 1940s, the pier was in a poor state with gaping holes in the decking, although that did not deter fishermen venturing out on it to enjoy a spot of fishing, or local children clambering over the entrance gate. Yet even in its derelict condition the pier was designated in October 1950 as a building of special architectural or historic interest under the Town and Country Planning Act of 1947.

Sadly, any faint hopes of restoring the pier to its former glory were dashed when the fourth span of the structure and one of the towers was washed away in the early hours of 27 December 1951 during a fearsome storm that battered the south coast of England throughout the Christmas period. The pier was reported to have violently trembled and shaken before the span crashed into the sea. Two nights later, further heavy seas fanned by hurricane force winds washed away the majority of the rest of the pier, strewing timber onto the beach and esplanade. The two tollhouses at the pier entrance were lifted bodily by the violent wind and hurled into the grounds of the Pier Hotel. All that remained was 100 feet of the shore end, two of the towers and the isolated pier head and, by the summer of 1952, they had all been cleared away by Messrs Dowding of Southampton.

It was a sad end to a unique pier.

BEMBRIDGE

A small and – for a time – fashionable resort that flourished following the reclamation of Brading Harbour and the opening of the railway from Brading in 1882. The nearby Royal Isle of Wight Golf Club at St Helens was patronised by royalty and Bembridge had its own sailing club and exclusive hotel, the Royal Spithead. A number of large houses for the wealthy were built in the village. Steamers from the mainland called at the harbour until it began to silt up in the 1920s and the railway closed in 1953. These days Bembridge is somewhat off the tourist map, but is noted for its long lifeboat pier.

Harbour Pier

A short wooden pier, 250 feet long and 6–8 feet wide, was erected in Bembridge Harbour in the 1870s as part of the Bembridge Railway, Tramway and Pier Act of 1864, authorising reclamation work of some 800 acres of marshes and sea between Brading and St Helens known as Brading Haven. However, work on building an embankment that would reclaim the area and link St Helens and Bembridge was not begun by the Brading Harbour Improvement & Railway Company until 1874. Numerous breaches of the embankment whilst under construction meant that the work was not finished until 1880 at a cost of £420,000. This enabled the railway to be extended from St Helens to Bembridge on 27 May 1882. The Royal Spithead Hotel was built close to the station as Bembridge began to be transformed into a quiet and select seaside resort.

A number of commercial vessels and paddle steamers used the pier, although the passage to it required constant dredging. Amongst the vessels that called were *Island Queen* in 1878, *Bembridge* (formerly *Princess of Wales*), *Sandringham*, *Lord Kitchener*, *Duke of York* and *Prince*. A new landing stage was added in 1910 and, four years later, there was a short-lived service between Bembridge, Seaview, Southsea and Portsmouth operated by the Seaview Steam Packet Company's *Alleyn*, which was interrupted by the start of the Great War and never recommenced. However, by then the harbour had begun to silt up and the pier could not be used by large vessels. The steamer service to the pier ended in 1924

2   BEMBRIDGE (Isle of Wight). — Pier and Club House. — LL.

The small wooden pier at Bembridge was built in the 1870s for commercial vessels and paddle steamers to call. Silting up of the harbour led to the last ship calling in 1924 and the pier was demolished four years later.

upon acquisition of the harbour by the Southern Railway and they demolished the structure four years later.

The railway to Bembridge was acquired by the Isle of Wight Railway in July 1898 for £16,500 and became part of the Southern Railway in 1923. Upon Nationalisation in 1948, the line became part of British Railways until closure on 21 September 1953. The harbour remained in railway hands until 1968.

Lifeboat Pier

Bembridge Lifeboat Station was established by the RNLI in 1867 when a boathouse was built at Lane End. In 1922, a 750-foot-long lifeboat pier, complete with boathouse, was erected to house the motor vessel *Langham*. The pier was constructed of concrete piles and could be used at all states of the tide, which resulted in the subsequent closure of the stations at Ryde, Brighstone and Brooke.

The *Langham* remained in service until 1939 when it was replaced by the *Jesse Lumb*. In 1964, the old lifeboat station was brought back into use when an inshore lifeboat was placed there, giving Bembridge the honour of two stations.

In 1970, the *Jack Shayler and the Lees* was placed on station and remained for seventeen years until the Tyne Class Lifeboat *Max Aitken III* arrived. The boathouse on the pier was rebuilt to house the new craft and, two years later, the slipway was extended to recover the boat at low tide. In 1996, the pier was rebuilt with pre-fabricated struts by Dean & Dyball under the supervision of consultant engineers Posford Duvivier. In September 2010, the Tamar Class lifeboat *Alfred Albert Williams* (replacing the temporary Mersey Class boat *Peggy and Alex Caird*) was placed at Bembridge, necessitating another rebuilding of the pier and boathouse. The £1m needed to carry this out was raised by a public appeal.

The pier has become an attractive landmark on the island and is usually available for those who wish to take a stroll upon it. During the summer months, the boathouse is open on certain days to the public.

1. A postcard showing the original South Parade Pier at Southsea, opened on 26 July 1879, but destroyed by fire during the afternoon of 19 July 1904. The pier was rebuilt by Portsmouth Corporation at a cost of £85,000 and reopened on 12 August 1908.

2. The current pavilion on Southsea South Parade Pier was erected following the destruction of the 1908 building on 11 June 1974 during the filming of Ken Russell's *Tommy*. The pavilion currently houses an amusement arcade, bars and two function rooms.

Clarence Pier, Southsea.

3. A *c.* 1900 picture of Southsea Clarence Pier – one of the shortest and widest of all seaside piers. The large round pavilion was opened by the Prince of Wales in 1882 and was destroyed, along with the rest of the pier, by enemy bombing on 10 January 1941. Note the cannon close to the Bovril sign.

4. Following its wartime destruction, the Clarence Pier at Southsea was rebuilt during the 1950s and reopened on 1 June 1961 with a distinctive 60-foot-high steel tower. The entrance to the pier is seen here on a bright summer's day in July 2005.

5. A postcard issued by F. G. O. Stuart showing Lee-on-the-Solent Pier in around 1906. The pier was opened in 1888 but was demolished in 1958 after it was badly damaged during the Second World War. On the right of the photograph, standing close to the beach, is the railway station, open to passengers from 1894 until 1930.

6. The railway and ferry pier at Stokes Bay, as pictured on a postcard from 1906. The pier was opened in 1863 to provide a ferry service to Ryde on the Isle of Wight, which ceased in 1915. The Admiralty then took over the pier, but eventually it became derelict and was demolished in 1975.

7. An iron pier was built in 1865 to act as a landing stage for military patients arriving at the Royal Victoria Hospital at Netley. By the time of this postcard (c. 1904) the pier was mainly in use as a recreational centre and promenade for the patients. The pier later fell into disuse and was demolished by 1955.

The Royal Pier.   Minuette don't foget, I love you yet,   Southampton.

B. 1676. 3.   M. J. R.

8. A colour postcard of the Royal Pier at Southampton in 1904, featuring the railway station on the left and the pavilion in the centre distance. Originally built in 1833, the pier was extensively enlarged during the 1890s when the pavilion was added. The station was officially closed in 1921 and the pavilion was destroyed by fire in 1987, by which time the pier was derelict.

9. The long iron pier at Hythe, built in 1881, is used as a landing stage for the ferry service to Southampton and features a charming electric train dating from 1922. This photograph shows the pier and train in the late 1960s.

10. Lymington Pier railway station in November 2010 with the Yarmouth ferry seen in the background. The pier was originally opened by the London & South Western Railway on 1 May 1884.

Ryde. I. W. General View from Pier Pavilion.

11. A bird's-eye view from 1904 showing the 'three piers in one' at Ryde. On the left can be seen the railway pier and pier head station dating from 1880, whilst in the centre is the tramway pier opened in 1864. On the right is the promenade deck, the first section of which opened in 1814.

12. Ryde Pier Head station in July 2005, showing one of the former London Transport tube trains that have operated the service between Ryde Pier Head and Shanklin since 1966.

13. The elegant chain pier at Seaview is seen here on a postcard issued in 1902. The pier, opened in 1881, was sadly demolished after sustaining storm damage in December 1951. The Pier Hotel is also no longer standing.

14. The striking lifeboat pier at Bembridgem following its reconstruction in 2010 in order to house the Tamar Class lifeboat *Alfred Albert Williams*. The £1 million needed to rebuild the pier and boathouse was raised by a public appeal.

15. Sandown Pier was opened in 1878 to a length of 360 feet and was extended to 875 feet in 1875 when the pavilion was added. The pier is seen here *c.* 1905 with a steamer just leaving the landing stage and Clifford Essex's Pierrots advertised as performing in the pavilion.

16. Sandown Pier photographed from the landing stage in the late 1980s. The large building at the shore end of the pier was added as a theatre in 1934, but since 1999 has been used as an indoor bowling centre and amusement arcade.

17. Shanklin Pier was opened to a length of 1,200 feet in 1890 and it is seen here on a postcard issued c. 1905. The attractive kiosks at the entrance are of note, as is the curvature of deck leading from the entrance.

18. A photograph taken in 1982 of Shanklin Pier, showing the Mayneland amusements building along with customers relaxing in the deckchairs on a sunny day. The pier was damaged in the Great Storm of 16 October 1987 and the remains were demolished in 1993.

The Pier, Ventnor, Isle of Wight. (Showing Tugs.)

19. The pier at Ventnor was first opened in 1872 to replace a harbour that was quickly wrecked by stormy seas and can be seen here on this postcard from 1903. The pier stood on iron piles and was 683 feet long with a horseshoe shaped pier head for luck.

20. A lady walks her dog along Ventnor Pier in June 1981. The pier had been rebuilt in steel in the 1950s but later, in 1981, the pier was closed when it was revealed that £750,000 would be needed for repairs and maintenance work. Efforts to preserve the pier failed and its demolition was completed in 1993.

21. An iron pier was constructed at Alum Bay in 1887 (replacing an earlier wooden structure) to bring visitors by steamers to see the famous coloured sands (on the right). However, the pier had to be closed in the 1920s after it was damaged by storms and in the succeeding years the remains were slowly washed away.

22. Totland Bay Pier was opened in 1879 to serve a small resort and the Totland Bay Hotel. This postcard of the pier, issued in around 1920, shows a steamer calling at the landing stage. However, in 1931 the calls had to cease when the stage was declared unsafe. The pier survives, although the majority of it has been closed for some years.

23. The Grade II wooden pier at Yarmouth was opened in 1876 and is seen here in 1998 looking much the same as it did when it was first built. Now 609 feet long, Yarmouth is one of last remaining wooden pleasure piers in the country and is interestingly made up of three different types of timber – Douglas fir for decking and handrails, greenheart for the piles and *barcilata balau* for the latticework on the handrails.

24. A view of Yarmouth Pier, looking towards the town on a wet day in 2008. The sponsoring of planks on the deck has helped fund the pier's restoration in recent years and some of the sponsor's names can be seen. The pier remains a popular promenade and fishing centre ,and boats still call, including the ferry to Keyhaven and Hurst Castle.

The Esplanade and Pier   Cowes (Isle of Wight)

25. The Victoria Pier at Cowes was opened on 26 March 1902 and this postcard shows it around that time. Measuring just 170 feet in length, the pier acquired shelters in 1903 and a pavilion was built the following year. The pier was eventually demolished in 1961 after having lain derelict since the Second World War.

Wreck of Pier — Southbourne

26. Southbourne Pier was erected in 1888 as part of the development of a new resort by Bournemouth doctor Thomas Compton. Three years later, the pier was wrecked in a storm and left in a derelict state until its demolition in 1909. This postcard shows the ruined pier c. 1905.

Boscombe.   On the Pier

27. Boscombe Pier was opened in 1889 and in 1897 the skeleton of a whale, which had been washed ashore locally, was placed upon it. This postcard shows the skeleton shortly before it was removed in 1903.

28. Boscombe Pier in 2008, looking very different from its Victorian predecessor. The pier was extensively rebuilt in 1958–62, and again in 2007–08 when it was refurbished at a cost of £2.4 million.

The Pier   Bournemouth

29. An iron pier was opened at Bournemouth on 11 August 1880 following the failure of a wooden pier built in 1861; it can be seen here, pictured on this postcard from 1902. Measuring 1,000 feet in length and featuring an ornate wrought-iron and glass entrance building, the pier was a busy port of call for steamer services along the south coast.

30. Like its neighbour at Boscombe, Bournemouth Pier currently bears no resemblance to when it was first built. In 1979–81, the structure was extensively rebuilt in concrete, although the pavilion seen here – dating from 1959 – was retained and is still used for summer shows.

31. A postcard of Swanage Pier, taken from the upper deck of the pier head *c.* 1905. The pier was opened in 1897 to replace an earlier one built in 1859, although the latter was to remain in use for a number of years. The structure of the pier consisted largely of wood, but with ornate wrought-iron side panels and globe lamps.

32. A view along Swanage Pier in the summer of 2005, showing the splendid restoration work that was carried out during the 1990s to return it to its Victorian splendour. The attractive wrought-iron side panels and globe lamps are a particularly noteworthy feature.

In 1922, a 750-foot-long concrete pier was erected to enable the motor vessel *Langham* to be used at all states of the tide. This postcard shows the lifeboat pier in the 1930s.

In September 2010, the Tamar Class lifeboat *Alfred Albert Williams* was placed at Bembridge, necessitating another rebuilding of the pier and boathouse. The £1 million needed to carry this out was raised by a public appeal.

SANDOWN

One of the island's most popular resorts, Sandown, grew in popularity following the arrival of the railway in 1864. The town's location on the relatively sheltered Sandown Bay led to it soon gaining a fine reputation for sea bathing and by the 1870s bathing machines and marine baths were well-established. A pier was one of the earliest attractions to be provided, although until 1895 it was too short to receive steamers.

Sandown Pier

Following aborted schemes to provide a pier in association with the Isle of Wight Eastern Railway in both 1860 and 1863 (*see the Piers that never were chapter for further details*), a new pier scheme was proposed in 1874 by the Sandown Pier Company, which was incorporated on 20 February with a capital of £6,000 to be raised with 1,200 shares of £5 each. A 700-foot pier was authorised under the Pier and Harbour Order 1874 and the beach and foreshore upon which it would stand was acquired from the Board of Trade on 2 September 1875. A design for an iron pier 640 feet in length was drawn up by W. Binns and the contractors Jukes & Coulson of London commenced work in April 1876. However, lack of finance meant that only 360 feet of the pier was actually built, which was opened by Lady Oglander on Wednesday, 29 May 1878. Two attractive square toll booths, with hipped roofs and small spires, fronted the entrance and a small shelter was placed on the pier head. Continuous seating ran along both sides of the pier, which had cast iron piling, wrought iron girders and timber decking.

The already cash-strapped Sandown Pier Company soon discovered that the pier in its current state as a short and bare promenade was never going to pay its way. An Act of Parliament was passed in 1884 to extend the pier, but the company had no finance to do it as only 388 shares of their issue had been taken up. On 2 October 1885, the decision was taken to wind up the company and the pier passed into the hands of the Sandown Pier Extension Company, formed in 1886 with a capital of £10,000 (500 preference shares of £10 and 1,000 ordinary £5 shares) by the island's MP Richard Webster, later Viscount Alverstone. Webster,

The seafront at Sandown in the 1880s showing the original short 360-foot pier, opened in 1878, along with a fine array of bathing machines.

Sandown Pier photographed on the official opening of its extension to 875 feet on 17 September 1895. In addition to the pier being decked out in bunting, an illuminated sign bearing the words 'Forward Sandown' was placed across the entrance.

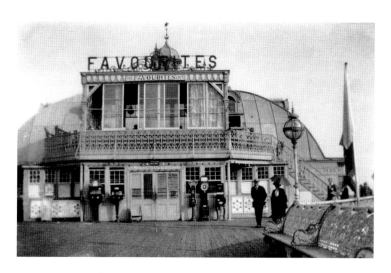

A fine photograph of Sandown Pier Pavilion, erected in 1895, when the pier was extended. At the front of the building on the first floor can be seen the Favourites café and on the ground floor a selection of chocolate, amusement and weighing machines.

Crowds line both sides of the pier to view the Sandown Bay Regatta on 22 August 1905.

The landing stage and sea end of Sandown Pier seen from a steamer *c.* 1910. The pier was a regular port of call for steamers from the mainland and those on 'Round the Island' cruises.

A postcard showing the entrance to Sandown Pier during the 1920s. Information boards list what the pier has to offer, including Round the Island cruises, concert parties, Bernard Stebbings' Orchestra, Grand Confetti Fête and the Sandown Bay Regatta.

Sandown Pier photographed in the late 1940s, showing the defensive gap blown in the structure in 1940. The pavilion at the shore end of the pier was officially opened by Lord Jellicoe, Admiral of the Fleet, on 23 October 1934.

A 1960s postcard of the Islander bar, situated in the old pavilion on Sandown Pier. The bar was closed in 1968 when the pier was declared unsafe and the old pavilion was demolished three years later.

A photograph of Sandown Pier taken in July 2005. The Pavilion was closed as a theatre in 1997 and converted into an amusement, bowling and indoor golf centre. The pier is now the only one on the Isle of Wight with such leisure activities on it.

The sea end of Sandown Pier in July 2005, showing the site of the old pavilion – demolished in 1971 and now given over to amusements for children. The concrete landing stage remains in use, mainly for fishermen.

who virtually financed the company on his own, announced he was to extend the pier to 875 feet and erect a 400-seat pavilion on a three-sided pier head surrounded by a landing stage for steamers. An order to extend the pier was granted in 1893 and the sea bed was sold by the Board of Trade on 23 July 1894. The appointed contractors, Messrs Roe & Grace of Southampton, commenced work in the early autumn of 1894 and the extended pier and pavilion were opened at a cost of £13,000 on 17 September 1895 to great celebration in Sandown. The pier, along with most of the town, was decked out in bunting and across the entrance was placed an illuminated sign bearing the words *Forward Sandown*. Following the official opening, Richard Webster treated the assembled dignitaries to a grand luncheon before they assembled to watch an afternoon regatta. Tea was then taken in the pavilion.

The extended pier initially proved to be more successful than its predecessor and an admission charge of 2d was levied to use it. Customers were greeted by the cheery Pier Master Samuel Edwards who was always ready to dispense a good yarn! He was also something of a poet and sent an ode to Queen Alexandra on the occasion of her fifty-first wedding anniversary in March 1914. Concert party and pierrot shows took place in the pavilion, which was leased out; in 1898 the lessees were the Island Pavilion Syndicate. The pier's landing stage was a port of call for 'Round the Island' cruises and for services to the mainland. In 1904, a new bathing house was added to the attractions the pier could offer.

The years 1904 to 1917 proved to be fairly profitable for the Sandown Pier Extension Company. A gross revenue average of £10,235 was obtained during the period, against an expenditure (excluding income tax) of £7,124. However, all profits were used to pay off interest on loans or for repairs, which included a refurbishment of the landing stage in 1911 at a cost of £1,070 and, following the death of the major shareholder Viscount Alverstone in 1915, the company was left moribund. Another great supporter of the pier, Pier Master Samuel Edwards, also passed away.

Following an agreement with the executors of the viscount's estate, Sandown Council acquired the pier on 1 June 1918 for only £2,500. They reduced the pier toll from 2d to 1d and gave the structure a much-needed refurbishment, particularly the pier head, which had suffered damage in November 1916. Following the amalgamation of Sandown and Shanklin councils in 1933 (despite great opposition in both towns), work was started on a new 980-seat pavilion at the shore end of the pier, designed by Ernest Latham. The pavilion cost £26,000 to build and was officially opened by Lord Jellicoe, Admiral of the Fleet, on 23 October 1934. The Sandown-Shanklin Municipal Orchestra, led by Ernest English, became a feature of the new pavilion as did summer shows, such as the Fol-de-Rols in 1938. The old pavilion on the pier head continued in use as a ballroom. Pleasure cruises continued to call at the pier's landing stage during the summer from the mainland and on 'Round the Island' cruises.

Following wartime breaching, the pier was restored in 1947 by the council, who contracted the work to the Harbour & General Works Company Limited at a cost of £10,677. The council was entitled to compensation from the Government for the wartime damage, although this was slow in coming and led to a delay in restoring the landing stage. Work on a new two-level concrete landing stage was finally begun in 1950 by Messrs Richard Costain Limited, but was not completed until 1954 when the final bill amounted to nearly £60,000.

The Pier Pavilion was re-branded the 'Pavilion Theatre' and hosted summer shows, music festivals and local functions. Between 1947 and 1957, Bill Scott Gordon's 'Revels' was the summer show in the pavilion and the Bournemouth Symphony Orchestra visited twice a year. Don Moody, Entertainment and Publicity Manager for Sandown-Shanklin UDC, successfully managed the pavilion until the 1970s. In the meantime, the old pier pavilion was converted into the 'Islander Bar' restaurant and amusement arcade by the leaseholders HMF Restaurants and HMF Amusements. The landing stage remained in use by Red Funnel steamers and Cosens and, in 1957–59, a short-lived ferry service to Portsmouth using motor launches was operated by the Sandown Company of Mursell and Kemp. During a two-day visit to the island in 1965, the Queen boarded the Royal Barge from the pier.

However, in 1968, the pier beyond the Pavilion Theatre was declared unsafe and closed; although those using the landing stage could still use the pier if they signed an indemnity form declaring they were using it at their own risk. The leaseholders of the old pier pavilion, HMF Restaurants and HMF Amusements, were each granted £7,000 in compensation for the early termination of their seven year leases granted in 1963. An examination of the pier found that the steel lattice girders supporting the 1895 extension were in a very poor condition and the concrete structure under the Pavilion Theatre was unsafe and had to be temporarily supported with timber baulks. The council initially proposed demolishing the pier beyond the Pavilion Theatre, not only due its unsafe condition, but because it never paid its way. However, a number of loans were obtained from the Ministry of Agriculture, Fisheries and Food (because the pier was technically classed as a 'fishing harbour') which enabled full restoration to be carried out. Work began in 1970, and in the following year the old pier head pavilion was demolished after suffering fire damage. The main body of the restoration work was carried out by contractors Westridge Construction Company of Ryde, although repairs to the landing stage were undertaken by Wessex Diving & Dredging Contractors. The Pavilion Theatre remained open during the work, which also saw it upgraded with new changing rooms, sun lounges, café and bar and a widening of the pier entrance. The total cost of the restoration work was £400,000 and, on Sunday 22 July 1973, the total length of the pier was reopened by Earl Mountbatten of Burma, the Governor of the Isle of Wight.

From 1970, the council presented in the Pavilion Theatre its own summer show 'Showtime' for a few years, before engaging John Redgrave Productions to manage the entertainment, who attracted household names such as Des O'Connor, Jimmy Tarbuck, Norman Wisdom and Frankie Howard. Admission to the pier was now free and Mursell & Kemp continued to operate cruises from the landing stage to Southsea and Shanklin, until their retirement in 1994. Their business was sold to Wightline Cruises of Ryde, which had been operating services from Sandown Pier since 1987.

In 1974, Sandown-Shanklin UDC was absorbed into the new South Wight Borough Council, who based their Tourism & Leisure Services Department in the Pier Pavilion for a time. In 1983, they engaged Nick Thomas Entertainments to take over the management of the Pavilion Theatre, and in his first year he managed to attract a number of household names such as Cilla Black, Jim Davidson and Jimmy Cricket. However, the pier changed hands in 1986 when it was sold by South Wight Borough Council to Sandown Pier Leisure Company, whose founder, George Peak, had operated the pier's amusement arcade for the past twenty years. The council retained a ten-year lease to run the Pavilion Theatre and spent £500,000 on refurbishing it. In 1989, the building was damaged by fire but was repaired at a cost of £2 million and reopened on 19 June 1990. Three years later, the theatre was contracted out to Isle of Wight Theatres, who struggled to make it pay, leading to closure at the end of the 1997 season. The Sandown Pier Leisure Company then converted the building into an indoor bowling and golf centre, which opened in 1999.

Sandown is now the only fully-fledged pleasure pier on the island and offers amusements, a funfair, gift shops, refreshment outlets, fishing, bowling and pleasure cruises.

SHANKLIN

Mentioned in the Domesday Book, Shanklin is one of the island's oldest settlements, but remained relatively undiscovered until the first quarter of the nineteenth century when its picturesque thatched cottages began to attract visitors, including the poet John Keats. A feature of the village was the wooded ravine, known as the Chine, which ran down to the sea, and three chalybeate springs that were said to cure rheumatism, eczema, anaemia and nervous exhaustion.

Development on the seafront remained small until the arrival of the railway from Ryde in 1864, when, in less than a decade, the population grew from a few hundred to over two thousand. Fine villas were built along the cliff top and the Osborne Steps were constructed to connect the village with the beach. William Colenutt provided bathing machines and opened up a path to the Chine.

During the Edwardian period, Shanklin became popular with the German and Russian Royal Families. The Crown Prince of Germany stayed at the Royal Spa Hotel in 1913 and, in the following year, the Kaiser's youngest son, Prince Joachim, only left the town twenty-four hours before the start of the First World War.

Shanklin Pier

The earliest proposal for a pier at Shanklin was in 1864, when the Shanklin Bay Pier Company received a Board of Trade order for a 1,200-foot pier. However, the company quickly foundered without doing any business. A further attempt to build a pier at Shanklin, by the Shanklin Pier Company in 1877, also met with failure (*see the Piers that never were chapter for more details of the 1864 and 1877 pier schemes*).

The incorporation of the Shanklin Esplanade & Pier Company on 22 December 1885 proved to be third time lucky for Shanklin, although it was to take nearly five years before the pier was opened. The new company had a share capital of £12,000, consisting of 2,400 shares of £5 each, and the site for the pier was leased to them for an annual rent of £5 and term of 999 years on 11 November 1885. The Act of Parliament for the construction of the pier was passed on 11 March 1886, but escalating costs led to an increase of the company's capital to £30,000 (6,000 x £5 shares) in 1887. Plans for a pier 1,200 feet in length were drawn up by

Shanklin Pier was opened on 18 August 1890 to a length of 1,200 feet and is seen here in the late 1890s with a bandstand situated in the centre. A paddle steamer can be seen leaving the pier heading towards Ventnor.

On 28 July 1909, a pavilion was added to Shanklin Pier by Alfred Thorne at a cost of £9,000, as seen on this postcard. The publishers of the card have superimposed the sailing boats onto the scene.

The interior of the pavilion was provided with a maple floor so that it could be used for roller skating during the off-season months. This rare postcard shows skaters in the pavilion in the winter of 1909.

An aerial photograph of Shanklin Pier in the 1920s shows the burnt out pavilion, following a fire on 29 June 1918. The remains of the landing stage can also be seen; this had been largely dismantled in 1915 after suffering storm damage.

HAROLD READING'S 1924 "MIRTH" CONCERT PARTY,
SHANKLIN PIER.

A postcard showing Harold Reading's Mirth concert party, who performed in the pier head concert area on Shanklin Pier in 1924.

In 1925, Shanklin Pier was acquired by H. Terry Wood and he rebuilt the pavilion as the Pier Casino, which was opened on 4 June 1927. This souvenir brochure was issued in 1929 when Ronald Frankau's Cabaret Kittens were the attraction in the Pier Casino and the Metronomes Band occupied the Dance Pavilion on the pier head.

A postcard commemorating the arrival of the first steamboat at the new landing stage at Shanklin Pier, erected in 1931. The landing stage was constructed in reinforced concrete by Concrete Piling Limited.

The entrance to Shanklin Pier in 1982; it was under the ownership of Fred Sage, who tried some novel attractions to entice custom. These included his secretary Joan Yule acting as the DJ for the pavilion discos, where she became known as the 'Disco Granny'. The pier also had a puppet theatre, cinema, bars, large slide, aquarium and an amusement arcade run by Mayneland.

A 1982 photograph of the pier pavilion at Shanklin, built in 1927 to replace the similar 1909 structure, which was destroyed by fire in 1918. Lack of space meant that the first floor of the building had to span across the whole of the pier deck.

During the Great Storm of 16 October 1987, large sections of Shanklin Pier were washed away and this photograph of what remained was taken on 6 August 1989. Various proposals to rebuild the pier came to nothing and the remains were removed in 1993.

Messrs F. C. Dixon and M. N. Ridley; a traditional design featuring cast iron piling, wrought iron girders and wooden decking. Two attractive kiosks were designed for the pier entrance and shelters were placed on two widened sections on the deck. A 90- by 60-foot pier head, along with a 150-foot-long wooden landing stage with a depth of 9 feet of water at the lowest spring tides, were to be placed at the end of the pier, which was to be inclined up from the esplanade to allow for high spring tides and bathing machines to pass easily underneath. The contractors John Dixon and Alfred Thorne commenced work in August 1888. Dixon had previously built the piers at Douglas and Llandudno, whilst Thorne would go on to construct a number of piers over the following twenty years. A formal agreement was drawn up with Thorne on 26 February 1889, agreeing to a contract price of £23,240, of which part payment was to be taken with the allotment of 687 of the company's shares. To help pay for the contract, the company mortgaged the pier property and undertaking on 21 October 1890 to Mr W. H. Willis of Lennox Lodge, Shanklin, for £6,500 at 6 per cent interest. Willis had already subscribed to 618 of the company's shares out of the 1,199 so far taken up.

The pier took two years to build before being officially opened on 18 August 1890 when the steamer *Flying Falcon* called during a cruise around the island. On 6 October, *Victoria*, belong to Cosens of Weymouth, called from Bournemouth and Swanage. The pier proved to be successful during its first two years of operation but the company fell behind on the interest payments on the mortgage and, in February 1892, Willis obtained an order to appoint a receiver to take over the pier. The Shanklin Esplanade Pier Company was to be eventually dissolved on 2 August 1904. Of the 6,000 shares of the company, only 1,886 had been sold and this included a further 78 given to Thorne and his family in lieu of payment.

The pier was put up for auction, but remained unsold and in the hands of the receivers. They kept it open and added a number of additions, including a bathing stage in 1893, shelters and lavatories in 1894 and a bandstand in 1897. The bandstand featured a stage and sheltered seating to accommodate 500 people and a canvas awning for covering. The pier's popularity enabled small payments off the mortgage to be paid to Willis although £8,500 was still owed to him in 1899 when the Extension Pier (Shanklin) Limited was formed to take over the pier. The new company were formally registered on 23 April 1900 with a capital of £13,000 and agreed to purchase the pier for £12,500: £1,000 in cash and the remainder in debentures of £100 each, redeemable in twenty years. An agreement was also reached with Willis to take on the existing mortgage payments.

Under its new ownership, the pier became a steadily earning asset during the Edwardian period. A profit of £537 1s 11d was made during the 1901 season, enabling a dividend of 3 per cent to be made to shareholders. The following years proved to be similarly consistent with £521 3s 3d profit in 1902 (3 per cent dividend), 1903 – £466 12s 11d (3 per cent dividend), 1904 – £586 12s 8d (3½ per cent dividend), 1905 – no figures, 1906 – £605 15s 5d (3½ per cent dividend), 1907 – £603 0s 2d (4 per cent dividend) and 1908 – £501 17s 1d (4 per cent dividend). The reasonable financial state of the company led them to provide a much needed pavilion on the pier, which was to be placed on a widened central section. Alfred Thorne was engaged to carry out the work and it was completed in 1909 at a total cost of around £9,000 (the original contract price for just the pavilion, less seating and lighting, was £2,652). The pavilion was formally opened on 28 July 1909 and featured a maple floor which could be used for roller skating during the winter months. The Extension Pier (Shanklin) Limited made a £691 3s 2d profit in 1909, paying out a 4 per cent dividend. The main items of expenditure and income make interesting reading:

EXPENDITURE

Repairs and Renewals	£256 6s 4d
Salaries and Wages	£244 0s 5d
Pavilion Expenses	£353 0s 2d
(percentages paid to performers and attendance)	
Skating Expenses	£126 10s 5d
Gas and Electric Light	£31 18s 8d
Entertainments	£43 11s 0d

INCOME

Tolls (at 2d)	£361 8s 0d
Landing Tolls	£555 13s 10d
Rents – kiosks, machines and advertisements	£63 16s 0d

Lavatories	£16 3s 3d
Pavilion – concerts	£561 6s 11d
Pavilion – skating	£260 13s 7d

The figures show that the pavilion proved to be a great success in the limited period it was opened during its first year. The roller skating boom would last another couple of years but was virtually over by 1911. The pavilion became home to the popular 'Burlesques' concert party until the building was destroyed by fire on 29 June 1918 and was left as a charred ruin, although the girders were subsequently reused in the construction of a cinema in the town. The pier's landing stage had also largely gone, having been dismantled in 1915 after suffering severe storm damage. The pavilion's destruction led to the pier toll being reduced to 1d in 1918. To compensate for the loss of the pavilion, a concert area had been erected on the pier head in place of the bandstand.

Following the fire, the pier was left as an eyesore with the pier company claiming they had no funds to repair it. Fortunately, the pier was acquired in 1925 by Horace Terry Wood, who had run the Theatre Royal in Ryde, and he arranged for Messrs Lysaght (ironwork) and Messrs Rousell & Sons (general work) to rebuild the pavilion to almost the same design as before, which was reopened on 4 June 1927. The new pavilion was christened the Casino and could seat 1,000 people. Anna Pavlova and the Corps de Ballet were visitors during its first season, although concert parties proved to be the staple fare. During the 1930s, Clarkson Rose's 'Twinkle' was the resident summer show and theatrical and musical stars of the day also came to the pier. On the pier head, the concert arena became known as the Dance Pavilion. Terry Wood also arranged for the landing stage to be rebuilt in reinforced concrete by Concrete Piling Limited. The new stage was opened in May 1931 and was to be kept busy throughout the 1930s with pleasure cruises. A favourite caller at the pier was the paddle steamer *Lorna Doone*, which did round the island cruises. The popular and reliable *Balmoral* offered trips to Cherbourg with 2½ hours ashore, while P&A Campbell's *Devonia*, *Waverley* and *Glen Gower* sailed to Brighton and Eastbourne. Sailings were also available to Bournemouth, Southampton, Portsmouth, Southsea, Hastings, Swanage, Weymouth and Bognor Regis. Four companies offered services from the pier: Southern Railway, Cosens of Weymouth, Southampton & Isle of Wight Steam Packet Company and P&A Campbell.

Terry Wood's commitment to the pier ensured that it was at its height during the 1930s when it rivalled Butlins in the number of attractions on offer. The pier even had its own tannoy system announcing the arrival of steamers, the service of meals and times of attractions, but Terry Wood had to turn it down after complaints from residents and holidaymakers along the seafront. A dancing pavilion was added in 1933 and three daily dance sessions were provided along with a carnival dance every Wednesday. There were summer shows in the pavilion, including Clarkson Rose and Olive Fox's 'Twinkle' for the 1934 season. That same year saw a Johnnie Walker cricket scoreboard installed for the last three England–Australia Ashes matches. Other attractions included the Palace of Fun amusement arcade, rifle range, voice recorders, novelty competitions, dancing, speed boats and divers: including the one-legged Montague Wesley who dived off the pier in flames. The pier even had its own social club named the Shanklin Pier Sporting Club, which had over 1,000 members. Admission to the pier was 2*d*, although fishermen had to pay 6*d* per day for each rod and line.

The onset of the Second World War saw the fun on the pier come to an end, and in 1940 a hole was blown in the structure to prevent it being used in the event of a German invasion. In 1944, one of two PLUTO (Pipe Line Under The Ocean) pipelines was laid from a pumping station to run along the pier and under the English Channel to supply oil for the Normandy landings. The gap in the pier was bridged for the purpose but in the event the pipeline was never used.

The wartime gap was eventually repaired using concrete piling and decking, which stood out like a sore thumb from the rest of the pier. Mr Terry Wood continued to provide a variety of attractions, including dancing on the pier head (band concerts on Sundays as dancing wasn't allowed) and speedboat trips from the landing stage, which was also popular with fishermen. The Casino Theatre continued to host the old-style summer shows, in addition to other entertainments.

Following Terry Wood's death, his widow continued to run the pier for a further decade until her retirement in 1970. There then followed a quick succession of owners – Pennix Limited, Pier Amusements Shanklin Limited and the Haven Marine Company – before the pier was closed for the whole of the 1975 season. Fred Sage then took on the pier in 1976 and tried some novel attractions to entice custom. His secretary Joan Yule acted as the DJ for the pavilion discos and became known as the 'Disco Granny'. There was also a puppet theatre, cinema, bars, aquarium, large slide and other rides on the pier deck and an amusement arcade run by Mayneland. The landing stage still saw occasional pleasure cruises operated by Mursell & Kemp and Wightline Cruises.

In 1980, Shanklin was transformed into 'Smallhaven' for the delightful Southern Television musical comedy *The End of the End of the Pier Show*, which was broadcast on May Day 1981. The programme focused on the attempts to save a resort's run-down pier and relived its past glories through song, dance and comedy. Unfortunately, the programme rather mirrored the state of Shanklin Pier and, in January 1982, the Shanklin Pier Preservation Society was launched to try and ensure the future of the privately owned pier in the face of rising maintenance costs. A lifeline for the pier appeared to come in 1986 when it was acquired by the Southampton-based Leading Leisure Company, although Mr Sage retained a 25 per cent stake. The new owners planned a multi-million pound leisure and conference complex, until their dreams were shattered by the Great Storm of 16 October 1987 when the majority of the pier was destroyed. Leading Leisure announced that they would rebuild the pier to two-thirds of its former length, with work to begin in 1989, but when this failed to take place it was purchased by South Wight Borough Council for demolition at a cost of £25,000. A further £189,000 had to be spent on the demolition itself, which was carried out by Graham Attrill of Arreton from February 1993.

VENTNOR

Ventnor was a popular convalescent resort due to its south-facing position 400 feet above sea level and protection by St Boniface Down, which rises 400 feet above. The town was laid out on a series of terraces down to the sea and, in 1826, Sir James Clark, in his paper on Organic Diseases, described the Undercliff as a 'highly favourable residence for invalids throughout the year', which led to the opening of a large Royal National Hospital for Consumption[10] in 1869 by Dr Arthur Hill Hassall. The curative properties of the resort led to members of the nobility and distinguished persons coming to stay at Ventnor, including Charles Dickens and Sir Edward Elgar, who spent his honeymoon there in 1869. The railway arrived in Ventnor in 1866 but a simultaneous harbour development proved to be a great failure. The replacement pier proved to be longer lasting and became the focal point of a popular resort.

Harbour Piers

Proposals to build a pier at Ventnor in 1843 and 1854 came to nothing, before the Ventnor Pier and Harbour Company was incorporated in 1861 with a share capital of £15,000 in £20 shares. The appointed engineer was Mr J. Saunders, who drew up a plan for two wooden piers to form an enclosed harbour, which would be able to handle imports of coal, timber, iron, slates and other goods. The western arm was to be the principal pier, running for 300 feet in a southerly direction before turning south-east and extending for a further 100 feet. The eastern pier was to extend south-west for 300 feet and the enclosed harbour would have a frontage of 180 feet. The two piers were to be constructed of timber, in-filled with rock, hardcore and soil.

---

[10] Consumption is an old name for tuberculosis and was so named because victims of the disease were 'consumed' by it and wasted away. Now commonly known as TB, the disease is caused by a highly contagious bacterial infection and about three million people around the world still die from it each year.

The western arm of
Ventnor Harbour
completed in April
1864. Constant storm
damage quickly led to
the harbour becoming
unusable and the
wreckage of the two
piers was largely cleared
away in 1867, although
sections remained until
1873.

To replace the failed
harbour at Ventnor, an
iron pier was erected
and the first stage was
opened on 5 August
1872. Lack of finance
meant that the pier
was not completed to a
length of 520 feet until
1876.

Ventnor Pier, as seen
from a paddle steamer
in 1894. Following
storm damage in 1881,
the pier was rebuilt to
a length of 683 feet
and fully opened on
19 October 1887. It
was hoped that the
horseshoe shape of the
pier head and landing
stage would bring the
pier good luck.

Ventnor Pier decorated for the regatta in 1912. Note all the small rowing boats surrounding the paddle steamer. The pavilion at the end of the pier was officially opened on 1 July 1907.

A wonderful photograph of children at Ventnor posing on the beach in front of the pier *c.* 1912, where a paddle steamer can be seen berthed.

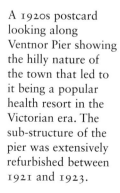

A 1920s postcard looking along Ventnor Pier showing the hilly nature of the town that led to it being a popular health resort in the Victorian era. The sub-structure of the pier was extensively refurbished between 1921 and 1923.

The Act of Parliament for the harbour was passed in 1862 and the capital increased to £20,000. Work began in April 1863 with a force of sixty men and, just two months later, a 260-foot section of the western arm was officially opened on 29 June 1863, when passengers were disembarked from the Portsmouth steamer *Prince Consort*. Unfortunately, disaster struck just two days later when the steamer *Chancellor* settled on a rock whilst attempting to use the pier and pierced its hull. The sea flooded into the boat and it broke in two. Work continued on the western arm and it was completed in April 1864.

Excursions from the harbour commenced on 10 May 1864 and included trips to Littlehampton on the converted tug *Antagonist*, where a connecting train could be caught to get you to London in four hours. The vessel often returned to Ventnor carrying coal to sell on the beach but this hardly made it conducive to passenger comfort. A second vessel, *Ursa Major*, was employed on the Littlehampton route, but she was also barely adequate for the job and there were a number of complaints about her. Steamers also called from Portsmouth and Southampton, including the cargo ship *Medina* from Southampton, operated by the Southampton, Isle of Wight & South of England Royal Mail Steam Packet Company (still operating now under the name Red Funnel). On fine days, the Ventnor Temperance Band sometimes performed on the pier, which by the end of August 1864 had seating along its length. A toll of 2*d* was levied for those wishing to use the pier, reduced to 1*d* on Sundays.

A start was made on the eastern arm, but storms continually damaged both arms by washing out the soil infill and by 1865 they were both in a bad state of repair with bits of timber breaking off and floating about in the sea. Sailings to the harbour had already apparently stopped. To add to the woes of the Ventnor Pier & Harbour Company, locals strongly complained about the smell of rotting seaweed accumulating in and around the harbour. In 1866, the company was wound up and the piers were advertised to be auctioned off on 19 July 1866 at the London Tavern, Bishopsgate Street, London. However, it appears that they were eventually sold by local firm Francis Pittis & Son in February 1867. The western arm was sold to brewer John Burt for £460 and the eastern arm to Mr Norris the butcher for just seventy guineas. However, in 1869 there were complaints that the piers had not been fully removed, although this had been carried out by 1873.

Royal Victoria Pier

In 1870, the Ventnor Pier & Esplanade Company was formed by Messrs Burt and Moore, with a capital of £35,000 to erect an iron pleasure pier on the site of the failed harbour. Messrs Roe and Grace drew up a design for a pier 520 feet in length and work began in December 1871, with the first 200-foot section being opened to the public on Monday 5 August 1872. The pier was extended as funds allowed: to 300 feet in June 1873 and 478 feet by the following September. Mr Rennick of Ventnor continued the work throughout 1874/75 and by 1876 the

A postcard from the late 1940s showing the hole blown in the pier as a defence measure in 1940. The decision was taken to condemn the structure and rebuild the pier.

The new Royal Victoria Pier at Ventnor was officially opened on 28 May 1955, having cost around £100,000 to build. On the pier head was placed a sun deck pavilion with bandstand, cafeteria and licensed bar, while at the shore end was the Calypso coffee bar, which claimed to be the first on the island to sell espresso coffee.

Ventnor Pier photographed in June 1981. The pier was closed that year when a survey revealed that £750,000 would be needed for repairs and maintenance work, although the entrance building remained open.

After £800,000 had failed to be raised for its restoration, the decision was taken to demolish Ventnor Pier and in November 1992 contractors Graham Attrill of Arreton commenced demolition at a cost of £225,000.

pier was virtually complete. *Jenkinson's Guide* of 1876 described it as 'a new pier, which is its (Ventnor's) favourite promenade, the charge for admittance is 2d per person, periodical tickets are also issued. A band of music usually plays at the end of the pier during the summer months.'

Landing steps were added to the pier in 1876 but it was not until July 1881 that the finance had been raised to build a landing stage. On 8 August 1881, the Southampton steamer *Prince Leopold* called at the partially completed landing stage to take passengers to the Bournemouth Regatta and, on 15 September, the *Heather Bell* landed passengers from Portsmouth and Southsea. However, on 27 November the landing stage and 40 feet of the pier were destroyed in a storm. A report stated that the 'pier was a light and elegant structure 520ft long and 22ft broad, containing a platform in the centre, and a large head with glass windscreens, but a heavy and unsuitable landing stage was built which offered so much resistance to the waves that it was washed down and carried with it the head and part of the stem of the pier.'

The Ventnor Pier & Esplanade Company was unable to afford the cost of repairing the pier and it was dissolved. The structure lay derelict until it was acquired by the council for £2,600 and a Royal Assent was granted in July 1884 for a pier designed by Henry Wallis, which was to utilise the iron piles of the old structure and extend it 80 feet further. However, in March 1885, the Board of Trade refused to give their approval for the reconstruction of the pier as the deck level was lower than stated in the Act of Parliament. It took until September for the council and Wallis to submit an amended design, which was approved. The contractors, Messrs Trehearne & Company, finally began work in the autumn of 1885 and the first section was opened to the public on Easter Monday 1886. On 19 July 1887, the steamer *Bangor Castle* called at the pier on the occasion of the contractor handing over the pier to the council. Two days later, the horseshoe-shaped pier head (which was hoped would bring the pier good luck) received the excursion steamers *Princess Beatrice*, *Prince Leopold* and *Albert Edward*. The council received the consent of Queen Victoria to name the pier 'Royal Victoria' and on 19 October 1887 it was officially opened by the Attorney General Sir Richard E. Webster QC MP to a length of 683 feet, having cost £12,000 to build.

Pleasure steamers were once again able to call at Ventnor, although the town council refused to let them visit on Sundays until 1909 when a referendum of local residents showed that the majority were in favour of Sunday sailings[11]. During the landing stage's first full season in 1888, 3,000 people arrived on steamers from Bournemouth, Portsmouth and Southampton, which increased to 10,000 the following year. In 1892, the *Sea Breeze* became the first steamer to call at the pier from Brighton. Seeing the popularity of the steamer trips to and from the pier, a group of local businessmen formed the Southsea, Ventnor, Shanklin & Sandown Steamboat Company in 1888 and acquired the steamer *Dandie Dinmont*. However, she proved to be a troublesome vessel, which was often laid up for repairs, and the company was unsuccessful.

During the Edwardian period, steamer traffic using the pier was at its height with the following companies using it and fiercely competing for custom: P&A Campbell (*Glen Rosa* and *Cambria*), Southampton & Isle of Wight Company (*Balmoral*, *Bournemouth Queen*, *Lorna Doone*, *Solent Queen*, *Lord Elgin*, *Queen*, *Stirling Castle* and *Duchess of York*), Bembridge Steamers (*Sandringham*, *Lord Kitchener*, *Duke of York* and *Prince*), London, Brighton & South Coast Railway and London & South Western Railway Joint (*Duchess of Richmond* and *Duchess of Norfolk*), Bournemouth & Swanage Steam Packet Company (*Monarch*, *Empress*, *Albert Victor* and *Emperor of India*), Cosens of Weymouth (*Majestic*), Brighton, Worthing & South Coast Steamboat Company, Sussex Steam Packet Company, R. R. Collard of Newhaven and Hastings, St Leonards & Eastbourne Steamboat Company. However, the pier was one of the trickiest for the steamers to berth at safely and during stormy weather they often cancelled their calls to the pier and terminated their journeys at Shanklin.

The pier was described as 'a handsome structure. It is 650ft long and 25ft broad with a large diamond shaped head, and a landing stage running the whole way round adapted for steamers landing at all stages of the tide. Commodious glass shelters are provided on the head and centre, with ladies and gentlemen's lavatories at the foot of the pier. The Town Band performs on the pier most evenings of the week.' The Ventnor Temperance Band also played on the pier head three evenings per week. The year after the pier had reopened, in 1888, the Thompson's Patent Gravity Switchback Company had approached the council to erect one of their switchback roller coasters along the length of the pier. The company had successfully erected switchbacks on the piers at Ramsgate and Weston-Super-Mare, but were unsuccessful at Ventnor where the council were intent on providing amusements rather more genteel. In 1903, they expanded the bandstand and sheltered seating on the pier head with a small stage and dressing rooms under an awning, which was converted into a pavilion four years later at a cost of £980. The pavilion was officially opened on 1 July 1907 with a concert by the Evening Stars concert party and during the summer months it was host to summer shows, band concerts and confetti battles, whilst wintertime saw the building used as a roller skating rink. Nevertheless, the pier was proving to be a loss-making concern for the council; or so they said when they wrote to the Board of Trade in 1910 asking for permission to reconstruct the landing stage. A new high level stage was designed by Borough Engineer H. Hughes Oakes and opened in 1913 at a cost of £6,236.

Maintenance of the pier was somewhat neglected during the First World War, which led to major repairs of the sub-structure in 1921–23. During the inter-war period, the pier pavilion remained a popular entertainment venue. In 1921, 'Bunny' Bennett and his Colour Concert Party proved an immense success, enabling the pier company to make a profit of £538. They were not so successful the following season and, in 1924, it was decided to have fortnightly concert party residences rather than one summer show. That season's entertainment included the diver Captain Lawson Smith, who donned full diver's helmet and suit and was lowered to the sea bed where he gave a commentary of what he could see through a special megaphone. In 1930, the pavilion was leased by W. J. Board, who presented the Gwen Lewis Entertainers nightly at 8.15; admission prices 3s, 2s 4d, 1s 10d and 1s 3d. There was also tea, children's matinee shows and morning coffee in the vestibule lounge. During the 1930s dancing became increasingly popular in the pavilion and sports were played out on the pier deck. The Southern Railway's *Southsea* and *Whippingham* and Red Funnel's *Balmoral*, *Lorna Doone*, *Queen*, *Princess Elizabeth* and *Gracie Fields* steamers called at Ventnor during the inter-war years if the weather conditions were suitable, but often terminated their services at Sandown or Shanklin when it wasn't. In addition to the sailings to Bournemouth, Southampton, Portsmouth, Brighton and other resorts on the island, there were trips to Cherbourg and 'Round the Island' cruises.

Following wartime breaching, the pier was left in a poor state and was condemned in 1948. The council were keen on rebuilding the structure, however. Following a grant for 90 per cent of the costs from the Ministry of Health, they were able to proceed with the scheme. The design of Basil Phelps of Shanklin was chosen and, in 1950, Messrs Wall Brothers of Wootton, who had submitted a tender of £76,267, commenced the reconstruction of the pier. The wartime gap was closed in 1951 and the pier was reopened as a promenade the following year with the addition of a new entrance building. In 1953, the old pavilion was demolished and on Whit Monday of the same year, P&A Campbell's *Cardiff Queen* became the first vessel to call at the pier since the 1930s. The Red Funnel steamers also returned to the pier in the guise of the new twin-screw motor vessel

Balmoral (2) and Cosens of Weymouth called with *Embassy*. The rebuilding work continued for a further two years until 28 May 1955 when the pier was officially reopened by Commodore R. L. F. Hubbard R.D. R.N.R. retired. Around £100,000 had been spent on the new structure, of which £17,000 was allocated for the superstructure. The pier now measured 683 feet long with a main deck width of 23 feet, a central widening of 53 feet and screen shelters in 30-foot units. The decking of greenheart was laid upon welded steel girders, and concrete beams where it was widened, which were supported by cast iron piles. The landing stage was constructed of greenheart and pine with elm rubbers and cast iron grids. On the pier head was placed a sun deck pavilion with bandstand, cafeteria and licensed bar, while at the shore end was the Calypso coffee bar, which claimed that it was the first on the island to sell espresso coffee. The pier was leased to Messrs Nuthall (who also leased the Winter Gardens), who appointed R. A. Gammons to act as General Manager. He organised a variety of entertainments on the pier: including concerts, dance evenings, beauty contests and a small fun fair. There was an admission charge of 2d to use the pier, 1s if you were a dog! Fishermen were allowed to use the landing stage and it became noted as a place to catch large conger eels, but in 1968 it was damaged by storms, curtailing both the fishing and calls by steamers.

The Pleasurama group eventually acquired the lease of the pier and covered in the shore end to provide an amusement arcade. Mayneland Amusements took over in 1976 but, following a structural survey in 1981, the pier was closed when it was revealed that £750,000 would be needed for repairs and maintenance work. The pier was left to deteriorate as arguments raged about its future and in September 1985 the shore end buildings were destroyed by fire, allegedly started by arsonists. Various proposals for the pier's restoration came and went, but a legal dispute between the council and the pier's leaseholder ensured that the structure remained in a bad way. The Ventnor Town Trust expressed an interest in taking over the pier if they could raise the £800,000 need for its restoration. They received £250,000 from the council to get their fund up and running but the response to their appeal proved disappointing. The pier was doomed and in November 1992 contractors Graham Attrill of Arreton demolished it a cost of £225,000. The shore end of the pier is now marked by a waste water treatment building.

ALUM BAY

Situated on the far west of the Isle of Wight, Alum Bay is famous for its coloured sands and close proximity to the Needles headland. The coloured sands began to be recorded around 1780 and within fifty years were an established feature of the island holiday scene. Shaped bottles were filled with the different coloured layers of the sands and were sold to tourists. The Royal Needles Hotel was built in 1860 and a pier followed ten years later to cater for visitors arriving by steamer. The establishment of the Needles Park, based around the surviving part of the hotel, ensure that Alum Bay and its coloured sands remain on the tourist map today.

Alum Bay Piers (Wood and Iron)

The first pier at Alum Bay was a wooden structure, 340ft long and 8ft wide, erected in 1870 by Mr. J. White of Cowes for the Alum Bay Pier Company. The company had a share capital of £1,500 in 150 x £10 shares and their registered office was at the Royal Hotel in Alum Bay. Vessels called at the pier from Portsmouth, Southampton and on 'Round the Island' cruises. On Whit Monday, 10 June 1878, the Cosens steamer *Premier* visited on her first public cruise from Weymouth and vessels of the Bournemouth & South Coast Steam Packet also called. In 1879, Messrs Sharpe operated in competition to Alum Bay with the Bournemouth Company and slashed the fare from 3s to 1s, but in August they withdrew their sailings following a debilitating price war. The steamer *Heather Belle* called three times weekly in the early 1880s.

In 1883, the Board of Trade was informed that the pier was unsafe due to the eating away of the wooden piles by the marine toredo worm. The Alum Bay Pier Company responded by claiming they had inserted additional piling into the pier head during the past three years and had acquired some of the iron piles from the recently demolished Kernot's Pier at West Cowes. The pier was closed during the winter of 1883/84 and never reopened due to the Alum Bay Pier Company going into receivership in November 1884. On 26 October 1886 they were wound up.

A new company, the Needles & Alum Bay Pier Company, was registered on 7 September 1886 with a capital of £3,000 in shares of £1 each to build a

The first pier at Alum Bay was a 340-foot wooden structure erected in 1870 and demolished in 1886/87 to make way for a replacement iron pier. Beyond the pier the famous Needles rocks can be seen.

Alum Bay's iron pier was opened to a length of 370 feet on 5 August 1887, having cost £2,135 to build. The pier, along with the refreshment hut, is seen here from the cliff *c.* 1902.

A postcard of Alum Bay Pier with two visiting steamers *c.* 1907. Steamers run by Cosens of Weymouth and the London & South Western Railway from Lymington called at the pier until the First World War.

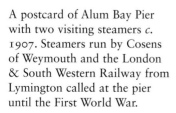

4 ALUM-BAY (Isle of Wight).
Steamers at the Pier. — LL.

The Needles can be viewed through the broken section of Alum Bay Pier after the storm of 13 February 1928. The pier was not restored and was left to progressively disappear over the following twenty years.

The shore end of the pier was left intact after the 1928 storm and was used for a time to provide tables and seating for customers using the refreshment hut on the shore. The famous coloured cliffs can be seen – enhanced a little by the postcard publisher!

In 1987, a small jetty with a floating pontoon was constructed at Alum Bay for use by motor launches that run trips to the Needles Lighthouse and rocks.

replacement 370-foot iron pier designed by James Lemon of Southampton. The company's first meeting was reported by *The Isle of Wight County Press* on 8 January 1887: 'The Needles and Alum Bay Pier Company held its first ordinary and public meeting at Southampton on Thursday. Chairman John James Burnett reported that the capital consisted of 3,000 shares of £1 each and that the money has been more than subscribed. The contract for the construction of the pier has been given to Mr I. Saunders, the price being £2,135. The pier, which is to be wider (it was 12ft wide) and 30ft longer than the old structure, is to be completed by the excursion season.' The pier was opened on 5 August 1887 and featured ornamental railings with seating and a large pier head for the steamer traffic. It may also have incorporated the iron piles from the former Kernot's Pier at West Cowes, which had lain unused on the beach since their purchase in 1883.

Up until the First World War, steamers run by Cosens of Weymouth and the London & South Western Railway from Lymington called at the pier. The Pier Master was Alfred Isaacs who ran fishing boat trips from the pier and craft servicing the Needles Lighthouse[12]. He kept his lobster pots on the pier and ran a café at the entrance where a glass of water set you back 1d. Isaacs was also the local Bird Protection Officer and reared, acclimatised and released ravens and falcons. Among the visitors to view the birds was novelist and broadcaster J. B. Priestley. On 5 September 1894, a match between *Britannia* and *Vigilant* for the Cape May Challenge Cup was started by Royal Yacht Squadron officials from the pier.

In the years prior to the First World War, the Needles & Alum Bay Pier Company had begun to sustain yearly losses and, by the early 1920s, this was amounting to around £1,200 annually, mainly due to steamer services having ceased. The last steamer to call at the pier was the *Queen* from Southampton in 1920; partially due to the path up to the chine from the pier having been declared unsafe after subsiding badly. Five years later, the pier itself was largely closed when the structure became buckled after a fierce gale. Hopes of restoring the pier were dashed when it was wrecked in a storm on 13 February 1928, as described by the *Isle of Wight County Press*:

> **ALUM BAY PIER WRECKED**. The pier at Alum Bay, which has been allowed to get into a bad state of disrepair during the last few years, was almost completely destroyed in the gale on Thursday. At about midday, the central portion of the structure gave way under the strain of the wind and heavy seas, and was swept on the beach to the northward, leaving some 30 yards of the structure at the shore end and the pier head still standing. The succession of heavy storms of late had weakened the piling, and the pier suddenly sagged in the middle during a particularly strong gust of wind, and, with a roar, both piling and decking were torn away from the rest of the structure, and it quickly disappeared into the raging seas.
>
> The pier was built just over 40 years ago by the Alum Bay Pier Company, and until four years ago it was regularly used in the summer by pleasure steamers landing trippers to see the famous coloured sand cliffs, but since that time it has been considered unsafe, and steamers have not called. It was a popular resort of island anglers, however, and they will keenly regret its end. The late Mr. Alfred Isaacs was pier-master from the time it was built until his death about 18 months ago, and since then his grandson has been in charge.

The Needles & Alum Bay Pier Company went into liquidation in 1925 but the Isaacs family kept the café open on the undamaged shoreward end of the pier for a time, although the rest of the pier was gradually washed away.

The remains of the pier were eventually removed by the 1960s, yet some fragments remained until the 1980s. In 1987, a small jetty with a floating pontoon was constructed for use by motor launches that ran trips to the Needles Lighthouse and rocks. The pier is commemorated by the Pier Head Shopping Emporium at Needles Park which claims: 'The design of the shopping emporium reflects the image and style of the nineteenth century Alum Bay pier which bought many visitors to Alum Bay by paddle steamer in Victorian times.'

TOTLAND BAY

Totland consisted of a few farms before the nearby bay was transformed from the 1870s into a quiet watering place by the Totland Bay Hotel & Pier Company. They erected a large hotel, pier and villas and bathing machines and rowing boats were available for hire on the beach. A Bill to construct an electric railway from Totland Bay under the Solent to the mainland was passed in 1901 but never built, thus preserving the bay's rather serene existence to this day.

Totland Bay Pier

The first pier at Totland Bay was a wooden structure 336 feet long, erected in 1864 for shipping stone used in the building of the Needles Lighthouse. The pier had become derelict by the time of the incorporation of the Totland Bay Hotel & Pier Company, on 24 July 1878, with a capital of 10,000 in 1,000 shares of £10 each. Formed by local landowners, led by Messrs G. Aman and G. Preece, the company intended to develop the area as a select seaside resort and an iron pier to receive steamers was seen as the first step. The land for the site of the pier was acquired from the War Office (who had the privilege to land stores on it if they so wished) in November 1877 for £150 and the Crown's interest was eventually purchased for £85 on 1 March 1879.

The Provisional Order to build the pier was granted by the Board of Trade in 1879, which stated that it was to be 550 feet in length and situated 624 feet north-east of the wooden pier. Proposed tolls to use the pier were 2d for those wishing to promenade, 6d for steamer passengers, 6d for perambulators and bath chairs and 1s for any calling vessels. There was also a large list of tolls for each type of goods landed. The pier was designed by Samuel Hansard Yockney, who took 75 shares as part payment when the capital of the company was increased to £15,230 (1,523 shares of £10). The pier was probably constructed by men directly employed by Yockney and opened in March 1880 with a pier head on the western end. The pier was described as 'a small landing pier of a light girder framework on cast iron columns and carrying a minimum of appointments. There is only a small shelter on the head and a tiny amusement pavilion at the shore end.' The pier as

3   TOTLAND BAY (Isle of Wight). — The Pier. — EL.

Totland Bay Pier decorated for regatta day *c.* 1907. The pier was connected with the Lymington and Yarmouth steamer services, and boats also ran to Bournemouth, Southampton, Portsmouth, Southsea and Cowes.

54675. Steamer leaving the Pier, Totland Bay, I.W.

A postcard of Totland Bay Pier in the early 1950s showing three motor coaches meeting the passengers, who have just arrived off the steamer. The pier was reopened on 17 June 1951 following wartime damage and *Lorna Doone* became the first steamer to call at the pier in twenty years.

TOTLAND BAY HOTEL I.W. FROM THE PIER

The Totland Hotel seen from the pier in the 1950s. The hotel was opened along with the pier in 1879 but was closed in 1970 and demolished soon after.

Totland Bay Pier as seen from the beach in 2008. The two wooden supports at the shore end replaced those of cast iron removed as a defence measure in 1940.

The entrance building to Totland Bay Pier in 2008, in use as a café.

A small section of the deck of Totland Bay Pier has been restored to accommodate tables and chairs for the café, as seen in this photograph from 2008.

built was 450 feet long (not 550 feet as stated in the Board of Trade order), 14 feet wide and the pier head measured 88 x 52 feet. The hotel was opened on the cliffs above the pier in 1879 and was enlarged in 1885 following a further increase in the company's capital to £20,000.

The pier was connected with the Lymington and Yarmouth steamer services and boats also ran to Bournemouth, Southampton, Portsmouth, Southsea and Cowes and on 'Round the Island' cruises, which cost 4s. The cost of admission onto the pier from the shore and the boats was 2d. Following the opening of the Freshwater, Yarmouth & Newport Railway in 1889, an omnibus service ran between the pier and Freshwater station. The railway company considered taking over the interests of the Totland Bay Hotel & Pier Company, but when that failed to happen, the TBH&P was reformed in 1898 with £10,000 each of preference and ordinary shares.

The pier was the focal point of the annual Totland Bay Regatta, when it was bedecked with flags by Pier Master Alfred Isaacs, who also looked after the pier at Alum Bay. In 1910, the regatta was honoured with a visit by HRH Princess Henry of Battenburg and local MP Douglas Hall. However, the connecting ferry service to the pier was reduced in 1918 and stopped altogether in 1927 due to declining passenger numbers. The poor condition of the pier led to pleasure steamers ceasing to call in 1931. Two years later, the beleaguered Totland Bay Hotel & Pier Company was involved in legal proceedings with Totland Parish Council following a long running dispute and on 8 September 1939 the cash-strapped company was wound up.

During the Second World War, two spans of the shoreward end of the pier were removed as an anti-invasion measure. They were restored after the war by Messrs Wall Brothers of Wootton using timber supports rather than cast iron. The pier was reopened on 17 June 1951 and *Lorna Doone* became the first steamer to call at the pier in twenty years. The Chairman of the Totland Bay Hotel & Pier Company, Mr G. A. Preece, welcomed the passengers as they stepped onto the pier and also went on to the vessel to speak to Captain T. Larkin. The ship was scrapped the following year but other steamers occasionally called at the pier until 1969.

In 1970, the Totland Hotel was closed (and soon demolished) and in the following year the pier was sold by the expiring Totland Bay Hotel & Pier Company to Trinity House for £10,000. The new owners used the pier as a base for their pilot boats navigating the large liners through the Needles Channel to and from Southampton. In 1975, a weather gathering centre was placed on the pier by the National Physical Laboratory. The condition of the pier was causing concern, however, and by the early 1980s it had been closed, save for the amusement arcade and café at the entrance. This was damaged by the Great Storm of 16 October 1987 but was reopened by owner Jack Shears.

In 1992, the pier passed to Henry Leeson and in May 1993 he briefly reopened the pier for a visit by the MV *Balmoral*. Four years later, it was purchased at auction for £19,500 by Andy Millmore, who rebuilt the pier head building and landing stage, but by 2001 the pier was in the hands of Derek Barran. He converted the building on the pier head into his own private art studio and, on 1–3 March 2001, staged a spectacular light show on the pier organised by Dear Productions of Chicago.

The pier has remained largely closed, although during the summer of 2006 the owner opened his studio to the public at a cost of £1 per person, the money going towards the restoration of the pier. In December 2008, the pier was put up for sale but failed to reach its reserve price.

---

[11] Although in August 1891 the steamer Comet did land passengers on two occasions on the same day but without approval from the council who locked the landing stage gates and placed a policeman on duty. However, they eventually unlocked the gates to prevent an accident.

YARMOUTH

Yarmouth is one of the Isle of Wight's oldest settlements; dating from Saxon times. The town gained its first royal charter in 1135 and became the main port for the west of the island as it was only three miles from Lymington on the mainland. A steam packet service was commenced between the two towns in April 1830, which operated from Yarmouth Quay and Harbour. In April 1876, a wooden pier was erected as a deep water terminal for the ferry, which remained in use for passenger services until 1959; it is now a Grade II listed building. Cars were ferried across the Solent by towing barges until the Southern Railway introduced a new car ferry service in 1938 and slipways were built in the harbour to accommodate it. The harbour was extensively rebuilt between 1964 and 1972 and can now accommodate 10,000 visiting craft, thus making Yarmouth a renowned yachting centre. Visitors are also attracted to the town by its unspoilt charm and Tudor castle.

Fort Victoria Pier

Fort Victoria was built in 1852–55 to defend the deep water channel off Sconce Point near Yarmouth and a pier was erected in 1856 to service it. In 1870, the pier acquired an 18-inch railway with a hand-propelled trolley for moving goods. In 1886, it was lengthened by 35 feet and widened to 60 feet. A further enlarging of the pier was carried out during the winter of 1897/98.

The fort was mainly used as a training base to instruct soldiers in the art of seamanship and this was put to good use on 25 April 1908 when members of the garrison swam out to rescue sailors struggling in the water following the collision of HMS *Gladiator* and SS *St Paul* off Sconce Point during a blizzard.

In 1920, the Royal Engineers left the fort and it lay largely unused, as did the pier, although occasional pleasure steamer trips called there. During the Second World, the fort was brought back into use when it received training regiments of the Royal Artillery. Torpedo tubes were placed on the pier as part of the Western Solent Defences and it was used for the transport of weaponry to the Normandy front.

The remains of the pier erected in 1856 to service Fort Victoria near Yarmouth. The fort is now part of the Fort Victoria Country Park and houses a marine aquarium, underwater archaeology centre, planetarium and model railway. The pier, however, is cut off from the shore and sadly derelict.

The military continued to use the fort until 1961, when the barracks were used as a holiday camp and the pier became the property of a security company. The fort is now part of the Fort Victoria Country Park and houses a marine aquarium, underwater archaeology centre, planetarium and model railway. However, the pier is cut off from the shore and sadly derelict.

Yarmouth Pier

Steamer services across the Solent from Lymington to Yarmouth were operated by the small wooden paddle steamer *Glasgow* before the Solent Steamship Company introduced a steamer service in 1850 using the vessels *Duke of Buccleugh* and *Solent*, which also ran to Portsmouth, Southampton, Ryde and Cowes. Traffic increased on the Lymington to Yarmouth route following the opening of the Brockenhurst to Lymington Railway in 1858 and the need for a new landing stage at Yarmouth became clearly evident, leading to a proposal by Yarmouth Corporation for a deep water pier in 1870. An Act of Parliament to build the pier was passed in 1874 and in the following year a tender of £4,097 was accepted from Messrs Denham and Jenvey of Freshwater for a wooden structure 685 feet in length. The corporation borrowed £4,000 of the cost (to be paid back over

The Pier,   Yarmouth (I. W.)   25414

A postcard view of Yarmouth Pier in 1902, taken from Pier Square, shows a group of horse carriages awaiting custom from passengers alighting from the Lymington steamer.

Yarmouth Pier, Isle of Wight.   Taunt & Co 3673

The entrance tollhouse and gate to Yarmouth Pier c. 1903 with the station master posing for the photographer. Admission to the pier was a penny, although bicycles were charged 2d, tricycles 3d, perambulators 4d and corpses 3s!

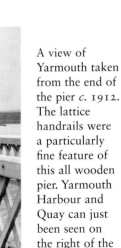

A view of Yarmouth taken from the end of the pier c. 1912. The lattice handrails were a particularly fine feature of this all wooden pier. Yarmouth Harbour and Quay can just been seen on the right of the picture.

Passengers walk along Yarmouth Pier after disembarking from a Lymington steamer in 1925. In May 1938, the Southern Railway opened slipways at Yarmouth Quay for the car ferry service, but passenger vessels continued to call at the pier until 1959.

Yarmouth Pier on a wet day in 2008 with the 30p toll 'honesty' box prominent. The pier was reopened on 26 April 2008 by Alan Titchmarsh, the patron of the fundraising appeal, following the replacement of piles attacked by marine worms.

This attractive wooden shelter has been a feature on the pier head of Yarmouth Pier since it was opened on 19 July 1876, and it is seen here in 2008.

fifty years) and work began on building the pier in June 1875. Just over a year later, on 19 July 1876, the pier was officially opened by Dr C. W. Hollis, Mayor of Yarmouth.

The early years of the pier proved to be troubled. Just a few weeks after it was opened the structure was damaged by the steamer *Prince Leopold*, which removed a 50-foot section. Furthermore, local seafarers had fierce objections to its construction, which intensified after the corporation erected the gates to keep the pier closed on Sundays and after the last steamer had departed. They claimed that the gates obstructed their access to the shore and in retaliation they smashed them up with an axe in the summer of 1877. To placate them, the corporation refitted the gates so as not to block the shore access and the opposition to the pier largely died down. Except, that is, from John Dore. He would row his boat alongside each steamer that came to the pier and tout for passengers to use his boat for a halfpenny to get to the shore rather than use the pier where they had to pay a penny toll. During fine weather, he often did a brisk trade with his cry of 'this way for the ha'penny boat', but when the weather was less kind his patronage was virtually non-existent. Finally, even John Dore accepted that the pier was here to stay and stopped going out in his boat, although he never warmed to it and enjoyed telling everyone how long it would take for the corporation to pay for 'the wretched thing'.

The Brockenhurst to Lymington Railway was taken over by the London & South Western Railway in 1879, and was extended to Lymington Pier in 1884 when a regular steam packet service was commenced from the new pier to Yarmouth Pier. Yarmouth acquired its own rail connection in July 1889 with the opening of the Freshwater, Yarmouth & Newport Railway, although this was not connected to the pier.

A new authority, the Yarmouth Town Trust, took over the pier's affairs in 1891 when the town lost its borough status. Three years later, access to it was improved when buildings were demolished by the entrance and Pier Square was created. Admission to the pier was a penny, although bicycles were charged 2*d*, tricycles 3*d*, perambulators 4*d* and corpses 3*s*! The pier remained busy during the Edwardian period with boat trips during the summer to Bournemouth, Swanage, Portsmouth, Southsea and the annual regatta at Cowes and, as a result, the opening hours were increased from 8 a.m. – 9 p.m. to 6 a.m. – 11 p.m. in July 1912.

Repairs to the pier had to be carried out after the barge *Shamrock* removed 50 feet of the structure during a storm on 26 October 1909. Although generally kept in good condition, the piling of the pier was constantly under attack from the dreaded marine worms and in April 1916 a survey revealed that nine of the piles needed replacing. As the pier was being used by naval vessels at the time, and it was thought they had also been responsible for damaging the piles, the Yarmouth Town Trustees applied for a grant from the Admiralty to pay for repairs. The Admiralty refuse however, claiming the town had more than enough money to pay for the piling to be renewed. Indeed, in 1924, the trust paid off the final instalment of the money borrowed to pay for the pier's construction and three years later added new waiting rooms and offices.

In October 1931, the pier passed into the hands of the newly formed Yarmouth Pier & Harbour Commissioners. However, patronage of the pier declined following the opening of slipways at Yarmouth by the Southern Railway, in May 1938, for the new car ferry service from Lymington. The passenger vessels continued to call at the pier until 1959. The pier remained in use as a promenade, angling centre and as a landing stage for boats to call, but maintenance was neglected and despite gaining a Grade II historic building listing in 1975 it was closed in 1980 after the commissioners were advised that most of the component parts of the structure had reached the end of their natural life and a complete restoration programme would be required if the pier was to remain open to the public.

An application by the Yarmouth (Isle of Wight) Harbour Commissioners for listed building consent to demolish the pier was refused in 1981 by both South Wight Borough Council and then on appeal by the Secretary of State for the Environment. The restoration of the pier was then carried out in three stages. The first stage was commenced in 1983 and completed by the winter of 1984–85 at a cost of £131,630, enabling the first 264 feet of the pier to be reopened to the public. Craft continued to call at the pier and in 1985 16,523 passengers were landed from 187 boats sailing from Bournemouth, Poole and Hurst Castle. In the ten years between 1983 and 1993, around £1 million was spent on refurbishing the old wooden structure. To assist with the cost of the restoration, 552 deck planks were engraved with the name of each person or organisation who had donated £25. In 2007, the pier was awarded a Heritage Lottery Grant of £350,000 towards the cost of replacing piles attacked by marine worms and the refurbished pier was reopened on 26 April 2008 by Alan Titchmarsh, the patron of the fundraising appeal. The leader of the project was Richard Gribble, who had an appropriate surname considering that the gribble is one of the marine worms that eat through the pier's wooden supports! Despite being the villain of the piece, the gribble has become something of a local celebrity and a gribble sculpture was placed on the quay. On 5 August 2008, HRH the Duke of Edinburgh visited the pier to unveil the final carved plank, engraved with his name.

Now 609 feet long, Yarmouth is one of last remaining wooden pleasure piers in the country and is interestingly made up of three different types of timber – Douglas fir for decking and handrails, greenheart for the piles and *barcilata balau* for the latticework on the handrails. The pier remains a popular promenade and fishing centre, and boats still call, including the ferry to Keyhaven and Hurst Castle, the Paddle Steamer Preservation Society's PS *Waverley* and MV *Balmoral* and smaller pleasure cruisers.

Bouldnor Jetty and Proposed Pier

Bouldnor is a quiet area situated just to the east of Yarmouth, but at one time there were big plans to develop the area. The scheme was first put forward in 1867 by the Bouldnor Pier & Land Company, led by Christopher Nugent Nixon and on

This 1875 map shows the little wooden pier built at Bouldnor as part of a grand plan to develop the area as a seaside resort. However, the resort, along with the proposed esplanade marked on the map and a larger pier, never materialised.

16 October 1867 the *Hampshire Telegraph and Sussex Chronicle* reported:

PROPOSED NEW TOWN AT BOULDNOR, NEAR YARMOUTH – A number of gentlemen having bought Bouldnor House and ground (late the residence of P. Farnall, Esq.) commenced laying it out some while since for building plots. Roads are laid down through the estate in various directions of a uniform width of 50 feet, a site whereon a church is proposed to be built has been marked out in a central situation, and large sea water baths are erected on the shore. The land being undulated, it presents charming sites for villas, the Solent forming a panorama on one side, whilst on the other the view of the country is delightful. As a whole this estate embraces all the requirements for a yachting man, there being good anchorage in the bay, and a pier will be built for landing upon. As a building speculation it will no doubt answer, and all the building frontage on the high road between the house and Lord Heytesbury's land is already taken up. There being an abundant supply of excellent water, we should not be at all surprised to see it brought into Yarmouth at some future time. In addition to all this there is to be an esplanade and sea wall along

---

[12] His grandfather was a lighthouse keeper who was apparently murdered by smugglers.

the front of the property, which, if Lord Heytesbury would carry it past his property, would form a most delightful promenade between Yarmouth and the new town of Bouldnor. R.J. Woodcock, Esq., is the architect and engineer.

The first portion of the estate, and the mansion, were put up for auction at the George Hotel, Yarmouth on 4 June 1868:

62 LOTS OF VALUABLE FREEHOLD BUILDING LAND, IN PLOTS with average frontages of 50 feet, by depths varying from 200 feet to 400 feet, situated on the high road from Yarmouth to Newport and Cowes, and on intended roads, to be called West Terrace, North Crescent, Park Road, Park Terrace, Park Crescent, South Crescent and Woodview Crescent, in all about 31 ACRES, also THE MANSION, with Orchard, Kitchen, and Pleasure Gardens and Grounds, as bounded by roads already made, containing upwards of 5 acres. The Estate is undulating, well wooded, and sloping towards the north-west to the Solent Sea, with extensive views of the Hampshire coast, and overlooking to the south the beautiful scenery of the island. Nine-tenths of the purchase money of the building plots may remain on mortgage or contract, at 5 per cent interest, to be paid in 9 years, by equal quarterly instalments, or the balance may be paid at any time without notice. Only thirteen of the plots were sold at the auction, at prices ranging from £65 to £105.

There were also plans for a Bouldnor, Yarmouth & Freshwater Railway with a branch to a pier at Bouldnor, and plans for the pier were deposited with the Board of Trade on 30 November 1868. The Bill to build the railway and pier came before a committee of the House of Lords on Wednesday, 14 April 1869 and the *Hampshire Telegraph and Sussex Chronicle* recorded: 'The pier is to commence at Shalfleet, at a point above high water mark, northward of and nearly opposite the brick works on the Bouldnor estate, and extending across the foreshore for a distance of about 300 yards into the sea. The railways is to be 5 miles 1 furlong 7 chains and 15 links in length, commencing at the southern end of the pier and terminating in the parish of Freshwater, at or near the eastern end of Beadon Warren, at or near the northern boundary of the meadow on the northern side of the Needles. The capital of the company is to be £50,000, in 5,000 shares of £10 each, and the company are authorised to borrow any sum not exceeding £16,600.'

The Act of Parliament for the Bouldnor, Yarmouth & Freshwater Railway and Bouldnor Pier Order was passed in 1873. All that was built, however, was a small wooden pier, erected in 1875 and described in Jenkinson's *Practical Guide to the Isle of Wight* (1875): 'One and a quarter miles from Yarmouth a small pier has been erected and close to it is a board stating 'site of Bouldnor Pier and Hotel'. At one time it was intended to build a little town here with money raised by a limited liability company, but the scheme has never arrived at maturity.'

Plans for an esplanade were also drawn up in 1875, but the company had no money. In 1879, the Bouldnor Pier & Land Company was reformed with a capital of £55,000 (5,500 shares of £10) and an application to extend the time of the

Provisional Order was granted in 1880. Nevertheless, the town, railway or even a larger pier never materialised, which is just as well as the area has been prone to serious coastal erosion. The Bouldnor Pier & Land Company was finally dissolved on 19 April 1887.

According to the *Hampshire Telegraph and Sussex Chronicle* on Saturday 5 November 1892, the abutment of the railway pier was constructed. The paper also recorded that a jetty was to be built:

> BOULDNOR-ON-SEA. FOUNDING A NEW TOWN – On Wednesday afternoon and evening interesting ceremonies took place at Bouldnor-on-Sea, an estate of about 200 acres, situated a mile to the east of Yarmouth. A portion of the estate was sold in lots by public auction a few months ago and on Wednesday the first pile of a new jetty 80ft long by 12ft 6in in width, was driven in by Miss Douglas, of Yarmouth. The place was gaily decorated with bunting, and the ceremony was under the personal direction of Mr. John Fowle, the architect, who has planned out the estate, and is conducting its development. A dinner was afterwards given to the workmen and a few invited friends, at the Bugle Hotel, Mr Fowle in the chair, and Mr H. Lee in the vice-chair, and several toasts were honoured. In the course of the evening Mr Fowle explained that it is intended by the owners of the estate to construct six groynes in addition to the jetty for the collection of a beach, to build a sea wall and form a carriageway along a sea front of about a mile and half, to lay out a portion of the estate for a recreation ground, another portion as a tennis lawn, and a wooded belt of land parallel with the carriageway as gardens. A pier is also a portion of the scheme, the abutment of which has already been constructed.

None of the aspirations for Bouldnor – town, railway, pier or resort – ever materialised and today it comprises of a small village. It is thought that the little jetty that was may have come to serve a gun battery and brickworks and its foundations may be seen at low tide, some way off shore.

COWES

Before its ascent into a renowned yachting centre and fashionable watering place, the chief industry of Cowes was shipbuilding. Yards were built on both sides of the mouth of the River Medina, which split the communities of West Cowes (plain Cowes since 1895) and East Cowes. In 1825, one of the world's premier yacht clubs, the Royal Yacht Squadron, moved to Cowes and two years later a guide recorded: 'Cowes is a very interesting watering place: it is furnished with almost everything that can attract the visitor: it has inns, lodging houses, libraries, ballrooms and the greatest facilities for bathing. In the height of the season, the vessels belonging to the Royal Yacht Club are engaged in a sailing match, this with the contest that succeeds it the next day with rowing boats, form a scene of great vivacity and attraction.' The fashionable status of the resort was enhanced further when Queen Victoria and Prince Albert acquired nearby Osborne House in 1845.

In 1820, a steam packet service was commenced between Cowes and Southampton and three years later the Fountain Quay was erected as a landing stage for the route, which is still in use today by Red Funnel. Cowes and East Cowes are connected by a floating bridge/chain ferry, the ferry rights of which were granted by the island's Governor to the Roberton family in 1720. They sold the rights to the Cowes Ferry Company, who built the floating bridge, in 1859. In 1868, the Southampton, Isle of Wight & South England Royal Mail Steam Packet Company acquired the rights to operate the bridge and continued to do so until 1901 when it passed to Cowes and East Cowes councils. It is currently operated by the Isle of Wight County Council. Cowes has also had two pleasure piers: the short-lived Royal/Kernot's Pier, and the Victoria Pier, which never reopened after the Second World War.

The town's tradition of yachting remains strong and Cowes Week, established in 1826 and the longest running regular regatta in the world, continues to draw in many visitors.

Victoria Pier

Following the destruction of Kernot's Pier by a storm in 1876, there were calls from the people of Cowes for a replacement pleasure pier. However, due to the restrictions imposed by the Admiralty (particularly on the length of the pier), companies were reluctant to undertake such a venture. In 1897, a proposal to convert the Watch House Slip into a pier foundered when another proposal for a pier at the Zig-Zag was put forward, although this was considered too far from the town and the idea was soon dropped. It was left to Cowes Urban District Council to erect a promenade pier and landing stage for excursion steamers (which were barred from the Isle of Wight Steam Packet Company's Fountain Pier and Quay). A site was chosen on the Parade near Bath Road in October 1899 and the Cowes Pier Act was passed in the summer of 1900. In the interest of 'Her Majesty's Yachts' the Admiralty limited the length of the pier to only 170 feet. A design for the pier by R. E. Cooper was accepted and contractor Alfred Thorne began work on its construction in 1901. The pier was completed early the following year at a cost of £12,800 and was officially opened on 26 March 1902 with the steamer *Monarch* calling at the landing stage.

Two elegant pagoda tollhouses flanked the entrance to the pier, which had wooden decking laid upon steel girders and iron piling. A generous amount of seating was provided along the sides of the pier and also in the centre of the

20   COWES (Isle of Wight). — Victoria Pier. — LL.

The Victoria Pier at Cowes was opened on 26 March 1902 and the pavilion was added two years later. Steamers called at the pier from Bournemouth, Southampton and resorts on the island, and one of them can be seen at the landing stage on this postcard from *c.* 1907.

The landing stage at the Victoria Pier, Cowes, photographed on a hot summer's day *c.* 1908 with a queue of people waiting to use the rowing boats. Note the young boys wearing only their underpants, quite risqué for the time!

Cowes Victoria Pier pictured during the 1930s with a fine array of cars parked along the esplanade. By this time, the pavilion was used mainly as a dance hall and refreshment room.

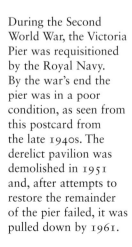

During the Second World War, the Victoria Pier was requisitioned by the Royal Navy. By the war's end the pier was in a poor condition, as seen from this postcard from the late 1940s. The derelict pavilion was demolished in 1951 and, after attempts to restore the remainder of the pier failed, it was pulled down by 1961.

deck and on the large pier head. Wooden landing stages surrounded the head and landing steps were also provided for small craft.

During its first year of operation, 100,000 people used the pier and steamers called on 300 occasions on services from Bournemouth, Southampton and the other island resorts. The pier would always be at its busiest during the famous Cowes Regatta weeks, when it was bedecked with bunting and large crowds gathered to watch the races, the diving performances and the fireworks during the evening. The pier was also used by the Island Sailing Club as a base during their annual races, and another sailing club, the *Medina*, commenced their races from it.

In 1903, two shelters were added on the centre of the pier and in the following year a pavilion was erected on the pier head. Concert parties, small orchestras and performances by dramatic and musical societies were the main entertainments provided, although during the winter the pavilion was rented by Miss Cust for roller skating. Divers were another attraction and, in 1910, W. Stanley, Secretary of the York Street Swimming Club, was given permission to play water polo from the pier. Bathing facilities were provided at the pier head, but apparently only for men; ladies were not permitted! Fishing was sometimes allowed from the pier and in February 1914 a record catch of 200 bass in an hour was made by three men fishing with rods and lines. The entrance to the pier was lined with sweetmeat and amusement machines, although this being Cowes they were not too racy!

During the First World War, the pier was used for the movement of troops but returned to full business after the end of the war, once repairs had been carried out. The pavilion continued in use for concert party entertainment, although dancing became increasingly popular as the 1920s wore on. The building also housed a well-liked refreshment room.

The pier was requisitioned once again during the Second World War when it was taken over by the Royal Navy. By the war's end the pier was in a poor condition and the derelict pavilion was demolished in 1951. Attempts to restore the remainder of the pier failed and by 1961 it had gone.

Kernot's/Royal Pier

The Fountain Pier was purely a functional steamer pier/quay and as early as 1839 the people of West Cowes were petitioning for a public promenade/landing pier. Their desire to erect a pier gathered pace following the Royal Yacht Squadron's move into Cowes Castle in 1858, and the subsequent influx of wealthy visitors. A doctor named Charles Noyce Kernot was to take up the baton of building such a pier when he erected what he called the 'Royal Pier' (although locals referred to it as 'Kernot's Pier'), an obscure pleasure pier of which little is known.

Dr Kernot was one of 127 signatories on a petition submitted to the Local Board on 17 February 1857 calling for a landing/goods pier:

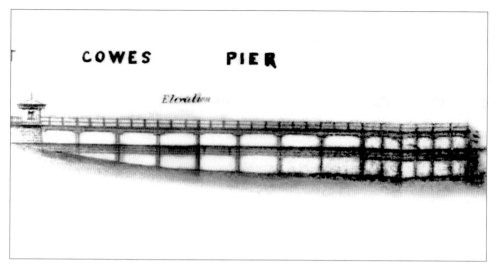

COWES PIER

Elevation

Soap manufacturer Charles Noyce Kernot was the driving force behind the building of the obscure and short-lived Royal Pier at Cowes, extant between 1867 and 1883. This plan of the pier shows it as originally built, with its plain deck on iron piling before the addition of a pagoda, ballroom and refreshment room.

A PETITION...to Local Board of Health at West Cowes, calling on them to consider the necessity of at once carrying out the clause empowering them to erect a TOWN PIER AT FEATHERS SLIP.

The reasons for the petition are that the only landing place is at a pier in an inn yard [Fountain] – the pier and yard being private property.

One steam boat company has by lease the exclusive privilege of bringing and taking passengers and luggage to and from the pier.

The neglect of the duty imposed upon the authorities of the town by the Act of forty years ago has caused the loss of a large revenue to the town. In the last ten years there has been a diminution in the number of passengers to Cowes.

Tolls...as well as from goods' vessels, now compelled to discharge their packages in the open harbour at increased cost and risk.

The Market House so near the pier will become a source of income and the establishment of a market (one of the objectives of the Act) an inestimable benefit to the poorer classes, as well as to the public at large...

Some of the signatories with their 'amount of rating':

Charles Fellows	£446
Sarah Goodwin	£648
Alfred Barton	£120
Max Geneste	£55
Robert White	£100
C. Hare Townsend	£54
Thomas Barnes	£69

Michael Ratsey	£110
Martha Turner	£99
M. A. Macnamara	£56
Jane Ratsey	£50
John Hewitt	£55
John Prangnell	£66
Henry B. Hillyer	£66
Thomas Lee	£150
Charles N. Kernot	£74
Charles Ratsey	£67
Ellen Aris	£133
George Marvin	£115
Charles Hanson	£75
Earl de Grey	£81
John Stuart Hippesley	£60
(A High Street shopkeeper between	£12 and £20)
Plan submitted by Mr Wyatt	

However, the Local Board replied that they were unable to comply with the memorial for a pier because the Admiralty were refusing to give assent to any projection into the harbour beyond the Admiralty Line.

In response to the pier proposal, improvements were announced for the existing Fountain Pier (actually more of a quay) by its owner William Ward. The proposed changes included the addition of two waiting rooms and the removal of existing buildings that obstructed the centre of the quay. Exclusive rights to use the quay were leased to Ward's Isle of Wight Royal Mail Steam Packet Company.

Dr Kernot resided at Gloucester House and in 1862 he sought permission to make soap there. The Local Board objected on the grounds it was injurious to the health of the inhabitants of the town. Kernot had a long list of patents, including a powder to be placed in water to keep meat fresh, another powder to keep beer from going sour and a method of embalming human bodies so they were kept fresh whilst in transit.

Despite the earlier setback, Kernot was still keen on the idea of a pier and in 1864 he formed the West Cowes Pier Company. An application was made to the Board of Trade under the General Pier and Harbour Act 1861 for the 'construction of a pier commencing at the back of Gloucester House, High Street, West Cowes, in the parish of Northwood…and extending there into the sea in a north-easterly direction for a distance of 350 feet.' The engineers for the project were stated as being Ebenezer William Hughes and William Bage of 5 Queen Street, Westminster.

The West Cowes Pier Provisional Order was sanctioned by the Board of Trade on 16 November 1864, but there were a number of objections to the plans. The West Cowes Local Board claimed it would be a 'great impediment' whilst the Southampton, Isle of Wight & South of England Royal Mail Steam Packet

Company, operating from Fountain Pier, said it would be a threat to navigation. A reformed West Cowes Pier Company was incorporated on 19 June 1866 with a capital of £8,000 (800 x £10 shares) and the Provisional Order to build the pier was passed on the condition that the structure was to measure not more than 250 feet in length. The first iron pile of the pier was driven in on 11 November 1866, but the cost of construction proved to be more than anticipated and in February 1867 the company increased its capital by a further £4,000. The pier was opened to the public in the summer of 1867 and as well as housing a 60-foot landing stage available at low tide, featured a pagoda, ballroom and refreshment room.

A description of the pier was given in the *Morning Advertiser* on 23 June 1870: 'The pier is situated near the Yacht Squadron Castle and adjoining the Parade, West Cowes, a splendid landing place of 60ft in width, capable of being reached at all tides and weathers, extending from Gloster House 250ft seawards by 60ft wide, with elaborate lounging rooms to protect the passengers and promenaders from the elements. There is also a pagoda erected in oriental style 50ft high.' The 1871 Hampshire and Isle of Wight Directory described it as the 'Royal Promenade and Steam Packet Pier'.

Although the pier proved to be reasonably successful, Dr Kernot and the West Cowes Pier Company struggled to make it pay and on 8 October 1873 the company was wound up. Kernot kept the pier going but on 29 September 1876 it was badly damaged by a tornado, as described in *The Graphic*: 'Yesterday's tornado travelled along the northern part of the island in a north-easterly direction. It blew down every tree in its path in Parkhurst Forest, leaving a clearance of about thirty yards wide, and went on to cause havoc in West Cowes.' The *Hampshire Gazette* recorded: 'the tornado swept Kernot's Pier away. Pagoda etc gone, only the bandstand remains.'

What remained of the pier was sold by Kernot, who was now in Calcutta, to William Ward in October 1877 for £5,500. However, it was left unrepaired and in February 1880 it was reported that the piling that supported the pier were to be removed as they prevented access to the Market Slip. In March 1882, Ward wrote to the Board of Trade announcing he was to remove the pier as it had fallen into disuse, and he had completed this by 1883. Some of the iron piles were sold to the Alum Bay Pier Company to repair their wooden pier and, although the restoration failed to happen, the piles may have been incorporated into the new iron pier.

Fountain Pier/Quay

The first pier to be erected at Cowes was the Fountain Pier, which was hardly deserving of the title 'pier', as it was more of an extended quay for steamer landings. The pier began life as a short 56-foot quay erected by George Ward outside the Fountain Inn in 1823. Ward, along with William Fitzhugh, had formed the Isle of Wight Royal Mail Steam Packet Company in 1820 and established the first steamer services between Cowes and Southampton. Ward also became

Above left: A postcard issued *c.* 1960 showing the Fountain Arcade leading to the Fountain Pier and Quay. One of the Red Funnel Steamers operating to Southampton can be seen at the end of the pier.

Above right: The Red Funnel terminal at the Fountain Quay, photographed in 2008.

involved with the Southampton-based Isle of Wight Steam Packet Company upon their formation in 1826 and allowed their vessels to use the quay on a renewable lease. The two companies soon co-ordinated their services and introduced a common timetable, and before long the Southampton company was providing the bulk of the steamer crossings.

Following Ward's death in 1829, his son, George Henry Ward, took over the business and built a wooden pier onto the end of the quay, increasing its length to 100 feet. Cellars were built into the quay to store coal for the steamers. In 1834, following the construction of a causeway at the pier, Ward was taken to court by Newport Corporation. A wooden pier was recorded as being built at the Fountain in 1841.

Upon the death of George Ward in 1849, the pier, steamer company, Fountain Inn and his other businesses passed to his nephew, William George Ward. In 1852, he erected iron gates to prevent locals going onto the quay and pier; an ongoing saga which was to cause great resentment and eventually led to legal proceedings. Five years later, proposals were put forward to provide waiting rooms for boat passengers and remove buildings that obstructed the centre of the quay. In 1857, the gates reappeared to close off the quay after William Durnford fell into the sea and drowned, leading to another petition from the locals. Ward also failed to enhance his popularity when he refused to allow troops to land at the quay except in the case of emergency, claiming it would interfere with the passenger traffic and his obligation to the steamer company. The lease of the quay was renewed to the company in 1858 for two years at a cost of £500 per annum.

On 10 September 1861, the Isle of Wight Steam Packet Company merged with the Isle of Wight & Portsmouth Improved Steamboat Company (established the previous year) to form the Southampton, Isle of Wight & South of England Royal Mail Steam Packet Company. The new company retained exclusive use of the pier by claiming it could not accommodate larger vessels than their own. In 1867, they acquired the lease of the floating bridge that ran between West and East Cowes and held it until 1901 when it passed to Cowes and East Cowes councils. They set up a Ferry Committee that divided the profits equally between the two councils and in 1915 they purchased the ferry foreshore and bed of the river for £2,500.

Plans were made to improve the Fountain Pier by building covered waiting rooms, enlarging the access to the quay and building a new pontoon to replace the old pier. The pontoon was opened in June 1873, increasing the pier/quay length to 120 feet, and by the following year all the improvements had been completed. However, the company's decision to erect further gates across the quay, therefore blocking access to it, caused local uproar and their decision to charge a 1d toll to use the pier/quay led to long drawn out legal proceedings. In 1880, Ward was found guilty of obstructing the right of way to the harbour from the Fountain Quay.

The early 1890s saw the pier further upgraded and in 1893 a new pontoon was added, bringing its length to 120 feet. Around thirty different paddle steamers were used on the Cowes to Southampton route before diesel vessels began to be introduced from the 1930s, which had side-loading bays for cars. In 1935, the Southampton, Isle of Wight & South of England Royal Mail Steam Packet Company became formally known as Red Funnel.

High speed hovercraft services were introduced in 1969 to counteract those introduced by British Railways three years earlier. Catamarans began to be introduced in 1991, the year that all vehicle ferries ceased to call at the Fountain Quay – all services being transferred to East Cowes. A half-hourly service on the Red Jet Hi-speed Catamarans is currently provided.

Dolphin Hotel Pier

The Dolphin Hotel adjoined the Fountain Hotel and Pier/Quay and during an auction sale of the property on 14 March 1871 it was stated that it had its own 84-foot-long pier 'affording a promenade and landing place'. The hotel now trades as a gift shop.

EAST COWES

Unlike its neighbour on the other side of the River Medina, East Cowes was never developed for tourism on a major scale and remained a small town largely concerned with the building and maintenance of marine craft. Following Queen Victoria's acquisition of Osborne House in 1845, an estate of grand houses was planned but very few were built.

East Cowes is connected to Cowes by a floating bridge/chain ferry and to the mainland by Red Funnel's car ferry service to Southampton.

Trinity Pier

This was a private pier used by Queen Victoria and her visitors to access her island retreat at Osborne House, purchased in 1845 and completely refurbished by September 1846. The pier was erected by the Admiralty in 1845 on the Trinity House wharf and consisted of a short wooden structure with a floating pontoon. However, it was reported in 1849 that the pier was little-used as the wharf was preferred as a landing stage.

In 1867, Trinity House extended the wharf 40 feet northward to provide a berth of 100 feet and the pier was extended by the Admiralty to 63 feet long. The structure at this time consisted of a 20 x 10-foot floating pontoon connected to the shore by bridle bridge 43 feet long by 10 feet wide. Further improvements were carried out in 1895/96 when a covered way and waiting rooms in the style of a Tudor house were erected in place of a wooden canopy with rounded roof. The new building boasted two waiting rooms, gas lighting and telephones.

The Royal Family normally decamped to Osborne twice a year: from 18 July to 23 August and close to Christmas. Apart from the Queen herself, members of her family and visiting European royalty also used the pier, including Napoleon III in 1857 and the German Kaiser in 1889, when troops lined the route from the pier to Osborne House. The visitors used their own private craft or the Royal Yachts. These included the *Victoria and Albert*; in service from 1843–56, before it was renamed *Osborne* upon being replaced by a second *Victoria and Albert*. In 1874,

The Trinity Pier was a private pier used by Queen Victoria and her visitors to access her island retreat at nearby Osborne House. The pier was erected by the Admiralty in 1845 on the Trinity House wharf and consisted of a short wooden structure with a floating pontoon.

A postcard issued in 1902 showing the Trinity Pier at East Cowes and waiting rooms erected for Queen Victoria in 1895/96.

Osborne was replaced by a new craft of the same name and the second *Victoria and Albert* was itself replaced in 1899. Other vessels included the Royal Barge *Alberta* and the screw steamers *Fairy*, *Elfin* and *Louise*. Upon Victoria's death on 22 January 1901, her body was placed aboard the *Alberta* for her last journey from the pier.

The Queen's successor, her son Edward VII, gave Osborne to the nation in 1902, although houses on the estate were retained by members of the Royal Family. Part of the estate became a junior training college for the Royal Navy in 1903 and the pier was used occasionally by them until the college was closed in 1921. The pier then passed into the hands of Trinity House in 1922.

The pier's entrance building was eventually sold by Trinity House for £10 in 1950 and re-erected as a public hall for the Parkhurst Horticultural Society. In 1961, it was purchased by the former Mayor of Newport, Alderman King, who moved it to the outskirts of Newport where it became a bungalow; later it was divided into two dwellings.

The pier itself was removed a number of years ago, but on 29 July 2006 a new pontoon pier, known as the Trinity Landing, was opened by Dame Ellen McArthur.

The Red Funnel car ferry pontoon at East Cowes, photographed from a departing ferry in 2006.

Ferry Pontoon

This was more of a pontoon than a pier, and was erected by Messrs Welch and Thornton in 1865 and leased to the Southampton, Isle of Wight & South of England Royal Mail Steam Packet Company. In addition to being used by vessels of the company on their services to Southampton, West Cowes, Ryde and Portsmouth, troops billeted at East Cowes Barracks were landed there. The Royal Yachts of Queen Victoria also used the pier during her visits to Osborne House. Soon after the pier was built, the Royal Yacht *Elfin* landed its passengers at the pier and the owners contemplated calling it the 'Royal Elfin Pier'.

A description of the pier/pontoon was given when East Lee was put up for sale by auction on 13 August 1872:

> East Cowes Pontoon Pier with small dwelling house, landing stage etc
> Large yacht store and extensive warehouse with granary above.
> Girder bridge about 60ft long
> 3-ton crane
> Pontoon 38ft 6in long x 17ft 6in wide
> Sea frontage about 60ft
> Part of this lot is leased to the Steam Packet Company for one year from August
> 1872 at £150 per annum

No sale appears to have been made as in the following year Welch and Thornton stated the pontoon would be closed as they were seeking a new tenant. However, it was eventually acquired by the Southampton, Isle of Wight & South of England Royal Mail Steam Packet Company and the same company – known as Red Funnel since 1935 – now use the pontoon for their hourly passenger vehicle ferry service between East Cowes and Southampton.

BOURNEMOUTH AREA
& SWANAGE

SOUTHBOURNE

Now a suburb of Bournemouth, Southbourne once had its own separate identity and was a purpose-built resort created by Bournemouth doctor Thomas Armetriding Compton. In May 1883, Dr Compton purchased 230 acres of land at a cost of £3,000 and then proceeded to bridge the River Stour to the east of Southbourne at a cost of £4,000. He then formed the Southbourne-on-Sea Freehold Land Company, who erected an esplanade and sea wall for a third of mile at a cost of £15,000, which was opened by Horace Davey MP in September 1885. The esplanade was fitted with gas lamps and was wide enough for a horse and carriage. A terrace of six grand houses was placed on the esplanade and the first attraction provided for visitors was a winter garden: the next one was to be a pier.

Southbourne Pier

A pier had first been proposed at a meeting in 1884, by Mr McEwan Brown, an estate agent from Boscombe, and on 8 November 1884 the Southbourne-on-Sea Freehold Land Company made an application to the Board of Trade to construct and maintain a pier of 800 feet with a pavilion, assembly rooms and shops. The application was remade in January 1885 upon the formation of the Southbourne Pier Company with a capital of £8,000 in £10 shares. The pier, which was designed by engineers Law & Chatterton and envisaged to cost £6,500, was approved by the Board of Trade in March 1885.

The Act of Parliament for the pier's construction was passed on 22 July 1885, but the money for it proved to be slow in coming and, on the evening of 6 November 1885, a meeting at the South Cliff Hotel launched a public subscription to raise funds. This proved to be a failure and in April 1887 an application had to be made for an extension of time to build the pier. Despite only 146 of the shares being taken up (65 by Edward James Woollaston, 18 by Compton), the decision was taken to start work on the pier in 1887. The original design was shelved in favour of one by Archibald Smith for a plain, modest, cast-iron structure 300 feet long and 30 feet wide, standing 17 feet above the high water mark. E. Howell of Poole erected the pier at a cost of £3,381 12s 6d and it was officially opened on

Southbourne Pier was opened in 1888 as part of Bournemouth doctor Thomas Armetriding Compton's creation of a new seaside resort. This photograph (later issued as a postcard) shows the pier within a few years of opening, before the pier abutment was washed away in a storm in November 1891.

Another retrospective postcard of Southbourne Pier – this time showing how it looked in 1898. The pier is basically intact but had not been used since the abutment and entrance had been washed away in November 1891. The houses in the foreground had been abandoned due to frequent incursion by the sea.

A close-up view of the wrecked Southbourne Pier *c.* 1904 shows the collapsed abutment of the pier, which has led to one side of it beginning to collapse. Although the pier is empty in this photograph, the more intrepid would endeavour to climb upon the structure.

This is how Southbourne Pier looked in around 1907 after some of the supporting piling had been washed away during the winter of 1900/01. The cellars of the houses on the promenade have been left exposed following their demolition in 1902.

A postcard commemorating the passing of Southbourne Pier, following its demolition in May 1909. A number of people can be seen on the wrecked pier.

The Vanishing of one of Bournemouths Landmarks.

Southbourne Pier erected 1888, Removed May 1909.   Chandler & Co.

The final stages of the demolition of Southbourne Pier can be seen in this photograph from 1909.

2 August 1888 with a steamer trip to Bournemouth aboard the *Lady Elgin*. The vessel left Bournemouth at 8.30 a.m., returning from Southbourne half an hour later. However, the afternoon sailing failed to take place due to rough weather. Around 1,200 people passed through the turnstiles on the opening day, overseen by Mr Legg the Pier Master, who was a retired sea captain.

The regular sailings between Southbourne and Bournemouth were due to have commenced four days later, with the *Lord Elgin* providing a daily service commencing at 9.30 a.m. and returning nine hours later. Return fares were to be 1s first class and 9d second class, whilst admission to the pier was 1d. However, the sailings were not advertised and a three times daily service by the *Nelson* between Southbourne, Bournemouth and Swanage in September 1888 foundered when the vessel soon left the district.

Dr Compton resigned from the directorship of the Southbourne Pier Company in February 1889 ahead of the company's first report the following month. This revealed that income had been derived from tolls (£8 8s 11d), yearly tickets (£3 3s) and boat moorings (10s 6d) and £13 had been spent on a Pier Master and £2 2s on a sweetmeat machine. The 1889 season proved to be equally modest, with income received from tolls (£21 15s 7d), yearly tickets (£8 4s 6d), monthly tickets (£2 18s 6d), weekly tickets (15s) and boat moorings (£2 2s), while the Pier Master was paid £26 for the year. The lack of support for the steamer services from the pier meant they were not renewed for the 1890 season and, furthermore, toll receipts fell to just £14 14s 5d that year. 1891 saw a further fall in tolls to £12 15s 2d. This was hardly surprising in view of the pier's short length and lack of attractions to entice anyone onto it.

Sadly, Dr Compton's grand resort of Southbourne-on-Sea was failing to take off and in November 1891 it received its death knell when a storm destroyed the pier abutment, the sea wall and esplanade around it, leaving the pier incapable of being accessed. As the Southbourne Land and Pier companies had no money to pay for repairs, there was no alternative but to close the pier, and after just over three years of use it was never opened to the public again. The houses on the promenade also had to be abandoned as they were now exposed to serious flooding. They became derelict and were demolished in 1902, the materials reused to build Ellerslie Mansions on Boscombe Hill.

The pier was left to the elements and those who were able could climb up on to it and enjoy a free promenade. The main structure itself remained fairly sound until the winter of 1900/01 when storms washed away the fourth (of six) set of supporting piles. During the next few years further piling was lost and the pier became twisted and buckled, with the front end of it eventually collapsing onto the beach. Nevertheless, the more brave-hearted still climbed up on it, despite warning notices, and because of its wrecked state the pier became something of a local landmark. Bournemouth Corporation, which had absorbed Southbourne in 1901, became concerned at the danger the pier presented and in October 1908 received a report on its condition:

> The length as originally constructed was about 277 feet from the wall of the promenade, which was constructed at the same time, and the width was 30 feet. At the sea end of the pier there was a landing stage constructed of wooden piles. The decking of the pier stood about 18 feet above ordnance datum. The structure was composed of iron lattice girders supported on cast iron screw piles. The pier has had practically nothing done to it since it was first erected about twenty years back. The main supports, viz: the iron columns, have mostly disappeared, and the abutment at the shore end of the pier, which supported the end of the lattice work girder, is washed away, and the main structure, or lattice work girders supporting the pier decking, is now only supported by about half the original number of iron columns. At the shore end where the abutment wall is washed away, the lattice girders have of course failed, and are now resting on the beach. Notwithstanding this state of affairs, the public climb on the structure which may collapse at any minute. The pier is not lighted at night, and this is of course a danger to navigation.

Nevertheless, the council refused to remove the pier, claiming it was not their responsibility. The Southbourne Pier Company was moribund, but still in existence, and in 1909 the directorship consisted of John Harvey, Alfred Blackford and James Edwards. They were ordered by the council to do something about the pier and in February 1909 they signed a contract with James Wells of Poole to remove it. The pier was cleared away by May 1909 and the Southbourne Pier Company followed it into extinction on 3 May 1912.

In 1913, it was reported that a few stumps of the pier still remained and presented a hazard to the public. They were eventually covered over by the silting of the sand, although the 'Pier Steps', a set of concrete steps that led down from the promenade by the pier to the beach, remained for a number of years.

BOSCOMBE

Despite being incorporated into Bournemouth as early as 1884, Boscombe has always managed to retain a semblance of a separate identity and still retains its own pier. Boscombe's development as a health resort was led by Sir Henry Drummond Wolff, who acquired nineteen acres of land and built his house, Boscombe Towers, in 1868. The remainder of the land was laid out for development and the provision of resort facilities, such as Boscombe Chine and Spa, and the plush Boscombe Chine and Boscombe Spa hotels. The area was further developed by land societies and private developers and Boscombe was soon merged into the eastern of area of Bournemouth.

Boscombe Pier

A proposal for a pier at Boscombe was first mooted in 1884; the leading advocate being Alexander McEwan Brown, who was the lawyer and land agent for landowner Sir Henry Drummond Wolff. Pressure was put on the Bournemouth Improvement Commissioners to build the pier, but they cast eight votes to five against the idea, having already used public money to build Bournemouth Pier. A number of public meetings were held in the spring of 1885 to discuss the setting up of a pier company and an application to build the pier was made to the Board of Trade in December 1886 upon the formation of the Boscombe Pier Company. Sir Henry Drummond Wolff was appointed chairman and many of the shares were brought by the poet Percy Shelley. The company was registered with the Board of Trade on 3 February 1887 and its prospectus was issued in July 1888 with a capital of £15,000, comprising of 3,000 shares of £5 each. The Bournemouth Commissioners originally opposed the building of the pier, but eventually gave it their approval in August 1888.

Although a length of 1,300 feet was originally proposed for the pier, this was reduced to 1,000 feet and then, through a lack of capital, to 600 feet. The chosen design of engineer Archibald Smith (who also designed nearby Southbourne Pier) featured 40-foot spans with a continuous wrought iron girder frame. The deck width was 32 feet and the pier head measured 120 x 38 feet with a landing stage on both sides.

Now a suburb
of Bournemouth,
Boscombe was once
an independent resort
in its own right and
opened a pier on
29 July 1889. This
postcard shows the
600-foot iron structure
in 1902.

Boscombe Pier acquired
a novel attraction
in 1897 in the form
of a 65-foot whale
skeleton which had
been washed ashore
close by. The skeleton,
which was enjoyed
by local children as
a climbing frame,
was removed after
the pier was acquired
by Bournemouth
Corporation in
September 1903.

THE WHALE.　　　　　　　　　BOSCOMBE.

A postcard of a paddle
steamer approaching
Boscombe Pier *c.*
1907. The steamer
trips called on their
way to Bournemouth,
the Isle of Wight and
Swanage, but it never
proved profitable for
the steamer companies
to use the pier and the
calls had largely ceased
by 1914 when the
landing stage needed
repairing and the sea
bed dredging due to
silting.

6　BOSCOMBE. — *The Pier.* — LL.

A fine old double-decker omnibus stands at the entrance to Boscombe Pier *c.* 1912. The ornate entrance building to the pier was added in 1904 by Bournemouth Corporation.

Boscombe Pier following the erection of the pier head in high alumina concrete in 1927. A pavilion was erected on the new pier head, which was home to W. H. Lester's Good Companions concert party.

A postcard of W. H. Lester's Good Companions concert party on Boscombe Pier in 1931. Lester, who can be seen sitting on the floor, provided the summer shows on the pier during the 1930s.

A photograph taken in February 1960 showing the rebuilding of Boscombe Pier following damage sustained in the Second World War. Messrs A. Jackaman & Son commenced work in 1958 and within two years the main body of the pier had been completed. Following the building of the Mermaid Hall, the pier was fully reopened on 6 June 1962.

Photographed in the 1980s, the entrance building to Boscombe Pier was erected in 1960 and was given Grade II listed status in 2005.

The Mermaid Theatre on Boscombe Pier, photographed in the 1980s when it was used as the Palace of Fun amusement centre. The building was opened in 1962, but closed in 1990 and demolished in 2007.

The sea end of Boscombe Pier in 2008 following the demolition of the pier head and Mermaid Theatre the previous year, and the erection of a new 18-square-metre head.

The contract for the erection of the pier was awarded to Messrs Howell of Poole, who had submitted a tender of £3,813. James Edwards of Southbourne was to build the pier approach at a cost of £938. The first pile of the pier was driven in by Lady Shelley (who pulled a red silk ribbon to start the pile driving engine) on 17 October 1888 following a grand procession of councillors and other dignitaries, local schoolchildren, the fire brigade and the Band of the Queens Own Dorset Yeomanry Company. All the children were given a bun and orange, as well as a one day holiday from school, and the sixty-six workmen engaged on the works were treated to a meal and tobacco by the visiting MP for Windsor, R. Richardson Gardner. Following the opening ceremony, the dignitaries went for a public lunch at the Chine Hotel.

The construction of the pier progressed well, although its final cost of £12,000 was a lot more than envisaged. The Duke of Argyll, accompanied by his son, the Marquis of Lorne, performed the official opening on 29 July 1889 on a day of great celebration in Boscombe. A grand procession worked its way from the Shelley Estate, Boscombe Manor, through the town to the pier and the route was bedecked with bunting, flags and banners proclaiming 'Advance Boscombe', 'Welcome to the Duke of Argyll and Marquis of Lorne' and 'Sir Percy welcomes the Duke of Argyll'. Crowds of schoolchildren, who had been presented with free buns, cheered the procession for all their worth. Arriving at the pier, the Duke presented his address and was given an album of Boscombe views by the Chairman of the Boscombe Pier Company. After declaring the pier open, the Duke went for a stroll upon it, followed by several hundred people, before partaking of luncheon in a gaily decorated marquee on the lower tennis court of the Chine Hotel.

During the opening day celebrations, the Cosens steamer *Premier* made several trips to the pier from Bournemouth and it became a regular port of call for both Cosens and the Bournemouth, Swanage & Poole Steam Packet Company's steamers. Most of the calls were on short-hauled trips to Bournemouth Pier, from where passengers could then catch the long-distance steamers, although boats sailing from the Isle of Wight or resorts east of Boscombe would call at the pier on their homeward journey to Bournemouth.

In 1893, Archibald Beckett, who was busy erecting shops, hotels and a theatre in Boscombe, leased the pier for four years at an annual cost of £500 with an option for two further years at a rental of £600 per year. The pier acquired a novel attraction in 1897 when the 65-foot skeleton of a whale was placed upon it. The whale had been killed after being run over by a tramp steamer just off Southbourne on 5 January 1897 and was eventually washed ashore close to Boscombe Pier, where it attracted a large crowd. On 8 January, it was acquired at auction for £27 by Bournemouth GP Dr Spencer Simpson, who arranged for the whale to be cut up where it lay as the smell had become so obnoxious. The council tried to remove the stinking whale but were defied by Simpson with help from the coastguard. A notice mocking the council was erected which read 'whale. 3*d* per 1lb, all sold, corporation too'. The council did eventually remove the whale and dumped it in the back of Powell's marine store in Victoria Road, Springbourne, before most of the blubber was dumped at sea off Brownsea Island and the remainder sold at Poole for a paltry 5*s*. Simpson was charged with assaulting Mr Cooper, the council's sanitary inspector, and fined £1 plus costs. The skeleton of the whale was put on the pier and was enjoyed by the local children as a climbing frame. This little verse became popular with the children:

Have you been to Boscombe?
Have you seen the whale?
Have you stood upon its back?
And smelt its stinking tail?

However, with little else on the pier apart from a small bandstand to attract customers, the Boscombe Pier Company could not make the pier pay and it was sold in September 1903 to Bournemouth Corporation for £9,000. The formal winding up of the Boscombe Pier Company took place on 26 August 1904.

The new owners set about refurbishing and renovating the pier at a cost of £3,380. The crumbling old whale skeleton was removed and ground down to make fertilizer, and a larger bandstand was erected on the pier head. The old bandstand was eventually re-erected in the children's corner of Kings Park in 1906. The small octagonal kiosks at the pier entrance were replaced by a new building containing public lavatories. The refurbished pier reopened to the public on 4 August 1904 and a section of the Municipal Band under the conductorship of Mr Hollis played twice daily. Reuben Moore, a well-known pierrot manager, was hired to present shows on the pier. However, box office takings were initially poor, so Moore travelled on the open top trams with his ventriloquist doll 'Tinker', attracting hordes of children onto the trams, who then pestered their parents to take them to the pier shows. Steamer trips were another attraction the pier could offer, with vessels such as the *Brighton Queen*, *Balmoral* and *Monarch* calling on their way to Bournemouth, Isle of Wight and Swanage. However, it never proved that profitable for the steamer companies to use the pier and they had largely ceased calling by 1914, by which time the landing stage needed repairing and the sea bed dredging due to silting. The council were reluctant to repair the landing stage, having spent £4,000 in 1910 on repairing the pier head. The pier was also used for fishing, particularly by the Boscombe and Southbourne-on-Sea Fishing Club following their founding in 1918. The first president of the club was Gordon Selfridge, founder of the celebrated London store, who lived at Hengistbury Head.

The pier was still proving to be unprofitable. At the end of the First World War, W. Gordon Wild ran concert party shows on the pier but gave up doing so in September 1920 after incurring losses of £338. He blamed the council for providing poor lighting and inadequate canvas cover. In 1924, the pier was re-decked and two years later the pier head was rebuilt once again, this time in high alumina concrete. A glittering ball by Dan Godfrey and the Municipal Orchestra heralded the reopening of the pier on 19 May 1927. A pavilion was erected on the new pier head, which was home to W. H. Lester's 'Good Companions' concert party during the 1930s.

The pier was breached as a defence measure in 1940 and by the war's end a large section of the neck had disappeared. The structure was left derelict as the council debated its future, but eventually £92,000 of government compensation was awarded for its reconstruction. The council added a further £18,224, which they borrowed over a period of three years, and a new concrete pier, complete with entrance building and pavilion, was designed in-house by John Burton. Messrs A. Jackaman & Son commenced work in 1958 and within two years the main body of the pier had been completed. Work on the remainder of the pier, including the Mermaid Hall on the pier head, meant that it was not fully reopened until 6 June 1962.

The Mermaid Hall was largely used as a covered roller skating rink until it was leased in April 1965 to Cleethorpes Amusements, who installed an amusement arcade. Boat trips also occasionally operated from the end of the pier: in 1967 the Cutler brothers ran a service from Boscombe to Swanage and Yarmouth using the yacht *Taurus*. A small craft named *Sapphire* operated from the pier to Bournemouth until 1975.

The Mermaid Hall reverted back to council control in 1988 but two years later the building, along with the remainder of the pier head, was closed on safety grounds. The rest of the pier remained open, but its future appeared regularly threatened during the 1990s, although it was repainted by a force of 2,000 volunteers during the weekend of 17–18 June 2000.

In 2003, proposals were outlined for the creation of a Boscombe Spa Village, which would include a revitalised pier. It was proposed to shorten the pier by 60 feet and build a three-sided decked platform on the end with a lookout tower and landing stage. At the shore end, a piazza area would have led to a large pavilion housing a restaurant and amusements. The plans also envisaged the creation of an artificial surf reef west of the pier. However, the granting of a Grade II listing to the pier entrance building in 2005 led to a scaling down of the plans, although the demolition of the pier head was carried out in 2007 and the £3m artificial surf reef was built. The pier was reopened on 23 May 2008 following a £2.4 million refurbishment, which included a new 18-square-metre head. A 'Friends of Boscombe Pier' group was formed to oversee displays and events on the pier. In 2010, the pier won the National Piers Society's 'Pier of the Year' award.

BOURNEMOUTH

Bournemouth is today a thriving, bustling resort, millions of miles away from its former dull image, which appeals to all ages and maintains a good selection of high quality hotels. Until the early years of the nineteenth century, Bournemouth consisted of just heath land in the parish of Holdenhurst and a beach used by smugglers. One of the Dorset Rangers engaged to protect this area of coast from the threat of Napoleonic invasion and to combat smuggling was Captain Lewis Tregonwell. Upon his retirement from the army in 1810, Tregonwell and his wife decided to build a holiday residence in the area close to the mouth of the River Bourne, and purchased 8½ acres of land from Sir George Ivison Tapps, Lord of the Manor of Christchurch, for £179 11s. A summer residence, named 'the Mansion', was erected in 1812, and between 1814 and 1822 further land was acquired to build residences for his family and staff. The Mansion was let out to the Marchioness of Exeter in 1820 and was later developed by Henry Newlyn into one of Bournemouth's top hotels, the Royal Exeter.

Following the death of Tregonwell in 1832, the impetus for the continued development of Bournemouth was carried on by Sir George Tapps-Gervis, who became Lord of the Manor in 1835. He wanted to create a select watering place and engaged Benjamin Ferrey to design detached villas standing in their own grounds amongst the pine woods. Westover Villas were erected in 1837, followed by the Bath (later Royal Bath) Hotel in 1838, and Belle Vue Boarding House (later Hotel) in 1840. The new resort – or spa as it liked to call itself – received a considerable boost by being included in Dr A. Granville's *Spas of England* in 1841, with the description: 'a perfect discovery among the sea nooks.'

Following the early death of Sir George at the age of forty-seven, in 1842, his estate was left in trust for his fifteen-year-old son, Sir George Elliot Meyrick Tapps-Gervis. The trustees continued the resort's development and engaged Decimus Burton as supervisory architect, who laid the pleasure grounds down to the sea. One of the first attractions for visitors was David Sydenham's Marine Library and Bazaar where, for a subscription of 3s 6d, the latest books and journals could be read and refreshments partaken. By the 1850s, the beach had twelve bathing machines and a few donkeys were available for hire. The Bournemouth Improvement Act of 1856 gave the town its first governing body and land was transferred to their control from the Gervis Estate. One of the main stipulations of the Act was to provide Bournemouth with a pier.

Bournemouth Jetty

The first proposal for a pier at Bournemouth was by Captain Denham, a friend of Decimus Burton who was laying out the new town for local landowner Sir George Gervis. On 3 December 1847, a meeting was held at the Bath Hotel where it was proposed to form a company to raise £2,000 in £10 shares. However, the scheme fell through due to lack of support and finance and the occasional boats that did call, including the *Princess* from Poole and Weymouth, had to land their passengers using small rowing boats. Joseph Cosens of Weymouth, owner of the *Princess*, suggested providing a moveable landing stage on wheels, as used at Lulworth Cove, but his suggestion was not acted upon. The decision was taken instead to build a small jetty. The first pile was driven in by contractor Samuel Ingram in July 1855 and the jetty was opened in 1856. It was described as a 'tramway on piles so that the top or platform is six feet wide and one hundred feet long, the causeway to it is ten feet wide, and contains a similar rail to receive the jetty platform when run off its bearing on the poles, the platform is protected by a cord run through iron standards.' Unfortunately, the structure was soon damaged by a storm on 20 August 1856, but was patched up and remained in use until a permanent pier was provided.

Bournemouth Pier (First Structure)

The Bournemouth Improvement Act of 1856 laid down that the pier must be built within five years and a Board of Commissioners was to oversee the construction. In 1859, George Rennie, brother of celebrated engineer John Rennie, came up with a design for a 1,000-foot wooden pier with a width of 16 feet and a T-shaped pier head. Contractor David Thornbury of Newcastle was engaged to build the pier, having estimated a cost of £3,418. However, such was the haste to build the pier; the first pile was sunk in on 25 July 1859 even before the contracts were sealed!

Disagreements between the engineer and contractor, along with bouts of bad weather, meant that the construction of the pier was not all plain sailing. Nevertheless, it was completed on time and officially opened by Sir George Tapps-Gervis on 17 September 1861, when a 'public festival and general holiday' was declared in Bournemouth. The day of great merriment included a procession, a twenty-one gun salute, a fair on the beach, a banquet, the berthing of visiting steamers *Prince* from Weymouth and *Ursa Major* from Poole, free teas in Cranborne Gardens and fireworks.

Admission to the pier was 1d with a resident's season ticket costing 5s to one guinea depending on the rateable value of their property. However, the great hopes expected of the pier were to be dashed when the wooden piles were attacked by the marine toredo worm. They weakened the piles to such an extent that 200 feet of the pier was washed away in 1866, followed by the disappearance of the T-head

Bournemouth in 1855
The Pier

A retrospective postcard of the jetty at Bournemouth. The first pile of the jetty was driven in by contractor Samuel Ingram in July 1855 and it was opened in 1856. Unfortunately, the structure was soon damaged by a storm on 20 August 1856, but was patched up and remained in use until a permanent pier was provided in 1861.

Work began on a 1,000-foot wooden pier at Bournemouth in 1859 and it was opened with great ceremony on 17 September 1861. This carte-de-visite photograph shows the pier after 200 feet of the neck and the T-head were washed away in 1866–67. A further 100 foot was washed away in November 1876 and the pier was demolished to make way for a replacement iron structure.

on 5 January 1867. In a bid to combat the marine worm, the wooden piles were replaced by those of cast iron.

Bournemouth Pier's strong association with paddle steamers started in 1868 when the Southampton steamer *Fawn* was chartered for a trip from the pier to see a review of the fleet at Spithead. The charterer of the vessel, David Sydenham, formed his own steamboat company and ran further excursions from the pier, but his loss-making company soon folded. Then, from 1871–76, George Burt of Swanage ran a service with the Clyde-built steamer *Heather Bell*, which could carry up to 146 passengers. Sydenham acted as the agent for the *Heather Bell* and served as local secretary for the steamer companies who served Bournemouth – including Cosens of Weymouth – from 1881 until his death in 1911.

In 1869, a toll-house for the pier collector was placed at the entrance at a cost of £30 (including stove). The pier collectors' wages were recorded as 12s per week and he was additionally provided with two suits annually and an overcoat every two years. An annual family ticket for locals (including servants) cost between 5s and one guinea. Visitors were charged 2s 6d for a monthly ticket or 1d a visit. In 1863, the Bournemouth Commissioners had decided to let the tolls, and Mr W. Roberts of the Baths, who tendered an annual income of a £170 a year, was appointed. In 1866, he was replaced by Mr Goodden, who submitted a tender of £235, which was reduced by £60 when the T-head was washed away in January 1867. Mr Roberts returned in 1869, and upon his death in 1871 his widow ran the pier until 1878. In 1874, the pier became gas lit, but on 11 November 1876 another 100 feet of the pier was washed away and it became too short to be used by steamers. The wrecked timber of the pier was found as far away as Swanage, and W. Hill was paid £17 19s 11d to recover it. The wood was used to build Joseph's Steps on the West Cliff. Mr Goodden returned to run the pier for one further year in 1878 before the structure was demolished.

Bournemouth Pier (second structure)

Plans had already been put in place for a replacement pier, but opposition to the plan from a group of townsfolk meant its passage was not as smooth as hoped. Furthermore, a rival company, the Bournemouth Promenade Pier Company, threatened to build the pier itself. They had been registered on 23 February 1875 with a share capital of £15,000 (1,500 shares of £10 each) and obtained provisional approval from the Board of Trade to build the pier as long as they acquired the Commissioners interests. The company soon failed, however, and was wound up on 27 April 1877 and formally dissolved on 17 July 1885. The commissioners suffered their own setback when the bank that held their funds failed. However, the National Provincial Bank offered to loan the money and the noted pier engineer Eugenius Birch was asked to submit three designs for a pier along with plans for a new promenade and an aquarium building also housing a swimming pool. In the meantime, Birch provided a temporary landing stage,

Bournemouth's second pier, which was formally opened on 11 August 1880 by Sir Francis Wyatt Truscott, Lord Mayor of London, cost £21,600 to construct. Seen here soon after it was built, the pier measured 838 feet in length and 35 feet wide for the first 250 feet and then 110 feet for the remainder.

A photograph of the ornate entrance building to Bournemouth Pier *c.* 1890. The clock in the tower was donated by local MP Horace Davey in 1882.

A busy day on and around the pier at Bournemouth during the Edwardian period. The pier was lengthened to 1,000 feet in 1894 and a pagoda bandstand, shelters and kiosks were placed on the enlarged pier head. An intensive steamer service operated to and from the pier and a vessel can be seen docking at the landing stage whilst another steams away west.

A pagoda bandstand was added to Bournemouth Pier in 1894 and this postcard *c.* 1907 shows a band concert in progress. During the summer months, a canvas awning was provided around the bandstand to shade patrons from the sun.

Bournemouth Pier on a fine summer's day during the Edwardian period with some customers enjoying a promenade along the wide walkway whilst others relax on the seating.

On 5 June 1909, the Lord Mayor of London, Sir George Wyatt Truscott, officially opened the new landing stage on Bournemouth Pier, which had been widened from 6 feet 9 inches to 15 feet 3 inches and additional berths provided.

The years 1908 to 1911 saw a boom in the popularity of roller skating and during the winter months the head of Bournemouth Pier was given over to those wishing to skate. This postcard shows skaters on the pier in 1910.

Passengers boarding the steamer *Monarch* from the landing stage at Bournemouth Pier, *c.* 1910. Operated by Cosens of Weymouth, the *Monarch* enjoyed sixty-two years of service to Bournemouth from 1888 to 1950.

Bournemouth Pier thronged with people during a regatta day in the 1920s. A steamer can be seen at the pier head. In 1928, the ban on steamers calling at the pier on a Sunday was finally lifted.

An aerial view of Bournemouth Pier from the mid-1930s, showing the new entrance building and pier head concert area added early in the decade. The pier's extensive landing stage can be seen to good effect.

A photograph, taken on 3 June 1946, shows the rebuilding work to Bournemouth Pier following wartime breaching and damage. The work was fully completed in 1953 at a cost of over £100,000. The temporary walkway to the landing stage can be seen on the left.

A postcard of Bournemouth Pier *c.* 1970. The Pier Theatre was added in 1959 and the central windscreen along the pier two years later.

Between 1979 and 1981, Bournemouth Pier was extensively rebuilt in concrete at a cost of £1.7 million, and this is how it looked in 2008.

A view of Bournemouth Pier and the Pier Theatre in 2008. In 2006, the theatre was leased to Openworld International and during the winter of 2009/10 underwent refurbishment before being officially reopened by Ken Dodd on 3 April 2010.

utilising the piles of the old jetty, from which steamer services commenced in July 1877. One of the vessels to call at the temporary landing stage was the *Criterion*, chartered by the Bournemouth Steam Packet Company, which had been formed with David Sydenham as secretary. The vessel operated trips to Swanage, Poole and the Isle of Wight and, on 19–21 August 1877, made a three-day sailing to Cherbourg. The company changed their name to the Bournemouth & South Coast Steam Packet Company for the 1878 season and commenced operations on Easter Monday, 22 March, with the chartered steamer *Lord Collingwood*. She ran until September when she was replaced by *Transit* but bookings fell away following the *Princess Alice* disaster on the Thames on 3 September when over 650 lives were lost following the steamer's collision with the cargo vessel *Bywell Castle*. George Burt was running *Lothair* to the pier from Swanage, but in 1879 both he and the Bournemouth Company faced competition from Messrs Sharpe Brother's 'new, powerful, swift and yacht-like paddle steamer *Royal Saxon.*' A price war followed with the Bournemouth Company cutting their fares by 25 per cent. In May, they introduced the larger steamer *Florence* and finally won victory in August when Sharpe withdrew, but at the cost of two seasons' profit being absorbed.

Birch's three submitted designs were: a 60-foot-wide pier costing £52,382; another (45 feet wide) cost £38,075 and a third for £27,500. The Bournemouth Commissioners opted for the middle quotation, but with modifications such as not building a pavilion. The plans for the promenade, aquarium and swimming bath were not proceeded with. Finally, in the autumn of 1878, Messrs Bergheim of London began work on the Birch design[13] (the same partnership was also engaged concurrently in erecting the pier at Hornsea on the Yorkshire coast). Two years later, after costing £21,600 to construct, the pier was formally opened on 11 August 1880 by Sir Francis Wyatt Truscott, Lord Mayor of London. The opening ceremony commenced with a grand procession featuring the local yeomanry, artillery and rifle corps and, in the rear, the Lord Mayor and Lady Mayoress in a semi-state coach, accompanied by a mace and sword bearer. The route was four miles long and was gaily decorated throughout. Following the Lord Mayors' address, the Lady Mayoress was presented with a golden key, giving admission to the principal entrance at any time. The Lord Mayor then formally declared the pier open and all the dignitaries made their way to a sumptuous luncheon for 500 people in the Winter Gardens. Following an afternoon of regatta sports, their stomachs were tested to the limit once again with another banquet at the Royal Bath Hotel. The day's celebrations were concluded with a display of fireworks on the pier.

The new pier was 838 feet in length and 35 feet wide for the first 250 feet, and then 110 feet for the remainder. The structure consisted of pitch pine decking, cambered to provide drainage, supported by pitch pine timber joists laid upon cast iron columns and screw piles. The landing stage was supported on greenheart piles, resistant to the attention of marine worms. At the entrance an ornate building boasting a clock tower was provided: the clock was donated by local MP Horace Davey in 1882. On the pier deck, covered shelters and a bandstand were added to the pier head in 1885. That same year saw the railway finally extended into the centre of Bournemouth, on the condition that the station was designed to resemble a winter garden!

During the new pier's first season in 1880 there was intense competition for its steamer traffic. The Bournemouth & South Coast Steam Packet Company operated *Carham* in competition with their former vessel *Florence*, run by its owner Mr Havelock following a dispute with the company. In addition, there was the Swanage steamer *Lothair*, the *Telegraph* from Poole, Mr W. Powell's *Sunshine*, the *Empress* from Weymouth and a 15-ton yacht called *Frederick William*. *Carham* and *Florence* were in direct competition with one other, offering similar trips to Alum Bay, Cowes, Portsmouth, Ryde, Swanage, Weymouth and Yarmouth. By September, the vessel's owners had finally reached an agreement not to compete on the same routes on the same days, but on 4 September *Florence* ran down a pleasure boat near the pier and drowned four of its occupants. The Master, Joseph Robertson, was convicted of manslaughter and the vessel was not seen at Bournemouth again. The Bournemouth Company was also in trouble, having lost a lawsuit against the owner of the *Florence,* and in February 1881 the company was wound up and the assets sold to Cosens of Weymouth.

The move to wind up the Bournemouth Company was met with opposition from those who wished to retain a local interest in the steamers using the pier. Sydenham in particular was criticised for his allegiance to Cosens, having become their local agent in return for 10 per cent of their Bournemouth income. The Bournemouth, Swanage & Poole Steam Packet Company was formed by those opposing Cosens and the steamer *Lord Elgin* was purchased from Scotland. In addition to sailing to Swanage, Portsmouth and the Isle of Wight, the new company also provocatively offered trips into Cosens' territory area of Weymouth, Portland and Lulworth. In opposition, Cosens used the vessels *Premier* and *Empress* and offered occasional sailings to Torquay, Cherbourg and even Brighton. This would be the established pattern of sailings for both companies throughout the 1880s as the Bournemouth steamer market steadily grew. Both Cosens and the Bournemouth Company employed bands to perform on their ships: Cosens the Royal Italian Band, whilst the Bournemouth Company stayed loyal to its local roots by employing the Bournemouth Town Band.

In 1884, the Bournemouth, Swanage & Poole Steam Packet Company's new vessel *Bournemouth* arrived on station after the company had rejected Cosens' offer of an amalgamation. The rivalry between the two companies intensified after *Bournemouth* began a competing cross-channel service to Cherbourg. In response, Cosens began a rival service to Alderney and introduced a new steamer of their own named *Victoria*. On their services to Swanage and the Isle of Wight, the vessels of the two companies could often be seen racing each other. However, on 27 August 1886 the Bournemouth Company suffered a bitter blow when *Bournemouth* ran aground on the rocks at Portland Bill during thick fog. The passengers were safely rescued aboard the ship's lifeboats and by the local fishermen, but the ship was abandoned after breaking her back and was stripped of anything salvageable.

The company endeavoured to carry on however, and for the 1887 season they acquired the Clyde steamer *Brodick Castle*. They even had the gall to announce that the first sailing of the new vessel, with the company directors and shareholders aboard, would be from Weymouth on 2 April 1887. The *Brodick Castle*, with its higher passenger capacity and faster speed, proved to be an immediate success, carrying 1,600 passengers on Easter Monday compared to a combined 1,300 on the Cosens' two vessels *Victoria* and *Empress*. In response, Cosens (who also styled themselves as the Weymouth, Bournemouth & Swanage Steam Packet Company) ordered *Monarch*, which was designed to outclass *Brodrick Castle* in almost every way. The *Monarch's* first official trip to Bournemouth took place on 7 July 1888 and throughout the summer the two vessels raced each other along the south coast with both sides claiming victories. In 1892, the Bournemouth Company introduced *Windsor Castle* with her faster speed and higher passenger capacity; but at a price, for her £32,000 cost was more than twice what Cosens paid for *Monarch*. The high running costs and fragility of the new vessel led to her being sold in 1895 after only three years service. By then, Cosens and the Bournemouth Company had entered into a running agreement in a bid to cut costs, but this failed to stop the Bournemouth Company going into liquidation in 1896 and being reconstituted as Bournemouth & South Coast Steam Packets Ltd. However, a new rival appeared in 1897 when P&A Campbell – the Bristol Channel steamer operators – based their fine steamer *Cambria* at Southampton and ran excursions to Bournemouth, as well as the Isle of Wight, Sussex coast, Swanage, Weymouth and Boulogne. The Southampton, Isle of Wight & South of England Steam Packet Company also ran excursions to Bournemouth and, alarmed by P&A Campbell's incursion move to Southampton, acquired the Cardiff paddle steamer *Lorna Doone*, which called at Bournemouth on her first public excursion on Easter Monday, 11 April 1898. P&A Campbell placed a second vessel, *Glen Rosa*, at Southampton for the 1898 season and, with so many steamers competing for the Bournemouth trade, a price-cutting war naturally ensued. In 1901, Cosens acquired *Brodick Castle* from the cash-strapped Bournemouth Company (who also agreed for Cosens to operate their other vessel *Lord Elgin*) and introduced the brand new steamer *Majestic*. On August Bank Holiday, 1901, no less than ten different steamers called at the pier, embarking between them around 10,000 passengers.

The pier's heavily used landing stage was damaged by steamers during the early 1890s and it was decided to provide extra berthing facilities on an enlarged pier head to cope with the ever-increasing number of calling vessels. Plans were prepared by Frank Robinson and the tender of contractor Murdoch & Cameron was accepted. Work began in the winter of 1893 and was completed on 26 June 1894, with an official opening to the public on 6 July 1894. The pier now measured 1,000 feet, and a pagoda bandstand, shelters and kiosks were placed on the enlarged pier head. During the summer months, a canvas awning was provided around the bandstand to shade patrons from the sun.

However, the new landing stage suffered extensive damage on its southern side on 12 January 1895. The contractor was blamed for providing piles shorter than proposed and for not driving them to the depths required. Repairs were carried out by the Borough Surveyor and his advisor Mr J. Lemon. Further work was carried out to the landing stage during the autumn and winter of 1908/09 when it was widened from 6 feet 9 inches to 15 feet 3 inches and additional berths were provided by Messrs Goddard, Massey & Warker Limited at a cost of £9,970. The work also included the addition of a refreshment outlet and shelters on the pier head at a cost of £1,216. The new extension was officially opened by Sir George Wyatt Truscott, the Lord Mayor of London, on 5 June 1909. A complete re-decking of the pier with teak was carried out in the following year at a cost of £1,000 and this was illuminated by eight electric lamps located along the centre and around the band seating area. Catlin's Royal Pierrots and Blackmore & Lindens' Pier Pierrots were popular attractions before the First World War, and the Municipal Orchestra and military bands performed in the bandstand. Divers performed off the landing stage, and during the winter the pier deck was used for roller skating.

By 1908, 90,000 people annually were disembarking at the pier and the competition between the steamer companies was as intense as ever. Sailings were available to Swanage, Poole, Boscombe, Southampton, Portsmouth, Southsea, Weymouth, Ryde, Sandown, Shanklin, Alum Bay, Totland Bay, Yarmouth, Cowes, Brighton, Worthing, Alderney and Cherbourg, provided by the following companies: Cosens (*Monarch*, *Empress*, *Albert Victor*, *Emperor of India*, *Victoria*, *Brodick Castle*, *Majestic* and *Lord Elgin*), Southampton & Isle of Wight Company (*Balmoral*, *Bournemouth Queen*, *Duchess of York*, *Queen*, *Lorna Doone*, *Stirling Castle*, *Lord Elgin* and *Solent Queen*), and P&A Campbell (*Glen Rosa* and *Brighton Queen*). The latter had moved their south coast fleet to Brighton in 1902 and their vessels now only called at Bournemouth on excursions from the Sussex coast. In December 1907, an agreement had been reached between the companies for a common scale of charges, which from Bournemouth was: to Southsea, Southampton, Ryde, Cowes, Sandown, Shanklin and Ventnor 3s; Weymouth 2s 6d; Alum Bay, Totland Bay and Yarmouth 2s and Swanage 1s 6d (saloon), 1s (otherwise). In 1912, the two main companies providing services to the pier – Cosens and the Southampton Company – came to the sensible economic agreement to alternate their departure times between Bournemouth and Swanage and not run long-distance excursions to the same places on the same days. However, the 1912 season proved to be a poor one, due to bad summer weather and the reluctance of some to use the boats following the sinking of the *Titanic*.

Upon Great Britain's entry into the First World War on 4 August 1914, the sailings from the pier continued in the face of restrictions and vessels being hired (and then commandeered) for Admiralty duties. In 1915, the Admiralty announced that excursion traffic was prohibited and boat traffic from the pier virtually ceased, although it remained open to the public.

Steamer services resumed from the pier in 1920 with Cosens running *Monarch* and *Alexandra*, although for most of the 1920s *Emperor of India* and *Monarch* were the favoured vessels. However, bad weather and the deteriorating national economic situation led to 1920 being a poor season and passenger levels would never return to their pre-war levels. The Southampton Company also returned to the pier with *Solent Queen* on the Swanage run, *Bournemouth Queen* sailing to the Isle of Wight and the flagship *Balmoral* carrying out the long-haul trips from Southampton and Bournemouth to Weymouth, Cherbourg, Torquay, Brighton, Dartmouth and the Round the Island trips. In 1928, the ban on steamers calling at the pier on a Sunday was finally lifted and they immediately proved to be very popular. The rising popularity of motor coach tours led to passengers on the Bournemouth sailings to the Isle of Wight being offered the option of a coach tour around the island. In 1929, the Southampton Company abandoned its services beyond Weymouth to Dartmouth and Torquay but during the 1930s sailings from the pier remained pretty much the same from year to year.

In 1925, the pier was re-decked in pitch pine at a cost of £15,000. A number of other improvements were carried out in 1931, including a new entrance building; brick built on a steel frame and faced with faience, at a cost of £19,000. The building provided accommodation for the pier offices and mess rooms, and incorporated shops and underground public conveniences. At the same time, a covered stage was provided on the pier head, complete with dressing rooms, at a cost of £2,039. These improvements were overseen by Captain Robinson, the popular Pier Master, who sadly passed away in February 1934.

During the Second World War, the pier was sectioned for defence purposes and much of the ironwork was salvaged to be used in the production of munitions. What remained of the structure was reopened with a temporary gangway in August 1945 to enable passengers to reach the pier head for the steamer sailings, which re-commenced in 1946. The cruises were very popular during the late 1940s, often leading to long queues along the temporary walkway. Both the Cosens and Southampton Company steamers returned to the pier: *Emperor of India*, *Monarch*, *Consul*, *Victoria*, *Embassy* and *Empress* for Cosens and for the Southampton Company *Bournemouth Queen*, a new *Balmoral* and *Queen of Kent* and *Queen of Thanet*; two steamers acquired from the New Medway Steam Packet Company that were renamed *Lorna Doone* and *Solent Queen*. In 1950, the long-serving and popular *Monarch* was finally retired after 62 years of service but her name was preserved and soon reused for the former Portsmouth–Ryde steamer *Shanklin* when she was acquired by Cosens and put into service in 1951. Motor boat services were also operated from the pier by Bolsons (later Crosons) to Poole and Studland. However, in July 1951 the Southampton Company withdrew their services from Bournemouth and scrapped *Lorna Doone* and *Solent Queen*, leaving Cosens as sole steamer operator from the pier.

Repairs to the pier were fully carried out between 1946 and 1953 at a cost of just over £100,000. In 1959, the Pier Theatre was added, supported by pre-cast and pre-stressed concrete piles. The pier could seat 600 and came complete with a stage, six dressing rooms, a bar and restaurant. The shows provided quickly became a popular summer show attraction. Further improvements were carried out to the pier; during 1960 the decking was renewed with the hardwood Jarrah and in the following year a central windscreen was erected at a cost of £8,500. In 1963 the handrails were all renewed.

By the early 1960s, boat traffic from the pier was declining with Cosens only operating two vessels from Bournemouth. In 1961, they entered into an agreement with Crosons for them to operate most of the Swanage sailings with their motor boats whilst the Cosens steamer *Empress* would work the Isle of Wight routes. However, a rival appeared for the Swanage traffic with the introduction of Mr Herbert Jennings' 'Blue Funnel' steamer *Swanage Queen* on 5 July 1961. Despite capturing some of the traffic from Cosens and Crosons, her stay proved to be short-lived. Jennings incurred a loss of £6,629 for the season and the vessel failed to return in 1962 and was scrapped. Cosens long link with Bournemouth Pier finally came to end on 22 September 1966 when *Embassy* called at the pier from Totland Bay before making her way back to Weymouth and the scrapyard.

By the mid-1970s, the pier once again needed extensive refurbishment and the decision was taken to rebuild it in concrete at a cost of £1.7 million, which included a new two-storey leisure centre at the entrance. The work was commenced in 1979 and a temporary walkway was provided to give access to the pavilion. The formal reopening was carried out by the chairman of the English Tourist Board in July 1981.

On 12 August 1993, there was an attempt by the IRA to blow up the pier when a bomb was placed on a girder underneath the deck. Fortunately, it failed to go off. Three years later, Bournemouth Council announced plans to erect a new hi-tech pier on the foundations of the existing structure at the cost of £13 million but the plan was rejected by the Millennium Commission. The landing stage was refurbished and heightened in 2000 to combat the threat of rising sea levels due to global warming.

In 2006, the Pier Theatre, whose future in hosting live entertainment had been in some doubt, was leased to Openworld International, who began the summer season with a four play repertory season presented by Charles Vance. Films were brought to the pavilion in 2009 following the purchase of a DVD projector and screen, but Openworld's suggestion that a Big Wheel and Viewing Tower be erected at the end of the pier to supplement the small fair and boost customer numbers was rejected by the council. During the winter of 2009/10, the Pier Theatre underwent a refurbishment and was officially reopened by Ken Dodd on 3 April 2010. There is currently a 50p toll to use the pier.

POOLE HARBOUR

Poole Harbour is Europe's largest natural harbour and the second largest in the world with a shoreline of around seventy miles. The harbour benefits from double high tides, which give fourteen hours of deep water daily.

The harbour was revealed to have been in use since at least 295 BC by the discovery in 1964 of a 33-foot-long log boat in the harbour mud. The Romans used the harbour to land goods at Hamworthy to supply a large fort near Wimborne. By the twelfth century, Poole had been established as a port, ousting Wareham, which was becoming difficult to reach due to the silting up of the River Frome. Poole became one of the largest and most prosperous ports on the south coast and managed to maintain this position until it was eclipsed by Southampton during the Victorian era. The coming of the railway to the town in 1847, and its extensions to Bournemouth in 1874 and 1888, also took away some of the seaborne goods traffic, although steady trade continued to be handled at Poole and Hamworthy quays until fairly recently. Excursion traffic along the south coast regularly called at Poole Quay and cross-channel services still operate to the Channel Islands and France. In addition, boats sail from the quay to Brownsea Island and a chain ferry runs between Sandbanks and Studland across the mouth of Poole Harbour. The harbour has been popular with private yachts since the late Victorian era, when a number of yacht clubs were established, and in recent years a number of marinas have been developed. Fishing continues to be carried out in the harbour, with a fleet based at Poole Quay.

A number of piers and jetties were built around the harbour for use by industries, ferries, yacht clubs and the military.

Sandbanks (North Haven)

An application to build a jetty at North Haven, Sandbanks, at the entrance to Poole Harbour, was made to the Board of Trade by Peter Tuck in 1880. The jetty was to bring people to a recently built hotel and proposed villas, and was to be sited next to the lifeboat house where a temporary jetty had stood[14].

The jetty was succeeded by a pier, sited 23 feet to the west of it at Panorama Beach, which had been proposed in 1895. The promoter was George Hapgood and

A small 92-foot pier was opened at North Haven, Sandbanks, on 6 April 1898 for the ferry service across the mouth of Poole Harbour to Shell Bay at South Haven. This postcard shows the pier in 1915 with notices advertising the ferry to Shell Bay and motor boats for hire.

In July 1926, a floating bridge/chain ferry was opened between North Haven and South Haven, which could carry fifteen cars in addition to passengers. The pier, which can be seen in the background, continued to operate a ferry service until it was removed as a defence measure in 1940.

he gained a Provisional Order to build the pier from the Board of Trade on 4 May 1897. A design for a pier of just 92 feet in length and 26 feet wide was accepted from architects and engineers Sanders & Goodger, and Fasey & Sons of Liverpool were contracted to build it. Work began in the summer of 1897 and the pier was officially opened by the mayor of Poole, Alderman J. H. Wadcott, on 6 April 1898. The mayor and his official party had arrived from Poole aboard the SS *Lord Elgin* and during the ceremony the Revd J. A. Lawson offered prayer and read Psalm 121. Mr Habgood then handed the Mayor the key to unlock the gates of the pier and as they opened the Poole Company of Artillery Volunteers played the National Anthem. Following a stroll on the pier, the official party were treated to luncheon at the Haven Hotel.

The pier was leased by James Harvey, whose ferries transported passengers between North Haven (Sandbanks) and South Haven/Shell Bay (Studland) across the entrance to Poole Harbour. However, vessels belonging to Cosens of Weymouth occasionally called at the pier on their journeys between Poole Quay, Bournemouth and Swanage. Benches were placed on the pier for passengers and a toll booth and waiting room were provided: it was also home to a Pilot's Lookout. In 1909, there was a proposal to build a new landing stage in a northerly direction for 33 feet. A fence erected across the entrance to the pier in 1912 led to complaints that people were unable to reach the beach, but the matter was resolved when steps were erected from the pier. In 1914, an extra red light was placed on the pier head to warn shipping of its presence.

By 1919, the pier and Haven Hotel were owned by Francois Poulain and Raymond Patenotte, who upset locals by restricting vessels landing at the pier and sailing in the area of the hotel. Two years later, they sold the pier and hotel to Edgar Dore for £15,000, who sold them on in 1925 to John Ruxton's Brownsea Island Estates (later Brownsea Haven Properties). However, the ferry service from the pier was hit hard by the opening of a chain ferry/floating bridge across the entrance to Poole Harbour between North Haven and South Haven in July 1926 by the Bournemouth–Swanage Motor Road & Ferry Company. Using a 150-ton, coal-fired, steam-driven vessel built by Messrs White of the Isle of Wight, the chain ferry could carry fifteen cars in addition to passengers. In its first year of operation, the chain ferry carried 12,000 vehicles and 100,000 foot passengers.

The ferry service from the Haven Pier continued to be operated by Harveys until the pier was blown up by the army as a defence measure in June 1940 and the area around it was heavily mined. The Pilot's Lookout was transferred to the old coastguard station. The chain ferry remained in use during the war to transport military personnel and hardware across Poole Harbour and continues to operate to this day using the diesel-hydraulic powered vessel *Bramble Bush Bay*, which can carry up to forty-eight cars.

Harvey's boats resumed their services after the war's end, but a proposal to rebuild the pier in 1949 was not carried out due to materials being in short supply. In 1962, the National Trust expressed a wish to buy the site of the pier to erect a landing stage for ferries to cross to Brownsea Island, which they had just purchased. A wooden jetty was erected for the ferries to the Island.

Remains of the pier's supporting piles were removed in 1962; nevertheless, some of the piles may still be seen at low tide.

Lilliput (East Dorset Sailing Club), Parkstone

The East Dorset Sailing Club was founded in 1875 and a small timber pier was provided. The pier received Board of Trade approval in 1896 to enable it to be extended a further 375 feet so it could reach the low water channel of Whitley Lake. The work was carried out two years later and a man was employed to look after it at a cost of 15s per week.

The pier still survives and remains in use by the club.

Lilliput (Salterns), Parkstone

Salterns was so named because the area had been used in the production of salt in the eighteenth century. However, by 1849 the salt was no longer being mined and in 1856 the successful London drainage engineer George Jennings took out a lease from Lord Wimborne's Canford Estate to open clay beds and build the South Western Pottery. The pottery soon became established as one of the leading businesses in the area, specialising in the production of bricks, stoneware drainage pipes and terracotta facing blocks.

Jennings shipped the finished goods from Poole Quay to his own private wharf at Lambeth in London. However, the three-mile journey over unmade roads by horse and cart from the works to the quay was slow and inefficient and, furthermore, Jennings resented paying the harbour dues at the quay. In 1866, he applied to the Board of Trade to build a pier adjoining the old salt works lagoon, which would free him from paying harbour dues. The pier was opened in 1867 and consisted of two sections: an embankment at the shore end comprising of old pipe and brick rubble (later concrete) and a timber section at the sea end. Adjoining the pier was the coal yard; as mentioned by Jennings in a letter to his son: 'Instead of ships taking our coal to Poole, they deliver it at once to my coal

The timber jetty that serves the East Dorset Sailing Club at Lilliput. A jetty was first built for the club in 1875.

One of the piers at Lilliput, Poole Harbour, can be seen on this postcard from the 1920s.

store at the Salterns, and I ship off my pipes from the same place.' A narrow gauge horse tramway, similar to that already being used in the clay beds, was built to ship the pipes and coal from the pier to the pottery.

In 1874, the pottery was connected to the new line opened between Poole and Bournemouth (West) by a standard gauge railway terminating in the goods yard of Parkstone station. An 0-4-0 saddle tank locomotive was acquired to work the line. By 1890, the narrow gauge line between the pier and the works had been converted to standard gauge, although the narrow gauge was retained on the pier as it was not strong enough to hold the larger locomotives and wagons.

During the First World War, the area around the pier and coal yard was developed into an engineering works, railway wagon repair shop, sawmill and woodworking plant by Alban Richards & Company. By the end of the war, the pier was rarely being used and in July 1918 Alban Richards announced plans to develop the area around the pier into a dock and shipyard. The proposal followed on from a failed scheme announced in 1917 to build a large shipyard at Salterns by the Dorset Shipbuilding Company. The pier would be incorporated by Alban Richards into the dock by building up its west side to form a new wharf with slipways and a large dock in the centre of the lagoon. A company called Salterns Limited was registered on 30 July 1919 with a capital of £20,000, and 115 acres of the area were acquired from the Canford Estate, including the pier. In addition to W. Alban Richards, the directors of the company included Florence van Raalte, owner of Brownsea Island, Poole shipyard owner Henry Burden and H. Wragg, a director of the South Western Pottery. In October 1919, the company

The small wooden pier at
Lake Beach, Hamworthy,
which once served
the Lake Clay Works
but is now enjoyed by
holidaymakers, fishermen
and members of the Poole
Harbour Canoe Club.

was floated on the stock market with the intention of raising £125,000 to cover
the development costs plus a further £35,000 as working capital. Some of the
money was indeed raised – £104,683 of it – but aside from the 1922 building
of a small dock on the south side of the pier (now utilised for the inner dock of
Salterns Marina) no work was carried out. In July 1923, the company went into
receivership and was finally wound up on 17 July 1931.

Following the failure of the dock scheme, the pier was utilised by the Poole
Harbour Yacht Club. In 1935, the railway from the pier to the pottery works
was lifted, although the section from the pottery to Parkstone station remained
in use until 1963. On 11 April 1963, the land around the pier and pottery site
was granted by the Crown Estate Commissioners to Harbour Properties (Lilliput)
Limited and the remains of the pier were subsequently demolished to make way
for the Salterns Marina and the pottery site and pits were filled in for housing.

Parkstone Bay (Weston Point)

The pier was opened in 1895 by the Parkstone Yacht and Pier Club, although a
proposal to extend it by a further 500 feet led to a dispute with Lord Wimborne,
who claimed the rights to the foreshore and wanted an annual payment of 2s 6d.

The club still operates as the Parkstone Yacht Club but the pier has been
replaced by a berthing marina.

---

[13] In his catalogue of piers Birch referred to the pier as 'Pier No. 49'. Presumably that was the
number of pier designs he had submitted for building, of which only some of course were
built.

Lake (Ham Common) Beach, Hamworthy

A small wooden pier remains as a remnant of the Lake Clay Works, which were situated close to the shore of the harbour west of Hamworthy. A narrow gauge railway once ran for a half mile to connect the works and the pier, from which the clay was transferred to barges.

The pier is enjoyed by holidaymakers, fishermen and members of the Poole Harbour Canoe Club. A nature reserve (known as Ham Common or Hamworthy Common) has been established on the clay works site and features a lake in one of the disused gravel pits.

Rockley

The Royal Naval Cordite factory at Holton Heath was opened in 1915 to supply the navy with explosive shells for its ships; a standard gauge railway was built to transport the cordite to a pier known as 'Rockley Jetty', from where it was transferred into barges. A further railway connected the factory to the nearby Poole–Weymouth line (where a station for the factory workers was opened on 3 April 1916) and from 1938 the line became the preferred method of transporting the cordite. The pier became steadily less used, although the line to it remained open until 1961 when part of the old cordite site was being used by the Admiralty Materials Laboratory. Thereafter the pier became derelict but was still standing in 1975. Now, just a few supports visible at low tide show where it stood.

Goathorn Point

On 17 November 1853, the Admiralty approved a plan submitted by the Isle of Purbeck clay mining company, Fayle & Company, to construct an open-pile wooden pier on the southern shore of Poole Harbour, at Goathorn Point, for the transportation of clay by barges. Another pier for the transportation of clay was situated nearby at Middleberry Farm.

A narrow gauge railway of 3-foot 9-inch gauge was added in 1868 and ran from Newton Heath onto the pier, where a chute at the end emptied the clay into barges. The railway was later extended to Norden, close to Corfe Castle station on the Swanage branch. In September 1876, Fayle's applied to the Board of Trade for permission to rebuild the shore end of the pier as a solid structure by infilling it with rubble.

By the 1930s, most of the clay was being shipped out via the Swanage line trains and the railway to the pier became disused. In 1940, the pier was removed to prevent it being used as a landing stage in the event of an invasion.

A small private pier has since been built at Goathorn.

This pier at Rockley was built to serve the Royal Naval Cordite factory at Holton Heath, opened in 1915. The pier has been demolished but a few supporting piles are visible at low tide to show where it stood.

In 1853, the Isle of Purbeck clay mining operators Fayle & Company constructed an open pile wooden pier on the southern shore of Poole Harbour at Goathorn Point for the transportation of clay by barges. The pier survived until 1940 when it was removed to prevent it being used as a landing stage in the case of invasion.

A wooden landing pier featuring castellated watchtowers was added to Brownsea Island following its acquisition by William Waugh in 1852, in order to exploit the clay deposits to manufacture high quality porcelain. The pier is now used for the ferries to the island from Sandbanks and Poole.

Brownsea Island Castle

Brownsea Island is the largest of the eight islands in Poole Harbour and is owned and maintained by the National Trust. The main feature of the island is Brownsea Castle, which was built during the sixteenth century and converted into a residence by William Benson in the early eighteenth century. In 1852, the island was acquired by William Waugh, a retired colonel in the British Army, in order to exploit the clay deposits to manufacture high-quality porcelain. A clay works was opened and Waugh built a village for the workers (named 'Maryland' in honour of his wife) and St Mary's Church. In addition, Waugh added a new gateway and tower to the castle and a wooden landing pier close by, which featured castellated watchtowers.

The island is chiefly known for the establishment of the first ever scout camp in 1907 by Robert Baden Powell, who was a friend of the island's then owner, Charles van Raalte, responsible for altering its name from Branksea Island to Brownsea Island. However, following the purchase of Brownsea by the reclusive Mary Bonham Christie in 1927, visitors to the island were largely banned until after her death in 1962 and its acquisition by the National Trust the following year. The island is a popular visitor attraction today with visitors eager to spot the population of rare red squirrels along with the Sika deer from Japan that were brought to the island in 1896.

The castellated watchtowers still survive as an impressive backdrop to the current wooden pier ,which receives the distinctive yellow boats of the Brownsea Island Ferries Limited that sail from Poole Quay and Sandbanks.

Brownsea Island Pottery

The development of a pottery works on Brownsea Island was undertaken by William Waugh following his acquisition of the island in 1852. He formed the Branksea Clay & Pottery Company and had a clay pit dug on the north-west of

William Waugh's development of a pottery works on Brownsea Island in the 1850s led to the construction of a mile-long narrow gauge railway from the works to a wooden pier where the pottery was transferred onto the ships and coal and coke were received for the kilns. The original pier of the clay and pottery works fell into disuse following its closure but a small wooden pier, known as the 'Pottery Pier' can be still seen on the site and is used by private craft to land on the island for a fee of £4.20.

the island, which was connected to the pottery works on the south shore by a mile-long narrow gauge railway that hugged the coastline. The line ran onto a 'substantial' wooden pier where the pottery was transferred onto the ships, and coal and coke were received for the kilns.

Unfortunately, Waugh's dream of creating high-class porcelain was dashed when the clay was found to be of poor quality. The development of the island had led him into huge debt and, in 1857, he fled to Spain to escape his creditors. Following much legal wrangling, the island was sold in 1873 to Hon. George Cavendish-Bentinck MP and the pottery ceased all production four years later.

The original pier of the clay and pottery works fell into disuse following its closure but a small wooden pier, known as the 'Pottery Pier', can still be seen on the site and is used by private craft to land on the island for a fee of £4.20.

Studland (Pilot's Jetty)

In 1931, a jetty was erected by the Poole Harbour Commissioners for use by their pilot boats. The jetty no longer survives but the remains of its wooden supporting piles can still be seen.

SWANAGE

Swanage is mentioned in the Doomsday Book as 'Swanic' and 'Swanwick'. Earlier, King Alfred defeated the Danes in a sea battle off the port in 877, which is commemorated by a granite column on the sea front erected by John Mowlem in 1862. Thereafter, Swanage settled down to become a fishing centre and port for the export of Purbeck stone and marble and was described by Thomas Hardy as 'Knollsea' in *The Hand of Ethelberta* (1876): 'a seaside village, lying snugly within two headlands as between a finger and thumb. Everybody in the parish who was not a boatman was a quarrier, unless he were the gentlemen who owned half the property and had been a quarryman, or the other gentleman who owned the other half, and had been to sea.'

The quarryman who owned half the town (called by Hardy the 'King of Swanage') was George Burt, the nephew of John Mowlem. Local man Mowlem had made his fortune in London importing stone, including the local Purbeck stone, for building materials and he brought discarded and demolished parts of London to decorate Swanage. Burt took over the business on Mowlem's retirement and laid out an estate on Durston Head. Amongst the former bits of demolished London Mowlem and Burt brought to Swanage were the grandiose frontage of Mercer's Hall, Cheapside, to grace Swanage Town Hall, and three granite pillars, originally ordered by Sir Charles Barry for Trafalgar Square but deemed surplus to requirements, which Burt erected at his home, Durlston Castle. In addition, Burt had a Great Globe cut from eight blocks of stone, which he placed on Durlston Head.

Stone Jetty

In 1993, a stone jetty with a banjo-shaped head was built as part of a flood prevention scheme and features a clock tower shelter at its entrance and seating along its length. Unfortunately, the jetty has disturbed the northward drift of the sand along the bay, leading to a build-up of sand on the southern side of the structure and a reduction on the northern side.

In 1993, Swanage acquired a stone jetty with a banjo-shaped head as part of a flood prevention scheme. This photograph, taken in March 2004, shows the clock tower shelter at the entrance to the jetty and seating along its length.

Old and New Piers

The provision of a pier and tramway at Swanage was suggested by Captain W. S. Moorsom, Chief Engineer of the Southampton and Dorchester Railway, as an alternative means of exporting Purbeck stone to the high-wheeled carts that transported the stone to the boats at anchor in Swanage Bay. It was envisaged that the pier, which would extend out from the existing stone quay, would cost £6,500 and the tramway £8,500. John Walton of London promised to provide £12,000 if the remainder of the cost could be raised locally. This led to the formation of the Swanage Pier & Tramway Company, led by Chairman John Mowlem, and also consisting of Edward Castleman, George Burt, George Evans and William Tomes. A Bill was presented to parliament, which received the Royal Assent on 8 August 1859. Mowlem laid the foundation stone on Monday 5 September 1859 before the dignitaries retired to enjoy dinner at the Royal Victoria Hotel. A marquee was erected close to what would be the pier entrance so that workmen engaged on the project and the townsfolk of Swanage could also enjoy some refreshment.

James Walton of London was engaged to erect the 550-foot timber pier, which was to extend from a new 240-foot causeway. Work began on its construction in October 1859 and proceeded rapidly. At the second biannual meeting of the company in February 1860 it was reported that 'the full 790ft of the pier was now open for trade, with one crane working and the other about to be erected and

The first wooden pier at Swanage was opened in 1860 to transport Purbeck stone, and for steamer services to Bournemouth, Weymouth and the Isle of Wight. The pier was superseded by a new pier in 1896 but remained in use for goods and as a berthing station for steamers, as seen here in the 1920s. Only the supporting piles of the structure survive today.

11 SWANAGE. — *The Piers from Hotel Grosvenor.* — LL.

The old and new piers at Swanage can be seen in this postcard view from around 1907. The new pier was opened on 29 March 1897 to a length of 642 feet and it took over all steamer services to Swanage from the old pier.

The Pier & Toll Gate, 'Swanage.

The tollhouses to Swanage Pier *c.* 1902. The length of the pier including the stone and concrete shore section from the pier gates measured in total 1,400 feet. The pier was not conventionally straight, branching off with a western dog leg about halfway along.

8   SWANAGE. — On the Pier. — LL.

This postcard of passengers walking along Swanage Pier after disembarking from the steamer was sent on 4 August 1909. The wrought-iron railings provided by the builder of the pier, Alfred Thorne, were one of its most attractive features.

13 SWANAGE. — Arrival of S. S. "Balmoral". — LL.

The arrival of the S.S. *Balmoral* at Swanage Pier is captured on this postcard from around 1907, whilst the funnels of another steamer can be seen at the end of the pier. The *Balmoral* was the flagship vessel of the Southampton, Isle of Wight & South England Steam Packet Company and was often used on their long-haul journeys to the Channel Islands and Cherbourg.

THE PIER, SWANAGE.

K.6680.

The old and new piers pictured on a postcard from the 1950s. As can be seen, the old pier is largely derelict but a diving board has been set up on the end by the Swanage Swimming Club.

This photograph taken on 6 September 1987 shows the poor condition of Swanage Pier at the time, with the upper deck closed off. In January 1982, the remainder of the pier was also closed after sustaining damage during a blizzard.

The new pier at Swanage was fortunately restored between 1994 and 1998 but, as can be seen from this photograph from March 2004, only the supporting piles remain of the old pier.

A view along Swanage Pier looking towards the upper deck on the pier head in March 2004. The fine restoration of the side panels, lamps and seating is evident.

only the moorings and a few other items remained to be put in place, and some wagons are promised for next month. The esplanade has been continued for 250 yards from east to west with strongly constructed walls.'

In addition to the exporting of the Purbeck stone, it was hoped the pier could be used to import coal and receive passenger steamers. Prior to the pier's construction, the steamers had to berth at the old quay or were anchored offshore and the passengers brought in by small rowing boats. A paddle steamer service was commenced from the pier to the new pier at Bournemouth during the summer of 1861 and a toll of 1*d* was charged for each passenger and article of luggage. By 1864, steamers from Weymouth to Bournemouth called at Swanage twice a week and other vessels called from Lymington and Poole.

Although the pier had been built as proposed, the tramway had not. It was supposed to have run from the pier to connect to the stone quarries in the parishes of Langton Matravers and Swanage, but local opposition meant that only 375 yards of it was built along the promenade from the pier to the bankers of cut stone awaiting shipment. The tramway originally sported a standard gauge of 4 foot 8½ inches. Two cranes were also provided to assist in the loading and unloading of goods. The total cost of building the pier and tramway was £6,000.

The pier was purely a functional rather than ornamental structure and came in for some severe criticism by a visitor to Swanage in the *Poole Pilot* on 1 March 1869:

Swanage is a charming place; it praises are in many mouths, and it cannot help rising in public favour if fair chances be afforded it. Its inaccessibility is one clog which retards its progress. The appearance of its pier is by no means an attraction; its baldness and inconvenience discredit every inhabitant in the place. An uglier, bone-breaking trap I have never looked at, especially for weak or invalid people. No side walk where passengers may go without fear of tripping between the open transverse planking; an iron tramroad projecting upwards of four inches; no seat on which tired or weak people may rest whilst waiting to embark; no protection, not even a handrail, to prevent a child from falling overboard and being drowned. First impressions are, we all know, the most enduring, and I believe many a person has condemned Swanage immediately upon viewing this construction.

In addition to being unprepossessing, the pier was also only moderately successful in the quantities of stone loaded from it (on average 300–400 tons in 1868–71) due to the high tolls charged by the company.

Steamer services from the pier were improved in 1871 when George Burt began operating the *Heather Bell* to Bournemouth, Poole, the Isle of Wight, Weymouth and Lulworth Cove. During the first three days of the vessel's service, it was said that over 1,000 passengers were carried in it. The *Heather Belle* remained in service until 1877 and Burt's other ship, *Lothair*, until 1880. The Bournemouth Steam Packet's *Carham* in 1880 was another visitor and the *Princess* called at the pier on route from Weymouth to the Isle of Wight. The Bournemouth, Swanage & Poole Steam Packet Company began operating services to the pier in 1881 with *Lord Elgin* in opposition to Messrs Cosens of Weymouth with *Premier* and *Empress*. Sailings to Bournemouth were particularly popular from the pier as it was only 7¼ miles by sea compared to 25 miles by road. The miniscule *Telegraph* plied between Swanage and Poole during the summer, calling at Sandbanks on route. The Cosens vessels often berthed overnight at the pier and took on coal under the supervision of their local agent Henry Hixson.

Work was carried out on the pier in April and May 1872 when 100 feet of the wooden structure was rebuilt with stone and in-filled with concrete and gravel and the tramway re-laid. However, the condition of the pier often gave cause for concern and further improvements were carried out in April 1881 when new piles, cross pieces and decking were installed. In 1884, one of the pier's two cranes toppled over into the sea, sadly drowning its operator, and the pier structure suffered damage after it was crashed into by the Portsmouth schooner *Two Sisters* on 22 September 1886. A further section of the pier was rebuilt in stone in 1885 and shelters finally added but the arrival of the railway to Swanage from Wareham that year soon ended the transhipment of stone from the pier. A description of the pier at this time was provided by C. E. Robinson in *Picturesque Rambles in the Isle of Purbeck* (1882):

The wooden pier, built about 1860, is a rough, shambling timber jetty running out eastward into the bay more than a hundred yards in continuation of a stone-built quay. It is generally the centre of a picturesque muddle of drying nets and lobster pots, fishermen and more or less pallid passengers out of some noisy snorting Bournemouth paddle-boat, wrapped up in a cloud of its smoke, and gay with bright bits of bunting. A stone-hacker or two will be loading from the pier, and perhaps a coal cargo discharging there.

The 1890s saw intense steamer competition from the pier between the Cosens of Weymouth and the Bournemouth, Swanage & Poole Steam Packet Company. The two companies' vessels would often race each other and, on 13 April 1891, this led to the embarrassing situation of *Victoria* and *Lord Elgin* colliding with each other off the pier. The Bournemouth Company's *Lord Elgin* was held totally to blame for the collision and the company were ordered to pay for the full cost of repairs for the *Victoria* plus costs.

The rising popularity of Swanage as a resort led to calls for the provision of a pier that it could be proud of, one that would be a safe and graceful promenade for visitors and be able to receive the larger paddle steamers plying along the south coast. Plans were finally put in place for a new pier in the 1890s, which would be built just to the east of its predecessor. The old pier would be retained purely for handling goods. Richard St George Moore supplied the approved design for the new pier, which would have a length of 642 foot 6 inches on the centre line, with a width for the greater part of its length of 28 feet. However, the length of the pier, including the stone and concrete shore section to the pier gates, measured in total 1,400 feet. The pier was not conventionally straight as it branched off with a western dog leg about halfway along, and was widened at two points for the purpose of providing steamer berths. At the inner berth, the width was 50 feet for a distance of 60 feet, and at the outer berth 70 feet for a distance of 92 feet. The pier was to be supported on 170 greenheart piles, comprising of 166 single piles and two double piles. The depth of the water at the pier at high tide varied from 7 foot 6 inches at the shore end to 14 feet at the outer end. The estimated cost was £10,000 and the contractor Alfred Thorne commenced work on 30 November 1895.

Thorne made good progress driving the piling into the tough rocky foreshore and the unfinished pier was able to receive the steamer *Lord Elgin* on May Day 1896. The final pile was driven in on 26 July 1896 and following the completion of the decking and its adornments the pier was officially opened on 29 March 1897. The pier proved to be an immediate success with 10,000 people arriving from steamers in its first season of operation, paying 1s 6d for a return ticket from Bournemouth, of which the Swanage Pier Company took a penny royalty. The steamers *Monarch* and *Empress,* visitors to Swanage since 1880, remained regular callers until after the Second World War. Sunday sailings, however, remained banned until 1929. The steamers sometimes used the old pier as an overnight

---

[14] The Poole Lifeboat house was sited at Sandbanks upon its establishment in 1865 but was removed in 1882 to Poole Quay.

berth and were loaded with coal from it. The tramway was re-laid to 2 foot 6 inches gauge and occasionally transported a shipment of stone along the pier to a waiting ketch.

Although the main purpose of the new pier was as a steamer landing stage, it did also offer a fine marine promenade to visitors, who were provided with a shelter on the top deck of the pier head. The wrought-iron railings provided by Thorne (he also used them at Tenby's Royal Victoria Pier built at the same time) were the most attractive feature of the new pier, which was otherwise constructed largely of wood.

By the 1920s, the condition of both the old and new piers was giving cause for concern. The old pier had not been used as a berth for the steamers since the First World War due to its unsafe condition and was now used by fishermen to dry their nets and a local swimming club, who placed diving boards on it. The tramway was rarely used and in 1936 it was largely removed, although the rails set in concrete on the shore section still remain to this day. The greenheart piles of the new pier were decaying badly after 25 years of attack by marine worms and in 1927 they had to be encased in concrete. Further improvements were carried out to the pier in 1933 with the installation of two timber dolphins either side of the pier head in bid to reduce the frequent damage to the landing stage inflicted by the steamers.

Steamer services to the pier from Bournemouth, Poole, Weymouth and the Isle of Wight remained buoyant during the inter-war years although not on the pre-1914 level. In 1922, the steamers ceased to call for a time after the Swanage Pier Company, due to its rather precarious financial condition, demanded that every visiting steamer must pay a 10s toll. Cosens and the Southampton Company agreed not to pay it and withdrew their steamers from Swanage until the pier company backed down and withdrew the proposed toll, allowing the steamers to call again from Whit Monday, 5 June 1922.

Both the old and new piers were sectioned for defence purposes during the Second World War. The new pier was restored in 1948 and the old gas lighting was converted to electric. The old pier was not repaired and was left to decay; today, only some of the piles remain standing. Steamer services were resumed from the new pier, although by the 1960s they were in decline and the PS *Embassy* was the last vessel to call at the pier when the services ceased on 24 September 1966.

The 1960s saw the control of the Swanage Pier Company pass into the hands of the Butterworth family, owners of the Hotel Grosvenor. However the pier lost them money and it fell into gradual disrepair, despite being listed as a Grade II structure. The sea end was blocked off and in January 1982 the remainder of the pier was also closed after sustaining damage during a blizzard when two of the main supporting columns were washed away, leaving a sag in the pier decking and a repair bill of £16,000. The Save Swanage Pier Appeal (soon to become the Swanage Pier Trust) was instigated to try and save the pier and negotiations took place with the Swanage Pier Company with a view to purchasing the structure. In

1983, Swanage Town Council voted to assume ownership of the pier and hand it back to the trust to run but although the Swanage Pier Company offered to gift the wooden section of the pier to the council, the concrete shore end, used for car parking, would only be offered for lease on a 99-year basis. Talks then ground to a halt due to the Swanage Pier Company's insistence that the pier would only be sold in tandem with the Grosvenor Hotel. Eventually, in June 1986, the pier and hotel were acquired by Durrant Developments Limited, who proposed absorbing the pier into a yachting marina. David Durrant announced that £300,000 was to be spent on the pier's restoration and in September 1987 the pier was briefly reopened for the visit of the MV *Balmoral*. However, the marina scheme failed to get past the House of Lords and in 1992 the receivers of Durrant Developments (Swanage Yacht Haven) Limited sold the pier to Purbeck District Council for the nominal sum of £1, who in 1994 transferred management to the Swanage Pier Trust.

With the aid of Heritage Lottery money and other funding, the restoration of the pier commenced in 1994. The deck was renewed in Ekki wood and the concrete piles were replaced with greenheart ones. The Victorian shelter was restored and the hand railings, panels and lamp standards were recast in iron using the original 1896 moulds. A small landing stage, which had been removed in the 1950s, was restored halfway along the pier to be used principally by diving boats. The pier was officially reopened on 27 July 1998 by Lord Raglan, a Swanage Pier Trust patron, and by 2001 £1.1 million had been spent on restoring it to its Victorian splendour. During 2001 the pier was used by 82,894 promenaders, 15,734 divers and anglers, and 14,749 boat passengers. The attractions provided included a diving school, water sports centre, boat trips to Bournemouth, Poole and the Isle of Wight, café and souvenir shops.

PIERS THAT NEVER WERE

Hayling Island

In 1900, Henry Rigg proposed building a pier at Eastoke, South Hayling, to project 200 feet beyond the low water mark to allow small steamers to call from Southsea. However, parliamentary procedures to build the pier were not proceeded with.

Warsash

A pier was proposed by Fareham District Council in 1897 to be built out from the Hard for the ferry service to Hamble-le-Rice. However, nothing came of the proposal.

Swanwick Shore

Situated upstream on the River Hamble, close to the point where the M27 crosses the river, a pier was proposed in 1908 by C. P. Beasley and submitted to the Board of Trade by H. Davies, the Consultant Engineer for the Swanwick Engineering Works.

A public meeting regarding the pier was chaired by Claude G. Mont-Fiore of Coldeast, Locks Heath, in January 1909. W. Garton of Sarisbury offered to supply the timber for the pier, which was to be an open pile structure 380 feet long with a floating pontoon at the end.

The scheme was later downgraded to provide just a temporary landing stage before being abandoned altogether in October 1910. A marina now occupies the site of where the pier would have been built.

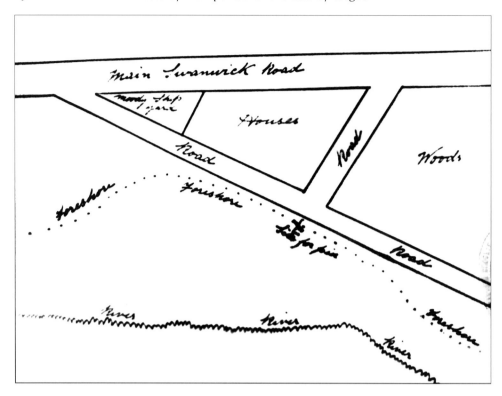

A diagram showing the site of the proposed pier at Swanwick Shore, on the River Hamble, in 1908. Within two years the scheme had been abandoned but a marina was subsequently built in the area.

Keyhaven

Keyhaven and Hurst Castle are the nearest points on the mainland to the western part of the Isle of Wight and, on 22 July 1936, the Isle of Wight Ferry Company's Pier and Harbour Provisional Order (Keyhaven) Bill was passed to provide a purpose-built car ferry service between Keyhaven and Fort Victoria near Yarmouth. At that time, cars had to be towed across on the route between Lymington and Yarmouth. The company announced that they were going to build piers and slipways at both Keyhaven and Fort Victoria, and would run the service using two redundant Mersey ferries. The Southern Railway expressed interest in the scheme and entered into negotiations with the company, but the latter's lack of capital led to its abandonment. However, realising the demand for a proper car ferry, the Southern Railway opened one between Lymington and Yarmouth on 1 May 1938.

 Keyhaven may not have got its car ferry pier but it does have a small jetty that provides a summer boat service to Hurst Castle and Yarmouth.

Milford-on-Sea

The Milford-on-Sea (Hants) Pier Company was incorporated on 5 February 1889 with a capital of £15,000 divided into 3,000 shares of £5 each. The company opened an office at 1 High Street, Lymington, but the share subscription was very poorly patronised and they were dissolved on 17 January 1893 with no work undertaken.

Ryde (Ryde New Pier and Railway Company)

The Ryde New Pier & Railway Company was formed in 1875 with a capital of £120,000 (12,000 x £10 shares) to build a new railway from St John's Road station to the end of a new 3,900-foot pier using a viaduct to cross the Strand and the Esplanade. The directors of the company included George Smith, Henry Granville Wright, William Edwin Cadman and Henry G. Wright. Engineer George E. Eachus estimated that the venture would cost in the region of £100,000. There

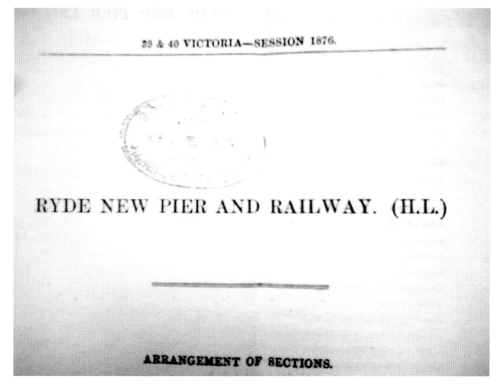

39 & 40 VICTORIA—SESSION 1876.

RYDE NEW PIER AND RAILWAY. (H.L.)

ARRANGEMENT OF SECTIONS.

The Bill placed before Parliament in 1876 for the Ryde New Pier, which would have provided a 3,900-foot-long pier with railway for the eastern end of Ryde. The scheme foundered when the LB&SCR and L&SWR companies threw their support behind an extension of the railway from St John's Road to a new railway pier alongside the existing Ryde Pier.

was some support on the island for the scheme as it challenged the monopoly of the Ryde Pier Company, but the residents of Ryde were not keen on the idea of a viaduct blocking their eastwards view and they voted against the plan by a slim majority.

However, the London, Brighton & South Coast Railway (who, along with the London & South Western Railway, jointly owned the railway at Portsmouth) expressed support for the New Pier idea and it gained favour in Parliament, who threw out an alternative scheme for a new line and widened pier by the Ryde Pier Company. In a bid to stop the New Pier proposals gaining steam, the Ryde Pier Company wrote to the LB&SCR and L&SWR Joint Management Committee offering to sell or lease them their tramway from Ryde Esplanade to St John's Road. On 10 May 1876, the mainland companies agreed to withdraw their support for the New Pier scheme on condition the RPC present a new Bill to parliament to build a railway from the St John's Road to Ryde Pier that would be acceptable to them.

The Ryde New Pier & Railway Company was promptly wound up but its plan had helped initiate the building of a railway between Ryde St Johns Road and Ryde Pier Head, which was opened by the LB&SCR and L&SWR Joint Committee in 1880.

Ryde Appley (Ryde Pier Company)

A proposal was put forward in 1874 by the Ryde Pier Company to build a railway from St John's Road station to a pier at Appley Beach. However, the line would have meant providing a tunnel under Appley Down and the idea was soon shelved.

Sandown (1860)

Sandown acquired a pier in 1878, but plans to build one had originally been mooted eighteen years earlier. In 1860, the newly-formed Isle of Wight Eastern Railway announced proposals to build five lines in the east of the island, one of which was a branch to Sandown Bay terminating on a 396-yard pier. Parliamentary approval was granted on 23 July 1860, but neither railway nor pier ever got off the drawing board.

Sandown (1863)

The Sandown Bay branch railway and pier scheme was revived in 1863, although the pier was to be built independently by the Sandown Pier Company. The company was formed by a group of local businessmen, headed by Chairman

Thomas Willis Fleming, and floated with a capital of £15,000 in 1,500 x £10 shares.

On 16 July 1863, the Board of Trade sanctioned a pier 1,500 feet in length, to commence at a point 90 yards north-east of the Kings Head Hotel, upon which the branch railway would terminate. The Sandown Pier Bill was passed in 1864 and the Bill for the railway came before a House of Lords Committee in May 1865, but problems in raising the finance meant that, once again, both the pier and branch railway were not built.

Shanklin (1864)

The earliest proposal to build a pier at Shanklin came in 1864 with the formation of the Shanklin Bay Pier Company. They proposed to build a 1,200-foot pier (the standard length all pier promoters initially gave to the Board of Trade) at a point near to Coastguard House. Approaches to the pier were to be improved with the widening of the road on the south-east side of Shanklin Chine and the making of a road to terminate on the cliff. Proposed charges to use the pier were 4d to promenade, 6d for landing from steamers, 6d for a bath or sedan chair and 2d for a perambulator.

The company was incorporated with the Board of Trade on 22 December 1864 with the required seven shareholders each holding one share. The company's plans must have been ambitious as they anticipated an expenditure of £24,000 but nothing came of them. After lying dormant for nearly twenty years, the Shanklin Bay Pier Company was eventually dissolved by the Board of Trade on 23 January 1883.

Shanklin (1877)

Following the failure of the Shanklin Bay Pier Company in 1864, a second attempt to provide a pier for Shanklin was made by the Shanklin Pier Company (Limited), incorporated on 20 December 1877 with a capital of £8,000 (1,600 x £5 shares). Engineers Davis & Emanuel drew up plans for a 1,200-foot pier, which they estimated would cost £7,000, and the Shanklin Pier Order was granted on 27 March 1878.

Unfortunately for the promoting company, there were a number of objectors to the pier, including the Shanklin Local Board and local landowner Francis Popham White. He eventually withdrew his objection in February 1881 and the Bill for the pier's construction went to Parliament, but with no finance forthcoming, the Shanklin Pier Company (Limited) quickly foundered and was eventually dissolved on 3 September 1886 with no work carried out. However, by that time another company had been formed, who were to prove successful at last in building a pier for Shanklin.

Yarmouth (Fort Victoria)

See the entry on Keyhaven regarding a proposal in 1936 to provide piers and slipways for a car ferry service between Keyhaven and Fort Victoria.

Yarmouth (Bridge Road)

Upon the opening of the Freshwater, Yarmouth & Newport Railway in July 1889, the railway company proposed building a branch from Yarmouth station to a new pier at the end of Bridge Road, from where ferries would run to the mainland. The plan was rejected by Yarmouth Corporation as they wanted to maintain ferry services from the existing pier.

Bouldnor

See the chapter on Bouldnor in the Yarmouth entry.

West Cowes (1891)

In 1891, W. Ashton Lever asked the Board of Trade if he could erect a 260-foot-long moveable landing stage opposite his house. This was to consist of a concrete causeway from high to low water, then a gangway leading to a floating pontoon.

The proposal met with a storm of protest from residents and the West Cowes Local Board of Health and was killed off in July 1891 when Ashton Lever was declared bankrupt, with liabilities of £9,222 on various Gentlemen's Clubs he had founded in London.

Cowes Millennium

Plans were put forward in 2000 for a pier on the site of the lost Victoria Pier to celebrate the Millennium. The Harbour Commissioners approved the plans but opposition to the development of the Parade (but not to the pier) killed the plan.

Boscombe (1885)

In 1885, the Bournemouth Commissioners announced plans to build piers at Boscombe and Alum Chine but soon grew cold on the idea. A pier was eventually opened at Boscombe in 1889 by the Boscombe Pier Company.

Bournemouth (1875)

The dithering of the Bournemouth Commissioners over providing a replacement for its storm damaged wooden pier of 1861 led to the formation of a rival concern, the Bournemouth Promenade Pier Company. They were registered on 23 February 1875 with a share capital of £15,000 (1,500 shares of £10 each) and obtained provisional approval from the Board of Trade to build a 900-foot pier adjoining the existing structure as long as they acquired the Commissioners' interests. Despite some local support, the company foundered and was wound up on 27 April 1877 and formally dissolved on 17 July 1885. A new iron pier was opened by the Bournemouth Commissioners in 1880.

Bournemouth (Alum Chine)

A pier was announced for this beauty spot in the west of Bournemouth by the Bournemouth Commissioners in 1885 but never got further than the drawing board.

BIBLIOGRAPHY AND
REFERENCE SOURCES USED

General

South Coast Pleasure Steamers by E.C.B. Thornton (T. Stephenson & Sons
    1969)
Piers of the Isle of Wight – a nostalgic review by Marian Lane (Isle of Wight
    Council 1996)
Piers – The Journal of the National Piers Society (various issues)
Isle of Wight County Press
Isle of Wight Observer
www.piers.co.uk
www.theheritagetrail.co.uk
www.simplonpc.co.uk
www.wikipedia.com

Hayling Island

I Remember when it was just fields: the Story of Hayling Island by Ron Brown
    (Milestone Publications 1983)
The Book of Hayling Island and Langstone by Peter Rogers (Halsgrove 2000)

Portsmouth and Southsea

National Archives BT 31/2382/11826
National Archives BT 31/3487/21180
National Archives BT 31/7463/53065
National Archives CRES 37/86
National Archives CRES 37/353
National Archives CRES 37/373
National Archives CRES 37/375
National Archives CRES 37/477

National Archives CRES 37/502
National Archives CRES 37/800
National Archives CRES 58/555
National Archives CRES 64/227
National Archives MT 10/328
National Archives MT 10/980
National Archives MT 10/1306
National Archives MT 19/108
Hampshire Telegraph and Sussex Chronicle
The Morning Chronicle 22 May 1856
The Growth of Southsea as a Naval Satellite and Victorian Resort by R.C. Riley (Portsmouth City Council 1972)
Southsea: Its Story by William Curtis (Bay Tree Publishing Company 1978)
The Portsmouth Papers No. 34: The Battle of Southsea by J.L. Field (Portsmouth City Council 1981)
Crossing the Harbour: The Portsmouth Harbour Story by Lesley Burton and Brian Musselwhite (Milestone Publications 1987)
Southsea Past by Sarah Quail (Phillimore 2000)
www.localhistories.org.uk/portsea
www.southparadepier.co.uk
www.clarencepier.co.uk
www.portsmouthnowandthen.com

Gosport

Gosport in old picture postcards by Peter Rogers (European Library 1985)
It's Shorter by Water: The Gosport Ferry 1875-2001 by Michael Wright (author 2001)
Goodbye to Victoria: the Story of Queen Victoria's Funeral Train by Peter J. Keat (Oakwood Press 2001)
Arming the Fleet: the development of the Royal Ordnance Yards 1770-1945 by David Evans (Explosion/English Heritage 2006)
The Railways of Gosport by Kevin Robertson (Noodle Books 2009)
Gosport Waterfront Trail Guide
www.gosportferry.co.uk
www.haslarheritagegroup.co.uk
www.gosportinfo.co.uk
www.gosport.gov.uk
www.priddyshard.co.uk
www.explosion.org.uk
www.hardwaysailingclub.co.uk

Stokes Bay

National Archives MT 10/1741
Hampshire Telegraph and Sussex Chronicle
To the Isle of Wight by Floating Bridge? By Eric D.G. Payne (*Sea Breezes* magazine December 1983)
The Piers, Tramways and Railways at Ryde by R.J. Maycock and R. Silsbury (Oakwood Press 2005)
Leisurely Gosport by Lesley Burton by Lesley Burton (Gosport Society 2006)
The Railways of Gosport by Kevin Robertson (Noodle Books 2009)
www.fortgilkicker.co.uk
www.remuseum.org.uk
www.gosportinfo/History/Stokes Bay Railway.co.uk

Lee-on-the-Solent

National Archives BT 297/696
National Archives MT10/418
National Archives MT 10/992
Hampshire Telegraph and Sussex Chronicle
The Story of Lee-on-the-Solent by Ron Brown (Milestone Publications 1982)
Lee-on-the-Solent by Lesley Burton and Beryl Peacey (Chalford 1997)
Leisurely Gosport by Lesley Burton (Gosport Society 2006)
The Railways of Gosport by Kevin Robertson (Noodle Books 2009)

Warsash

National Archives AIR 2/152
National Archives MT 10/716
National Archives MUN 4/6040

Netley

The Era 7 August 1864
Hampshire Telegraph and Sussex Chronicle 10 August 1867, 7 September 1872

Southampton

National Archives CRES 58/593
National Archives MT 10/584

www.davidstjohn.co.uk
www.townquay.com
www.plimsoll.org.co.uk

Hythe and New Forest Waterside

National Archives BT 297/737
National Archives BT 31/1589/5267
National Archives MT 10/252
National Archives MT 10/313
National Archives MT 10/712
National Archives MT 10/2047
The Hythe-Southampton Ferry including Hythe Pier Railway by Wm. A. Stearn
    and Bert Moody (Eltrac Publicatons 1970)
Hythe Pier and Ferry: a History by Alan Titheridge (Itchen Printers 1981,
    second edition 1996)
The Hythe Pier Railway by Peter A. Harding (author 2009)
www.hytheferry.co.uk
www.newforest.gov.uk
www.ports.org.uk
www.exxonmobil.com

Lymington

Lymington-Yarmouth: The New Generation by John Hendy (Wightlink 2008)
www.wightlink.co.uk

Ryde

National Archives AN 157/63
National Archives BT 285/422
National Archives BT 356/5378
National Archives BT 356/12548
National Archives MT 6/97/6
National Archives MT 6/157/1
National Archives MT 6/1594/13
National Archives MT 6/2489/3
National Archives MT 9/2871
National Archives MT 10/4
National Archives MT 10/118
National Archives MT 10/182

National Archives MT 10/232
National Archives MT 10/235
National Archives MT 10/250
National Archives MT 10/451
National Archives MT 10/734
National Archives MT 10/949
National Archives MT 10/1024
National Archives MT 10/1282
National Archives MT 10/1395
National Archives MT 10/1547
National Archives RAIL 330/144
National Archives RAIL 592
National Archives RAIL 648/446
National Archives RAIL 649/50
National Archives RAIL 1001/266
National Archives RAIL 1027/55
National Archives RAIL 1066/1413-15
National Archives RAIL 1110/398
The Portsmouth-Ryde Passage: A Personal View by John Mackett (The
　　Ravensbourne Press 1970)
The Railways and Tramways of Ryde by A. Blackburn and J. Mackett (Town
　　and Country Press 1971)
To Ryde by Floating Bridge? by Eric D.G. Payne (*Sea Breezes* magazine
　　December 1983)
Ferry Services of the London, Brighton and South Coast Railway by S. Jordan
　　(Oakwood Press 1998)
Ryde Postcards by Lynette Archer and John Woodford (Tempus Publishing
　　2003)
The Piers, Tramways and Railways at Ryde by R.J. Maycock and R. Silsbury
　　(Oakwood Press 2005)
www.wightlink.co.uk
www.historicrydesociety.com

Seaview

National Archives BT 297/759
National Archives MT 10/253
National Archives MT 10/1745
Isle of Wight Record Office H/SP
Seaview Pier: The Case History by Adrian Searle (Isle of Wight County Press
　　1981)
A Present from Seaview by Guy and Zuphie Parsloe (Falcon Press 2004)

Bembridge

National Archives MT 10/4
www.bembridgeharbourtrust.org.uk
www.mli.org.uk

Sandown

National Archives BT 31/1942/8114
National Archives BT 31/14857/23937
National Archives CRES 37/78
National Archives CRES 37/726
National Archives CRES 37/1897
National Archives MAF 209/2870
National Archives MAF 209/2871
National Archives MT 10/2
National Archives MT 10/159
National Archives MT 10/689
National Archives MT 10/1954
National Archives MT 10/2000
Sandown and Shanklin by Donald A. Parr (Alan Sutton 1996)
The Isle of Wight Railway by R.J. Maycock and R. Silsbury (Oakwood Press
    1999)

Shanklin

National Archives BT 297/760
National Archives BT 31/2391/11909
National Archives BT 31/3578/21940
National Archives CRES 38/728
National Archives CRES 38/737
National Archives MT 10/10
National Archives MT 10/316
National Archives MT10/441
National Archives MT 10/736
Isle of Wight Record Office H/EPS
Shanklin between the Wars by Alan Parker (author 1986)
Sandown and Shanklin by Donald A. Parr (Alan Sutton 1996)

Ventnor

National Archives CRES 58/647
National Archives MT 10/121
National Archives MT 10/385
National Archives MT 10/396
National Archives MT 10/471
National Archives MT 10/1260
National Archives MT 10/1279
National Archives MT 10/1292
National Archives MT 10/1385
National Archives MT 10/1548
Isle of Wight Record Office IWCC/ED/P/85
Royal Victoria Pier Ventnor Isle of Wight (Mayneland Amusements 1982)
The Piers and Harbours of Ventnor 1843-1988 (Ventnor and District Local
    History Society 1988)
Steamers into Ventnor 1863-1968 (Ventnor and District Local History Society
    n/d)
Ventnor and District in Old Photographs by Donald A. Parr (Alan Sutton 1996)

Alum Bay

National Archives BT 31/1509/4717
National Archives BT 31/14839/23115
National Archives MT 10/514
The Isle of Wight County Press 15 February 1928
Alum Bay and the Needles by John C. Medland (Coach House Publications 1995)
www.theneedles.co.uk

Totland Bay

National Archives BT 31/2444/12406
National Archives BT 31/31554/53752
National Archives CRES 58/613
National Archives MT 10/261
Isle of Wight Record Office BD/AC/65/22
Isle of Wight Record Office BD/AC 83/4
Isle of Wight Record Office AC 85/53
Around Yarmouth, Totland and Freshwater by Anthony and Olive Mitchell
    (Tempus Publishing 1998)
Cosens of Weymouth 1918-1996 by Richard Clammer (Twelveheads Press 2001)
www.totlandpier.com

Yarmouth

National Archives BT 31/2564/13385
National Archives MT 10/58
National Archives MT 10/188
National Archives MT 10/205
National Archives MT 10/295
National Archives MT 10/711
National Archives MT 10/1487
Hampshire Telegraph and Sussex Chronicle
Around Yarmouth, Totland and Freshwater by Anthony and Olive Mitchell
   (Tempus Publishing 1998)
Lymington-Yarmouth: The New Generation by John Hendy (Wightlink 2008)
Not the End of the Pier: saving the country's longest wooden pier (Brill Books
   2008)

Cowes

National Archives ADM 116/614
National Archives BT 31/1272/3142
National Archives CRES 37/39
National Archives CRES 37/1984
National Archives CRES 38/731
National Archives MT 10/6
National Archives MT 10/102
National Archives MT 10/231
National Archives MT 10/232
National Archives MT 10/385
National Archives MT81/86
Hampshire Advertiser and Independent
 (West) Cowes and Northwood Isle of Wight 1750-1914 by Rosetta Brading
   (author 1994)
Cowes: the Jewel of the Solent by John Groves (author 2004)
www.redfunnel.co.uk

East Cowes

East Cowes and Whippingham Isle of Wight 1303-1914 by Rosetta Brading
   (author 1990)
East Cowes and Whippingham Isle of Wight Book 2 1915-39 by Rosetta
   Brading (author 1993)
www.redfunnel.co.uk

Southbourne

National Archives BT 31/3430/20661
National Archives MT 10/512
National Archives MT 10/1677
Southbourne-on-Sea 1870-1901 by Dr. J.A. Young (Bournemouth Local Studies
   Publications 1982)
The Story of Southbourne by Dr. J.A. Young (Bournemouth Local Studies
   Publications 1989)
Southbourne and Tuckton Yesterday by Dr. J.A. Young (Bournemouth local
   Studies Publications 1990)

Boscombe

National Archives BT 31/3810/23895
National Archives MT 10/538
The Illustrated Police News 30 January 1897
Bournemouth: Then and Now by John Peters, David Couling and Michael
   Ridley (Blandford Press 1978)
A History of Bournemouth by Elizabeth Edwards (Phillimore 1981)
Bygone Bournemouth by Mary Davenport (Phillimore 1988)
Boscombe Pier – Its Two Centenaries by Elizabeth Edwards (Dorset Life July
   1989)
Boscombe: The Victorian Heritage by Dr. J.A. Young (Bournemouth Local
   Studies Publications 1993)
The Boscombe Whale (Dorset Life October 2000)
A History of Bournemouth Seafront by Andrew Emery (Tempus Publishing
   2008)

Bournemouth

National Archives MT 10/623
*The Spas of England and Principal Sea Bathing Places 2: the Midlands and
   South* by A.B. Granville (1841, republished 1971 by Adams and Dart)
Bournemouth: Then and Now by John Peters, David Couling and Michael
   Ridley (Blandford Press 1978)
A History of Bournemouth by Elizabeth Edwards (Phillimore 1981)
Bygone Bournemouth by Mary Davenport (Phillimore 1988)
Cosens of Weymouth 1918-1996 by Richard Clammer (Twelveheads Press
   2001)
Cosens of Weymouth 1848-1918 by Richard Clammer (Black Dwarf
   Publications 2005)

A History of Bournemouth Seafront by Andrew Emery (Tempus Publishing 2008)
Evening Echo, Bournemouth (various issues)

Poole Harbour

National Archives BT297/630
National Archives CRES 59/133
National Archives MT 10/36
National Archives MT 10/223
National Archives MT 10/654
National Archives MT 10/736
National Archives MT 10/1171B
National Archives MT 10/1487
National Archives MT 10/1739
National Archives MT 10/2027
National Archives MT 81/246
Rails to Poole Harbour by Colin Stone (Oakwood Press 2007)
Piers Information Sheet No. 56 – Sandbanks (Haven) Pier, Dorset by Lester
    Kitching (Piers Information Bureau 1990)
Lilliput's Industrial Past by Jeremy Waters (*Dorset Life* October 2009)
www.sandbanksferry.co.uk
www.eastdorsetsailingclub.co.uk
www.nationaltrust.org.uk/brownseaisland

Swanage

National Archives BT 297/629
National Archives C 16/58/A76
National Archives CRES 58/657
National Archives MT 10/397
National Archives MT 48/29
Swanage Past by David Lewer and Dennis Smale (Phillimore 1994)
Swanage Encyclopaedic Guide by Rodney Legg (Dorset Publishing Company
    1995)
Curiosities of Swanage by David Lewer and Bernard Calkin (authors 1999)
The Book of Swanage by Rodney Legg (Halsgrove 2001)
Cosens of Weymouth 1848-1918 by Richard Clammer (Black Dwarf
    Publications 2005)
Swanage: 125 Years of Railways by B.L. Jackson (Oakwood Press 2010)
Evening Echo, Bournemouth (various issues)
Western Gazette (various issues)
Swanage and Dorset Times (various issues)

Piers That Never Were

National Archives BT 31/1040/1771C Shanklin 1864
National Archives BT 31/2078/9236 Bournemouth 1875
National Archives BT 31/4342/28185 Milford-on-Sea
National Archives MT 10/211 Ryde New Pier
National Archives MT 10/803 Hayling Island
National Archives MT 10/1261 Swanwick Shore

ACKNOWLEDGEMENTS

Darlah Thomas (for the map)
Eamonn Rooney
Ian Jeffrey
David Maber
The National Archives, Kew

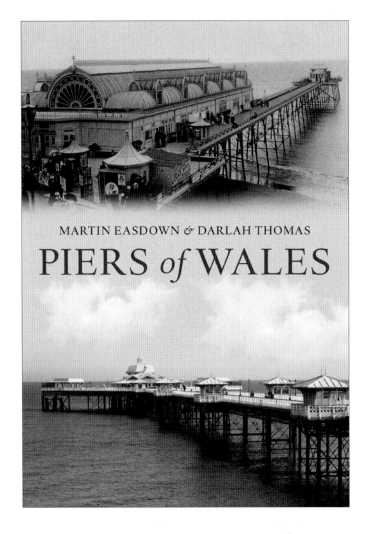